Literacy and Popular Culture

Literacy and Popular Culture

Using children's culture in the classroom

Jackie Marsh and Elaine Millard

P·C·P
Paul Chapman
Publishing Ltd

First published 2000

 Paul Chapman Publishing Ltd
A SAGE Publications Company
6 Bonhill Street
London EC2A 4PU

SAGE Publications Inc.
2455 Teller Road
Thousand Oaks, California 91320

SAGE Publications India Pvt Ltd
32, M-Block Market
Greater Kailash - I
New Delhi 110 048

British Library Cataloguing in Publication data

A catalogue record for this book is available from the British Library

ISBN 0 7619 6618 8
ISBN 0 7619 6619 6 (pbk)

Library of Congress catalog record available

Typeset by Dorwyn Ltd, Rowlands Castle

Contents

This book is dedicated to the memory of Winifred Whittaker, who taught three generations of children to read using *Woman's Own*.

It is also dedicated to Rita Marsh and Esther Riley, both avid consumers of popular culture.

Acknowledgements

We would like to thank warmly all the people who contributed to this book. Sharrow Nursery Infant School and Birley Spa Community School, Sheffield, and Hempshill Hall School, Nottinghamshire, have been most welcoming and we have been grateful for the opportunity to learn from their excellent practice. We thank the head teachers of these schools, Lynne Ley, Geoff Mawson and Marcia Puckey, for their support. We would also like to express our gratitude to the many teachers who have shared their work with us: Kate Barret, Joe Brian, Melanie Brown, Pauline Davies, Stuart Harrison, Matt Hayes, Mark Heaton, Marie Hill, Jackie Hines, Pam Hulme, Jill Ineson, Linda Scott, Huw Thomas and Phillipa Thompson. We know the children they teach love their creative ideas as much as we do, as we have seen the evidence and place some of it within these pages. Finally, we would like to thank the children who helped us to understand the power of popular culture and shared their private pleasures with us. Thanks go in particular to all the children whose work appears in the book, Angela Williams and Robert Fisher for their verses and Hannah and William Clark for their singing. Without the compelling voices of all these children, this book would not have been written.

Introduction

The study of popular culture is now quite firmly established in the upper stages of secondary schools, colleges and universities. For example, the University of Sheffield, where both authors currently teach, holds in its library collection 82 theses which address various facets of popular culture: 26 of these are concerned with advertising; 25 focus on television; 17 discuss film and video; six deal with aspects of popular music and eight focus on computer games and comics – including two theses on Japanese Manga.

It seems that for adults, popular culture, in its many manifestations, is a legitimate object of study. Postgraduate students are allowed wide choices when electing the topic for their work. However, the case is very different when we turn our attention to the sorts of texts that are commonly used with young children. Whenever the issue is debated as part of the drive to improve literacy in schools, the study of media other than print in its most rarefied form, the classic text, brings accusations of 'dumbing down' or trivialization, through a relativism that is no longer able to distinguish 'quality' in what it consumes. Here, Valentine Cunningham, Professor of English at Oxford and Senior English Tutor at Corpus Christi College, expresses his own distaste for popular and electronically mediated culture, an opinion which is shared by many of those who act as gatekeepers for the institutions which legitimize forms of knowledge:

> We are all bombarded with the bits and bites and bytes of current information. We are flooded with messages. And these signs never come simply, but always multiply. They are crazily synaesthetic, utterly over-determined. There is no song now without a video to go with it; no words – not even in the book sections of the posh newspapers – without a very large picture; no novel without a screen-adaptation coming up (and look how forcibly prescriptive, as well as skimming and wrenching they usually are).
>
> (Cunningham, 1998, p. 15)

Many schoolteachers experience similar feelings of discomfort with and distaste for the products of the mass market which, however much they are disregarded by teachers or excluded from the official school curriculum, find their way into nearly every classroom and certainly all playgrounds. Many teachers have also explained to us that they consider the products of popular culture to be unsuitable for their lesson planning because they are usually more transient than the literary forms of high culture and have only a short-term appeal to their users. In some cases, this latter charge is true, although some items, such as the early Disney films, for example, or the mystery and adventure stories of Enid Blyton, along with many 1960s pop lyrics, have thrilled at least three generations of children. The shelf-life of the artefacts we are about to discuss, however, is not the main consideration in our recommendations for their use. We are advocating an approach to cultural ephemera that draws on their linguistic and cultural appeal to motivate literacy learning, rather than suggesting that they have any currency in their own right. Put plainly, it is not a matter of choice between competing media narratives that we wish to promote, say, for example, the appeal of Teletubbies as opposed to Lara Croft of the Tomb Raider series, but a general sensitivity to children's culture that will allow teachers to create more powerful language work from the currency of pupils' own preoccupations.

The habitual rejection of popular texts for consideration in school, whatever the grounds, seems particularly paradoxical when we consider that our youngest children have been born into a world which is digitalized and wired to receive the products of mass culture, to an extent that even Walt Disney could not have imagined. Disney's first full-length animated feature film, *Snow White*, which was released on 21 December 1937, could be said to have heralded a childhood world where visual narratives began to take precedence over spoken and written ones. Nevertheless, even 60 years ago, long before the word 'digital' meant anything more than 'of, or pertaining to a finger',[1] children's literacy experiences through exposure to popular culture were much broader and more complex than was ever acknowledged in schooled versions of literacy. Children, whether or not they had been taken to see the Disney film, might have been bought the supporting picture book which required the famous red and green lenses to produce three-dimensional versions of key scenes, or taken to buy a packet of Snow White fruit pastilles, with a cut-out figure of the heroine inside. In the 1950s, the next generation to see the film could be offered a cut-out figure of the heroine to dress in paper outfits, or could buy a comic in which Disney figures were featured, or collect cards from cereal packets. Dressing-up clothes could be purchased for fantasy play at home and the songs from the film performed in concerts and pantomimes. Of course, today's children can now purchase the interactive CD-ROM of the Disney version, watch the video at home and visit the Disney website. The leisure pursuits of children have changed greatly over the years and this will, inevitably, impact on the way in which they read books.

Even the most ardent proponents of the supremacy of the book as a means of educating the young become nostalgic about other textual encounters when they look back to the fictions that fuelled their earliest pleasures. Eric Bolton (1998), former head of Her Majesty's Inspectorate (HMI), writing the introduction to *Literacy Is Not Enough* (Cox, 1998) a collection of polemical essays defending the work of literature from the encroachments of the media and other less 'demanding' texts, recalls:

> My memories of early reading are vague, but it seems to have been a rag-bag of legends and myths, *Rupert Bear*, Ridley's *Believe it or Not* and above all comics. The weekly editions of, first *The Beano* and *The Dandy*, and later *The Adventure*, *The Wizard*, *The Rover* and *The Hotspur*, were the common cultural capital and units of barter and exchange of all the boys I knew.
>
> (Bolton, 1998, p. 1)

But, of course, he considered the comics that he read then to be superior in quality to those published today: 'Unlike the comics of today, those for older boys consisted of page after page of columns of small print, which everyone then seemed able to read' (ibid.)

It has ever been the case that each older generation feels the culture of younger people to be less demanding in content and to mark a diminution of expertise, or complexity in presentation. This has been claimed for the movement from rock to punk music, radio serial to soap opera, film to video narrative or from written word on the page to image and text on the screen. These prejudices are often unfounded. Research, for example, has shown that the publications today's schoolboys choose for their leisure contain complex and often closely packed text, but that the topics that interest them have changed from the comic adventure narratives described by Bolton, to narratives, procedural texts and critical analyses focused on computer games or sport (Hall and Coles, 1999).

Eric Bolton and many of his fellow contributors to the Book Trust's sponsored collection, *Literacy Is Not Enough*, echo a fear of the fragmentation of the literary culture they love. This has been voiced repeatedly since the advent of mass education, mass literacy and mass culture, most memorably in the poetry of T. S. Eliot, who in *The Rock*, laments for, 'Those whose souls are choked and swaddled in the new winding sheets of mass-made thought' (Eliot, 1974, *The Rock*. Act I, 46). It is hard to dispute the persuasive arguments derived from the richness and power of the imaginative literature that has been central to the past schooling of most of today's educators. Yes, we agree that Dickens's description in *Bleak House* of Jo's helplessness in the face of a pitiless culture that has left him illiterate is very powerful; yes, Shakespeare's plays do catch the essence of experience and express human emotions in ways that have rarely been surpassed and we are not suggesting that children should be denied access to either of these authors. Neither do we suggest that they be prevented from analysing and discussing the importance of aspects of mainstream, or 'high' culture.

However, when it comes to developing a critical literacy, reading literary works is also not enough, nor do they hold the only key to effective entry into the kinds of empathetic and self-actuating encounters with human experience that its advocates would have us believe. Moreover, the cult of the book has often bypassed the experience and interest of a large number of pupils in school, who have not had a childhood surrounded by the kinds of stories and picture books that are the staple of most white middle-class homes and which are also the basis of early learning in schools. Shirley Brice Heath's work is the best known and most detailed account of the different experiences of early language and literacy events experienced by the children of diverse cultural groups in a southern state of America (Heath, 1983). She compares the home circumstances of a poor white working-class community, children from black sharecroppers' families and middle-class 'townspeople' to show how their particular patterns of literacy, experienced within their families, differ. She argues that the middle-class town children get a better educational start because their home experience with books and stories has more consonance with school than the practices of the other two groups. Similarly, the research of Taylor and Dorsey Gaines, carried out in Chicago, *Growing up Literate: Learning from Inner-City Families* (1988) reports that poor families do have effective literacy practices – but that these are not necessarily those of the school. Our concern is to make teachers more familiar with some of the literacy practices experienced by children in their homes and communities and to support teachers in using these to motivate positive learning experiences in school.

Moreover, we are currently living through a period of rapid transition from a linear, print-based and page-bound culture, which developed from the introduction of the printing press, to a screen-based, hyperlinked mode of communication. Here, information is in a constant flux and is only arrested for the moment of reception, when a deliberate act is made to save a semi-permanent version on disc or paper. These changes to the ways in which we communicate with each other to express our intentions and even feelings is having a profound effect on the way we respond to texts and make meaning from them. For the younger generation, particularly young men and boys, the new literacies appear to offer a world full of promise. For many of the older generation, an awareness of a changing consciousness that is more alert to the flow of messages has created anxiety, along with the desire to hold on even more firmly to the products of their conventional readerly ways which have endured the test of time. For them, the old literacy has greater currency, a literacy Freire (1972) would describe as bankable. Valentine Cunningham caricatures the products of the Internet as 'gab in, gab out' and contrasts its structuring of ideas unfavourably with that of the literary forms more familiar to him:

> What characterises, of course, the great democratic field of the Internet and the World Wide Web is precisely freehand jots, random thoughts, amateurishly rambling confessionalism, neo-epistolariness gone quite mad. And to be sure, ordered sequenced and connectedness of narrative and of concept and person, the great features of classic fiction and classic Western selfhood – of the book, no less – are bound to count for less when at the touch of just a few buttons, you can swiftly cut and paste everything to somewhere else.
>
> (Cunningham, 1998, p. 16)

What is most certain, however, is that increasingly, children are being exposed earlier and earlier to electronically and digitally produced texts, all of which they treat with the easy familiarity of those born to 'get digital'. The parents of very young children, surveyed by Marsh concerning their children's out-of-school literacy activities, detailed a wide range of access to popular culture. On a single day, three families recorded the literacy events in which their children had participated at home (Table I.1).

The wide range of texts recorded in Table I.1, which also form the focus of many other children's out-of–school literacy events, have enormous potential to engage their interests and inform their enquiries in nursery and school. From a utopian stance, access to the new

Table 1.1 Media consumption at home

Name	Video and television programmes watched	Computer games	Books shared	Comics and magazines	Other reading
Ansa	Pokémon and Looney Tunes		Read book on clay modelling with mum	Shared Pokémon magazine	Television subtitles
David	Beachcomber Bay Wipe Out	Spelling programme	Read nursery rhyme book with gran	Read Teletubbies Playdays	
Jack	Tweenies, Pingu, Tales of the Tooth Fairy	Zoo Animals	Read Roger Rabbit with dad	Bananas in Pyjamas Disney and Me	Pokémon book and cards

media has the power to educate and inform, as well as entertain and comfort. Indeed, much of the advertising about new forms, aimed at the family, emphasizes the educational gains to be had from computers, or other digital means of accessing the Internet. The electronic media are able to take children into new worlds, create new perspectives on their own and other people's lives and allow the stories of human experience to be shaped and reshaped into ever changing messages, which are yet able to retain something of the past. Consider, for example, the power of the World Wide Web to provide rapid access to a wide range of poetry and literature no longer available in conventional print, alongside biographical and critical materials which help with the study of particular writers. To adapt the title of George Lakoff's (1980) influential book, *Metaphors We Live By*, the new media are establishing contemporary forms of 'narratives we live by' in the way that parables, myths, fairy stories, epics and legends have done for previous generations. From a dystopian perspective, there is also a need to be on our guard about the new media's power to persuade and seek to control. There are powerful tools in the hands of propagandists, pressure groups, spin doctors and advertisers, who have designs, not only on our children's pockets, but also on their thought processes and opinions. For example, 'Got to catch 'em all!' is the persuasion to buy into the collector's cult that accompanies the current Pokémon craze, based on a Japanese computer game and its accompanying cartoon programme. The cultural forms which figure so largely in our pupils' lives are also embedded in larger discourses, some of which carry stereotypical messages of 'race', class and gender, most of them rooted in the commercial market. It is only with the development of our own awareness of the ways in which they attract and sustain interest, that we can engage our pupils more critically with the multiplicity of voices that surround them. Our view is that both a knowledge of the pleasure they arouse and an analytical eye for their positioning of the subject within their discourses are prerequisites for any teacher engaged in the use of popular culture in school.

In this climate of 'new times', we have written our book at the opening of the twenty-first century with two clear purposes in mind. We wish first to contribute to the debate about the role of popular culture in the education of the young and raise awareness of the important issues that are involved in both choice and presentation of the texts. Second, to offer a critique of the current primary school literacy curriculum, providing suggestions for changing practices related to the development of reading and writing. We therefore intend to confront current anxieties, hostilities, fears and downright prejudices which focus on not only the uses of popular culture in the primary school, but also its very presence as a seductive force in the lives of young school children. Then, having made what we consider to be a strong argument for teachers to take time to understand the ways in which a wide range of popular media already support literacy development in complex social settings, we will suggest practical ways in which particular aspects of each medium can be incorporated into classroom practice. The book, therefore, falls naturally into two complementary sections. The first, and shorter part, made up of two chapters, establishes the parameters of the debate, by defining exactly how the concept of popular culture has been discussed from the past to the present. Drawing on theoretical perspectives taken from postmodern, cultural and feminist theorists, it unpicks arguments used to reject the suitability of popular forms in the education of the young. This section is intended to stimulate discussion, rather than to offer conclusive solutions. It discusses how the concept of childhood itself has been constructed and how debates about the suitability of particular forms of cultural production for children have been contested. We intend that these two chapters should challenge our readers to grapple with some of the complexities of current critical theory, albeit only at an introductory level, and to provide some idea of the historical context within which views have been formed.

The second and more extended part of the book focuses more directly on pedagogical matters. It looks at the debates surrounding reading and writing in the classroom and illustrates how the knowledge that children bring with them to school about the content of the mass media and the cultural texts and artefacts designed particularly for them, can be used to confirm them in their self-confident use of language and act as the stimulus to thoughtful and constructive written work. Some practitioners may wish to concentrate their attention on finding out how to introduce work on particular media in their own classroom. For this reason, we have included some very specific examples of projects carried out in school and, where appropriate, pointed to other developmental work in the area. Teachers in English primary schools are currently working within the National Literacy Framework, which emphasizes the development of an understanding of literacy at word, sentence and text level. We have not followed this model to the letter, because the work we are suggesting can be adapted to contexts other than an English one. However, the reading of popular culture and the writing that emerges from it lend themselves to all three aspects of the framework and teachers will find a focus on word and sentence level in our recommendations in these chapters, as well as whole text and genre work. In addition, much of the work included as examples in the book has been produced within the framework of the literacy hour, either in shared or guided reading and writing sessions, or as independent work.

Finally, we have particularly enjoyed collaborating on writing this book, both with each other and with the teachers in whose classrooms many of the activities that are suggested were undertaken. Our pleasures have derived not only from sharing the recollections of our own childhood fads and fantasies, but also from encountering the sheer delight of school children when they were allowed to relate their own interests to their work in school. Our visits to schools have been marked by an excited curiosity that bubbles over into laughter and play and gradually settles into purposeful creativity, negotiated by teachers and children on the children's terms. It is a delight which has been given clear expression in the writing of Anne Haas Dyson, who describes children's assortment of popular cultural texts as a tote bag of 'symbolic material gleaned from the myriad of voices surrounding them' (Dyson, 2000, p. 362). She writes about its pleasures in opposition to the prescriptive frameworks of the state curriculum:

The state curriculum framework for the new millennium seems to have shut its textual door to keep out the noise of society at work and at play. I am standing outside that door, a tote bag slipping off my shoulder as lively children peek over its top. Those children are not blank tapes, waiting patiently for someone to select the voices they should record. Out from my bag come strands of love songs, sports reports, Godzilla adventures and orchestrated hybrids of varied voices. Wanting admission, feeling wary, I whisper loudly into the bag: 'SH!' But it's a bit late for shushing the children. No way I-we- are getting in that door.

(Dyson, 2000, p. 363)

We now are dealing with a framework for learning which, if not approached creatively, will also work to 'shut out the noise of society at work' and exclude the texts children value for themselves. Our hope is that the readers of this book will experience some of the same pleasurable shock of recognition of their own childhood delights when reading about aspects of the work we, and the teachers with whom we collaborated, created alongside children. Further, we hope that those who work directly with children will be prompted to seek out their own pupils' current cultural interests in order to devise ways of profiting from them in the classroom.

Note

1. This meaning was recorded being used in 1656 in the OED and the first application of the term 'digital' to a computer is recorded as having been made in 1968.

1

Exploring the Concept of Culture

Our first task, before attempting to identify the nature of the activities based on popular culture that we might want to introduce into the primary classroom, is to arrive at some understanding of what the terms 'culture' and, more particularly, 'popular culture' might encompass. Such an understanding is also essential in helping us to make sense of some of the debates and contested positions that surround the introduction of work based on various popular forms to school. This chapter, therefore, will explore the multifarious definitions of the terms 'culture' and 'popular culture' in order to provide a backdrop to the work outlined in other chapters. We begin by tracing historical constructions of culture and move on to deconstruct the idea of 'popular culture', specifically in relation to children as cultural consumers. But first, we will examine the concept of culture itself.

The concept of culture

'The concept is at least complex and at most so divergent in its various applications as to defy the possibility, or indeed the necessity, of any singular designation' (Jenks, 1993, p. 1). As Chris Jenks, a sociologist who has written widely on topics including childhood and culture, indicates, it is neither feasible, nor desirable, to arrive at a single definition of the term 'culture', which has been interpreted in many different ways by philosophers, anthropologists and social scientists over the centuries. In 1952, American anthropologists attempted the task of identifying the many different uses of the term in academic studies and found 164 distinct meanings (Kroeber and Kluckholn, 1952). Many of these definitions are embodied in a conception of culture as something detached from behaviour and action. In many of the definitions examined, it was an abstract concept that included the development of ideas and symbolic representation and ensured the distinction of humans from animals. However, this definition will not satisfy our purpose, as it is clear that

culture also include people's behaviours and actions. Jenks (1993) suggests that a classification of culture as a concept which refers to the norms, values, beliefs or expressive symbols of any particular group or society is more acceptable as a starting point for analysis.

It is, however, only that: simply a starting point. If we examine the trajectory of the term throughout history, it becomes clear that a single, linear approach to the concept is not possible. A brisk survey of the historical uses of the term 'culture' takes us from a concept which refers to a model of 'high' culture that celebrates the 'best' that has been produced in any given age, to a contemporary concept which acknowledges the complexity inherent in societies where distinctive cultures impact on each other. It is a development which culminates ultimately in a post-structuralist vision of cultures as socially constructed sites of shared discourses with fluid boundaries. However, we will begin by examining the tradition in which the term 'culture' is used to describe a tangible set of ideas and practices which are exclusive to particular groups of people.

One of the first significant staging posts in the journey towards a notion of an élite culture was Plato's *Republic*. Plato created a vision of a social order in which a group of men without family or personal wealth, described as 'philosopher kings', were specially trained to guard the moral integrity of society. These philosopher kings were expected to have a greater sensibility for the finer things in life than the rest of humankind: 'Only the man who has a taste for every sort of knowledge and throws himself into acquiring it with an insatiable curiosity will deserve to be called a philosopher' (Plato, *The Republic*, Book V, v. 475). This vision of culture as belonging to a highly cultivated, intellectual and artistic world, which could only be appreciated by exceptional individuals, was taken up prominently by a number of writers and philosophers in England in the nineteenth century. Their views were precipitated by intense changes to economic and social life as a result of the industrialization of the workplace. For example, Matthew Arnold and John Ruskin were concerned about the need to educate an upper middle class who would preserve a cultural high-life, which would in turn counterbalance the ignorance of the general masses. The rapid growth of urbanization and progress in technology, transport and communication all contributed to the unease felt by many, as they struggled to come to terms with the resultant changes in society. Some felt that it was essential to counteract these changes, which led towards increasing mechanization, by striving for an intellectual high-ground as an escape from this humdrum existence.

Amongst those who most influenced the thinking of later Victorian educationalists was the Romantic poet and critic, Coleridge, who described the notion of culture as a process of 'cultivation', an agricultural term which was hijacked in the attempt to account for the process of developing a refined sensibility. The cultivated mind, shored up with the fruits of the highest artistic and intellectual endeavour, would be able to resist the sullying influence of everyday life. Like Plato's philosopher kings, Coleridge proposed that an élite group whom he named the 'clerisy', should be accountable for ensuring the cultural heritage of the nation. In his work *On the Constitution of the Church and State*, he defined this clerisy as: 'members of the permanent learned class. . . the immediate agents and instruments in the great and indispensable work of perpetuating, promoting and increasing the civilization of the nation' (Coleridge, 1976, p. 50). This notion of culture as a process of the individual cultivation of mind which could influence civilization was prevalent in the nineteenth century and to some extent lingers today. In Johnson's dictionary (1755) the word ' culture' is used to designate both the act of tilling, or improving the soil, and the act of individual improvement. This meaning still holds some force as culture, like civilization, is frequently used to describe both a society's and the individual's spiritual and moral values.

This notion was taken up by Matthew Arnold who, as one of the first HMIs, appointed in 1851, had a significant influence on the development of the term 'culture' as it related to the 'high arts'. Like Coleridge, Arnold felt that traditional values were being displaced in the rush to mechanization and industrialization. His poem *Dover Beach* captures the profound sense of loss educated Victorians felt at the perceived threat to spiritual and moral certainty created by changes in society. Arnold attempted to hold on to visions of culture which had not been tarnished by the day-to-day issues of power and commerce. In *Culture and Anarchy*, first published in 1869, he asserted that culture seeks: 'to make the best that has been thought and known in the world everywhere; to make all men live in an atmosphere of sweetness and light, where they may use ideas, as it uses them itself, freely – nourished and not bound by them' (Arnold, 1963, p. 70). Thus, culture was defined as the pinnacle of human thought and achievement and associated with images of purity and Christian manliness. Arnold did not locate the ownership of this culture within the dominant classes; in fact, he condemned both the aristocrats as barbarians for their mindless pursuit of field sports, physical grace and prowess and the industrial manufacturers as 'philistines' for their provincialism and utilitarian materialism. Nevertheless, he did feel that the artefacts of high culture could only be appreciated by a particular kind of cultivated sensibility. Arnold thought that the general mass of the populace did not possess the taste or discrimination to recognize and exult in this culture, again celebrating an intelligentsia who would know better and so preserve cultural traditions.

This theme did not end as the roots of the Industrial Revolution dug in and Britain became accustomed to a modernized lifestyle. In the early years of the twentieth century, another celebrated poet-critic, T. S. Eliot, took up Arnold's argument and suggested that it was appropriate that culture could only be produced and appreciated by a select few; if it were to be more widely available, it would become tainted and worthless. In his work, *Notes Towards the Definition of Culture*, Eliot argues that the nation's cultural heritage must be upheld for the good of all in society. Eliot's work was strongly influential in shaping the English literary tradition in the earlier part of this century and his best known work, *The Wasteland*, records his sorrow at the disintegration of a greater cultural past. In Chapter 6, we will look in more detail at how literary critics, such as Leavis and Hoggart, extended and adapted Arnold's and Eliot's work to argue for the recognition of a canon of English literature that worked to exclude popular cultural texts from educational institutions.

In England, the forces of conservativism lead the flight away from those media (songs, ballads, novels and plays) that were popular amongst the working classes, whilst in Europe the work of radical Marxist critics had much the same effect, if from somewhat different perspectives. Arnold's and Eliot's vision of the working class as a mass of atomized beings, with little control over either the production or consumption of cultural artefacts, was shared by a group of German philosophers, working at the beginning of the twentieth century and known as the Frankfurt school. They were influenced by the work of Karl Marx who proposed that, 'The ideas of the ruling class are, in every age, the ruling ideas' (Marx, 1963, p. 93). This suggests that the culture of a society is determined by the ruling classes, not ordinary working people. The ruling class ensures its ideas hold a superior position to that of other groups and thus perpetuates its own dominant position over the masses. Marx developed the idea of 'base' and 'superstructure' to explain how cultural forms were produced. The base of a society is its economic structure, its material production. This is where the class structure of society is formed, as those with the material wealth control the working lives of others. Superstructure, on the other hand, refers to those structures that cannot be accounted for in the economic frame of the base and includes religion, education and culture. Marx stated that, 'The mode of production of material life determines the general character of the social, political and spiritual processes of life' (Marx, 1963, p. 67), thus suggesting that the workings of the base influenced the shaping of the superstructure. This notion has been contested by a large number of Marxist scholars ever since (see Storey, 1993; Strinati, 1995), as it is clear that it is not a simple matter of the economic structure of a society determining everything else, but that more complex dialogical processes are at play.

The Frankfurt school did refine the work of Marx and attempted to place a more central emphasis on the role of culture and ideology. The work of key members of the school, Adorno and Marcuse, led to the notion of a cultural industry which produced goods for consumption by the working class. They argued that capitalism had moved away from Marx's vision of it as an unstable system, to that of a stable system. As capitalist society raised standards of living for a greater number of people through the creation of wealth, it ensured that working-class people, now comfortable with the security they had acquired, bought into the system. Because working people's real needs of freedom and equality were being suppressed, the Frankfurt school argued that society created false needs which served to divert the masses from the conditions of their existence. In this sense, popular culture was not so much a release from economic pressures, it served as a means of masking these economic pressures.

The Frankfurt school suggested that the key to the creation of these false needs was the culture industry. It produced a range of cultural goods, which were then consumed by the masses and in turn made large profits for the capitalists, who ran the culture industry. In this consumption, the masses became passive customers of manipulative and profit-seeking capitalists. This is a very simplified version of a theoretical position that has become increasingly sophisticated. However, from this analysis, we can see that the élitist proponents of a highbrow culture, such as Coleridge, Arnold, Eliot *and* this group of Marxist scholars, all held reductive visions of 'the masses' and the cultural media that they consumed. Nevertheless, there are differences between the two positions, as Jenks has pointed out:

> The conservative explanation of the paucity of mass culture is in relation to the inadequacy, mundanity and 'low-brow' status of the general public's taste and receptive capacities – the Marxist explanation is in

terms of the intervention of the market, and the erosion of spontaneous folk-culture in the face of a mechanical and commercially exploitative popular culture imposed outside the control of the volition of the masses.

(Jenks, 1993, p. 108)

The 'folk-culture' referred to here is a concept which has served to describe the cultural norms, values, beliefs and expressive symbols produced and enjoyed by non-dominant classes in society, in contrast to popular cultural forms, which are commodified and led by market concerns. However, the term is sometimes used in a pejorative sense in that folk culture is suggestive of a naïve, simple and unsophisticated set of practices, which have been over-romanticized. The cultural theorist Raymond Williams (1963), however, was keen to preserve the notion of agency in relation to folk culture, as otherwise, as Strinati suggests, all that remains is a vision of the working classes as

a passive, supine, undemanding, vulnerable, manipulable, exploitable and sentimental mass, resistant to intellectual challenge and stimulation, easy prey to consumerism and advertising and the dreams and fantasies they have to sell, unconsciously afflicted with bad taste, and robotic in its devotion to the repetitive formulas of mass culture

(Strinati, 1995, p. 48).

The work of Williams (1963) was important in that, amongst other things, he suggested that the concept of mass culture was fundamentally flawed. He argued that, 'There are, in fact, no masses; only ways of seeing people as masses' (Williams, 1963, p. 289). His analysis led people to question the assumption that mass culture can be defined, or that we can determine who constitutes the masses. Society is not a concrete amorphous lump which can be neatly packaged into sections, but a complex web of constructed social identities which overlap and interrelate. The process of creating and consuming culture is much more complex and dynamic than the Frankfurt school had recognized and, in the latter half of the twentieth century, there was a move toward a vision of culture as a more complex entity. Cultural study is not defined as either a study of social activities or a study of social structures, but as the interplay between them. In fact, discipline boundaries are becoming increasingly meaningless as we study cultural concepts from works which draw upon history, communication studies, literacy theory, education, philosophy, economics and politics, as well as anthropology and sociology. Such an exploration leads us to a recognition that culture is 'a pattern of meanings embodied in symbolic forms (collective representations) which exist both in and outside the individual' (Swingewood, 1998, p. 55). Culture is constructed by groups as they build a shared discourse and it also shapes individuals in that we are born into a set of cultural values and norms acquired through social interaction. So as we move on from a vision of culture which consists of the 'best that has been thought and known' (Arnold, 1963, p. 70) to one which celebrates it as 'a contexted semiotic system' (Jenks, 1993, p. 168), we need to recognize that this plurality cannot be simplified or easily categorized.

Post-structuralism has contributed to the disintegration of any unifying concept of culture (as, for example, embodied in an agreed canon of 'great' writers or works of genius), although, as we have argued, there has only ever been the illusion of unification in explorations of the concept. Indeed, the notion of cultural pluralism is not new. Herder, a German philosopher, writing at the end of the eighteenth century, argued that European culture was not the highest point of civilization, but that there were other cultural forms that should be recognized and valued (Griswold, 1994, p. 8). In the latter part of the twentieth century, cultural studies has been strongly influenced by the work of Stuart Hall and others from the Birmingham Centre for Contemporary Cultural Studies. In the 1960s and 1970s, they developed the concept of cultural relativity by striving to tease out some of the complex connections between state, society and cultural forms. This work established a model of culture as a multifaceted, multilayered set of discourses, bound by hegemonic forces and subject to change when appropriated by the individual.

The last decades of the twentieth century have, therefore, brought further disintegration to the idea of an uncontested, single, national culture experienced by all, as post-structuralism has questioned the very basis of cultural formation. Indeed, the French philosopher Baudrillard argues that we can no longer distinguish cultural reality from fantasy and exist in a 'hyper-real' culture in which originals have been replaced by simulacra, copies of copies. This hyper-real culture becomes the reality: 'Disneyland is presented as imaginary in order to make us believe that the rest is real, when in fact all of Los Angeles and the America surrounding it are no longer real, but of the order of the hyper-real and of simulation' (Baudrillard, 1983, p. 29). This is the ultimate disintegration of culture into a shredded world of isolated and self-referential landscapes that have no connecting roads, with not even a map to locate significant features.

As national cultures become increasingly fragmented, there has been a growing perception of a globalized culture as geographical and national barriers become redundant in the face of multinational expansion. The 'McDonaldization' of societies (Ritzer, 1998) has meant that multinational companies have increasing control over what is produced and marketed across continents, with goods that have been successful in industrialized countries being sold in the developing world. Thus 'McDonaldization is . . . a largely one-way process in which a series of American innovations are being aggressively exported to much of the rest of the world' (Ritzer, 1998, p. 8). Many see this as a threat to indigenous cultures as people the world over crave for Nike shoes, McDonald's hamburgers and Coca-Cola. The move towards what McLuhan and Fiore (1967) characterized as the 'global village' has been precipitated by immense changes in communication through advanced technologies, as exemplified in the explosion of e-commerce. Thus, we can see that at the very point that the concept of 'high' culture is broken into a million post-structuralist pieces, global movements by multinationals are developing a communal cultural landscape ringing with the sound of cash registers and branded with the icons of a consumerist discourse. These are issues we will revisit more comprehensively in Chapter 2, where the question of consumerism and the exploitation of children within the market will be considered. The next step in this brief theoretical survey is to explore what is actually meant by the term popular culture itself.

The concept of popular culture

If the concept of culture has been difficult to trace historically in any coherent way, then the nature of popular culture is equally subject to slippage. It is generally accepted that popular culture refers to aspects of culture shared by a large number of people. However, things are not so simple. A large number of people share an interest in opera, but opera is not usually thought of as popular culture (except, of course, when its arias are press-ganged into the service of global football events). Inherent in the term 'popular' is an implicit understanding that the cultural text referred to (whether that is a belief, norm, value, practice or object) is not a cultural artefact which has been identified historically as being superior in quality to other forms, for example, as art, opera and classical music all have been. Nevertheless, as Strinati and Wagg (1992) point out, the boundaries between 'high' and 'low' culture are shifting all the time. If we take the work of William Shakespeare as an example, we can see that his plays were enjoyed by diverse groups of people in the seventeenth century and drew on a

comprehensive knowledge of their tastes in ballads, rumour and su-
perstitions. However, as we write this in the first years of the twenty-
first century, it is clear that Shakespeare has become the icon of 'high'
culture, with many people from working-class groups only ever
seeing his plays in the theatre as part of a school trip. So cultural forms
slip up and down a sliding scale of value but, as Rowe (1995) points
out:

> For all the interpenetration of high and low cultural forms celebrated
> by post-modernists, with opera-singers in the charts, vernacular
> styles of architecture on the street, avant-garde filmic techniques in
> television advertisements, and art exhibitions hyped like pop fes-
> tivals, there remains a widespread ideological enforcement of
> cultural hierarchies.
>
> (Rowe, 1994, p. 5)

Another feature which distinguishes popular culture from its more
élite counterpart is the relationship that exists between popular culture and the forces of power in a society which control key elements
such as government, education, media and economic production.
Gramsci's notion of hegemony is central to any exploration of this
dialectical relationship. Gramsci was a Marxist theorist who suggested that the ruling classes did not simply impose their will on
other groups. In fact, what happens is that 'subordinate groups and
classes appear to support and subscribe to values, ideals, objectives,
cultural and political meanings which bind them to, and "incorporate" them into, the prevailing structures of power' (Storey, 1993, p.
124). Hegemony therefore refers to the process by which dominant
groups impose and perpetuate their power: ideologically, politically,
economically and culturally. The degree to which popular culture is
the vehicle for ruling groups to impose their will, however willingly
that imposition is received by subordinate groups, has been the subject of much debate. Hall (1992) argues that popular culture, a site of
alternative traditions, is appropriated by the dominant forces for
commercial and ideological ends. He suggests that popular culture
is:

> the scene, par excellence, of commodification, of industries where cul-
> ture enters directly into the circuits of a dominant technology – the
> circuits of power and capital. It is the space of homogenization where
> stereotyping and the formulaic mercilessly process the material and
> experiences it draws into its web, where control over narratives and
> representations passes into the hands of established cultural

bureaucracies, sometimes without a murmur. It is rooted in popular experience and available for expropriation at the same time.

(Hall, 1992, p. 32)

However, as Fiske's work (1989) outlines, if popular culture perpetuates the oppressive ideologies of hegemonic forces, it can also offer resistant readings, according to the nature and circumstance of its production. Often these competing readings occur at the same time in the same popular text. Texts can also be read in different ways by different groups of people. Literary theorists such as Iser (1978), Fish (1980) and Eco (1981) (known as a group as 'reception' theorists) assert that the reader brings a particular cultural context to each new text and a personal reading history which influences how he or she makes sense of it. Robinson further suggests that 'reader, text and community are all involved in the constant interplay between culture, thought and language' (Robinson, 1997, p. 54). It is inevitable, therefore, that the texts of popular culture will provide a range of experiences for individuals, some finding particular texts oppressive, others liberating.

As an example, we would like to consider for a moment the meanings surrounding the superhero, Batman. It is evident that the *Batman* television series of the 1960s was 'read' in a number of different ways by a variety of people. Children generally made a literal reading of it, taking the programme and the adventures of the caped crusader at their face value. Yet Medhurst (1991) asserts that *Batman* programmes of the 1960s were especially appealing to gay audiences because the 'TV series was and remains a touchstone of camp' (Medhurst, 1991, p. 150). Popular cultural texts should, therefore, be recognized as polysemic, that is, having many different meanings. Further, specific cultural groups will have different forms of popular culture which they produce and consume primarily amongst themselves. These factors have led to a shift in the conceptualization of popular culture from that of a single 'mass culture' to a postmodern understanding of popular *cultures* (Strinati and Wagg, 1992). Of course, some complain that this, essentially post-structuralist, process has weakened the concept of culture: 'If culture was once too rarefied a notion, it now has the flabbiness of a term which leaves out too little' (Eagleton, 2000, p. 37). Nevertheless, it is clear that any contemporary definition of culture needs to accept its multifaceted nature and so it would seem appropriate to have a working definition of popular culture as a discourse, or set of discourses, which are shared by a group of people;

discourses which are complex in construction and often contradictory in the messages they give or readings they offer.

Children's popular culture

In the remaining chapters, we shall be turning our attention to an exploration of children's popular culture and its place in children's learning, recognizing that the beliefs, values, practices and objects that constitute that culture span a wide and varied set of sociological systems. Children's popular culture overlaps with that of adults in that the broad fields into which they can be categorized are similar: music, sport, computers and related merchandise, books, magazines, television and film. However, children's popular culture also incorporates such diverse artefacts as toys, games, comics, stickers, cards, clothing, hair accessories, jewellery, sports accessories, oral rhymes, jokes, word play and even food and drink. This list is not prescriptive; children's popular cultural forms are constantly emerging and disappearing.

This presents us with a special perspective on their 'use'. Popular cultural texts for adults are generally produced by adults, for adult consumption. Much of children's popular culture is also produced by adults and this circumstance changes the fundamental nature of the discourse. It leads many people to focus on the manipulative element of the popular culture industry for children. The fact that the multinational toy manufacturing industry, in collaboration with television and film companies, determine what many children's next desired object will be has led some people to argue that children are controlled by the needs of commercial interests. If we examine the way in which children's popular cultural icons are produced and consumed, it is clear that there are significant market forces involved. The production of a new cultural icon is usually carried out after extensive market research. Television programmes feature particular characters and the toy industry makes related plastic figures and accessories. Fast-food chains such as McDonald's are quick to capitalize on such crazes and significant deals are made with toy manufacturing industries to include small figures in children's meals. It is a particularly lucrative field, with the toy industry making a profit of around $30 billion, in the USA alone, during 1998.

The pursuit of bigger and bigger profit margins by the toy and game manufacturing industries throughout the twentieth century has led to a greater amount of television advertising targeted at children and marketing campaigns which play directly to their desires. The work of

Stephen Kline (1993, 1998) has been important in developing our understanding of the way in which the toy industry successfully analysed the market needs and developed products calculated to begin consumer crazes. This analysis drove him to conclude that 'children's culture has always been primarily a matter of culture produced for and urged upon children . . . Childhood is a condition defined by powerlessness and dependence upon the adult community's directives and guidance' (Kline, 1998, p. 95). However, this is suggestive of a perspective on childhood which is restricted in nature. Childhood, in Kline's analysis, is a 'condition', a term redolent with images of temporary illness or indisposition in which children are dependent on the whims of adults. This notion of childhood is concomitant with a view that children are merely the passive recipients of a culture created for them by others. Whilst it would be foolish to deny the economic exploitation involved in children's popular culture, it is necessary to acknowledge the complexities of the child as consumer. Some of the work on adults' popular culture has demonstrated how adults make alternative and resistant readings of discourses offered to them and are not the passive victims of hegemonic forces (Ang, 1985; Fiske, 1989). Similarly, children are agents in the construction of their own culture at the same time as being subject to hegemonic discourses of profit and consumerism. They both accept and reject the products offered to them. This issue will be examined in greater depth in Chapter 2.

Ultimately, it is important to recognize that, just as we deconstructed the concept of culture in order to acknowledge the plurality of cultures, so there is not one set of values, norms, beliefs, practices and objects which we can refer to as children's popular culture. Whilst the McDonaldization effect does mean that many cultural icons are shared across disparate groups, other popular cultural texts will be fashioned by the contexts in which children live and be subject to other cultural, social, economic and linguistic influences. Thus, in any one school community, there will be a number of different groups, each with their own set of popular cultural practices. This might just as readily involve watching Asian films or collecting car magazines (Dyson, 1996) as exchanging Pokémon cards. The practical activities based on popular cultural texts presented in this book rely heavily on discourses which are widely available. However, this does not mean that teachers should not also investigate and use the popular cultural forms specific to their pupils' particular communities.

As we draw this chapter to a conclusion, it has become increasingly apparent that it is not possible to reach closure on the term 'culture' and arrive at an absolute definition. Rather, we have offered a sketchy journey through changing cultural terrains in order to show that there are inevitably more questions than answers raised in any examination of the role and uses of both 'high' and popular culture. Not only, therefore, is it undesirable to arrive at any definitive classification of the concept, it is also inadvisable to suggest that our understanding can ever be anything more than provisional, made up of an *ad hoc* patchwork of interlocking patterns and threads. It is in the emergence of patterns and in the tracing of the threads that many of the pleasures inherent in any engagement with the topic lie. In the next chapter, we will move on to examine some of the cross-threads in this tapestry: those aspects of children's popular culture which many teachers find problematic and particularly challenging to the customary discourses of the classroom.

2

Challenging Racism, Sexism, Violence and Consumerism

If there is a single, most important reason why teachers do not include popular cultural texts in their classrooms, it is almost certainly because many feel uncomfortable with the ideologies which underpin many of these texts. These ideologies are often located in discourses of violence, racism, sexism and other forms of oppression. This chapter will examine ways in which children's popular culture is infused with such messages, but first we need to look at some of the forces which impact on adults' relationships with popular culture. Underlying adults' concern is the concept of childhood itself, one which has always been fraught with tension and unease. The first part of the chapter examines this relationship in order to trace how the construction of childhood throughout the centuries has changed and with it, adults' attitudes to childhood cultural iconography.

Changing view of childhood

Childhood is a construct which is shaped by economic, political, social and cultural forces in societies (James and Prout, 1997). Thus, childhood changes shape according to the needs of society. Ariès (1966) argued that in Europe, until the Middle Ages, childhood was not seen as a separate state of being from adulthood. Children were not excluded from the range of adult activities and no special consideration was given to their stages of development when making decisions about what they did or saw. As childhood began to be recognized during the eighteenth and nineteenth centuries in England as a stage separate from adulthood, two opposing views of what childhood might be could be seen to be informing social and cultural patterns. The first view, which threads through many cultural texts, is one of childhood as a state of innocence in which children need protecting by adults from the evils that surround them. The second view purports

23

that, in fact, children have the capacity to be wild, untamed and potentially evil if not constrained by adult rules and regulations. In some cases, these two views of childhood coexist, as in the nineteenth-century poet, Wordsworth's, major work *The Prelude*, or William Blake's *Songs of Innocence and Experience*.

If childhood is a state of innocence, then it can only be corrupted through interaction with elements in the adult world. Moreover, according to many sources, the elements relating to popular culture will be the most corrupting of all (Postman, 1983). On the other hand, if childhood is already a state in which corruption exists and children need to be protected from further degeneration, then it is even more important that children's leisure pursuits are policed. It is clear that both views of childhood can lead to the moral hysteria we have seen engendered regularly in response to a range of popular cultural artefacts, including television, video, computer games, music and toys. However, this bipolar positioning of childhood is oversimplistic. Children's identities are complex and contradictory in nature and cannot be reduced to neat formulae. Different cultural and social values give rise to different notions of what childhood is, making such judgements meaningless. In addition, the notion of moral panics needs further examination if we are to understand the complex issues at hand. 'Moral panic' is a term explained by Stanley Cohen, who explored the media reaction to mods and rockers in the 1960s. He observed that:

> Societies appear to be subject, every now and then, to periods of moral panic. A condition, episode, person or group of persons emerges to become defined as a threat to societal values and interests; its nature is presented in a stylised and stereotypical fashion by the mass media; the moral barricades are manned by editors, bishops, politicians and other right-thinking people; socially accredited experts pronounce their diagnoses and solutions; ways of coping are evolved or (more often) resorted to; the condition then disappears, submerges or deteriorates and becomes less visible.
>
> (Cohen, 1987, p. 9)

However, underlying moral panics is the sense that the media can manipulate an uncritical mass, suggestible to ideas. Walkerdine (1999) argues that studies conducted last century on the manipulation of crowds led to more recent work by social psychologists, which has focused on the irrationality of the masses: 'The importance of the twin issues of the mass medium and the vulnerable and suggestible mind cohere to produce a social psychology and psychopathology of groups in which mass irrationality and suggestibility have a central place' (Walkerdine, 1999, p. 5). Walkerdine suggests that this view of the masses, as being susceptible to corruption, is applied in particular to the working classes. Thus, although it is middle-class children who have the greatest access to video technology, computer games and other media discourses, it is working-class boys who are positioned as being most susceptible to the corrupting and addictive influence of this technology (for example, the killers of Jamie Bulger). In addition, some cultural theorists argue that 'Moral panics remain one of the most effective strategies of the right for securing popular support for its values and policies' (McRobbie, 1994, p. 198).

It is clear that the adult reaction to children's popular culture is complex and contradictory in nature. Buckingham (1998) argues that there are two conflicting positions which are evident in relation to popular culture and schooling. He suggests that, on the one hand, popular culture in the form of media has been seen as the site of dominant ideologies, messages which children should be armed to resist. On the other hand, Buckingham (1998) asserts that there is a position in which 'it is possible to regard teaching about popular culture as an extension of progressivism. From this perspective, popular culture is seen as an authentic part of students' experience, and hence as something teachers should seek to validate and even to celebrate' (Buckingham, 1998, p. 8). However, this neat positioning of two oppositional discourses could be misleading; in reality, things are not as clear cut. So for example, Stephen Kline, who has argued strongly that the commercialization of children's culture has been inherently damaging, has recognized that it has also brought some attendant benefits (Kline, 1993). Moreover, it is difficult to identify any work which suggests that teachers should unquestioningly celebrate children's popular culture in the classroom and use it as a liberating force. Thus, in any exploration of the relationship adults have to children's popular culture, we need to acknowledge that complex and contradictory strands are at work.

If adults' attitudes towards children's popular cultural texts are informed by specific socio-cultural constructs of childhood, they are also subject to the individual's sensitivity to issues of 'race', class, gender and other sites of potentially oppressive discourses. However, possibly the single most overriding adult objection to children's popular texts is the prevalence of violence. Superhero sagas, cartoons, action-adventure films and programmes, comics, magazines and video games have all been condemned for the level of violence which saturates them. In the following section, we examine some of these views and suggest ways in which children can be encouraged to engage with a critical analysis of the violence embedded within their favourite texts.

Violence

There is no doubt that children's popular culture is permeated with images of violence. Superheroes use kicks, weapons and tricks to overcome their enemies. Computer games often involve the player 'shooting up', 'zapping' or blasting opponents. Toy guns and war toys encourage an obsession with death on a large scale. Children regularly have access to films and videos which tolerate, even at times celebrate, violence. There has been much concern that an exposure to violence encourages its use by children. However, it has been stated many times that there is little conclusive evidence to suggest that there is a direct effect between the watching of screen violence and children's use of violence in everyday life (Barker and Petley, 1997). Nevertheless, we would want to caution against the desire to seek simple answers to complex questions. As McLaren and Morris (1998) suggest:

> television programs can help to produce specific economies of affect-mattering maps that need to be understood conjuncturally, in relation to the social and cultural settings where the viewers watch the show, the individual subjectivities of the viewers and the ways in which their subjective formations mediate, engage, or resist the show's many competing discourses (and this may involve the race, class, sexual orientation, and other characteristics of the viewers) and the specific articulations that are made among the structures of violence in the show and family violence, schoolyard violence, violence in organized sports, and so on.
>
> (McLaren and Morris, 1998, p. 118)

In other words, what is going on in children's lives will impact on whether the violence in television programmes and other cultural texts is one of the determining factors in their use of violence in real life. Moral panics about violence in popular culture ignore the fact that for many children, violence within the home or community is a regular feature of daily life. Many children are subject to emotional, sexual or physical abuse in the home by adults, with some estimating that such abuse affects 60 per cent of American children (Denzin, 1987). Yet, when the media focus on the violence of modern youth, such as we see regularly in the USA school-shootings, the violence children are exposed to in the media is blamed, rather than looking at more complex social, economic and cultural factors such as hegemonic constructions of masculinity or adult fascination with, and ownership of, guns.

The discussion of violence in cotemporary children's lives needs also to be tempered with a close look at the role violence has had in children's play throughout history. Both French (1987) and Rotundo (1998) outline how war games and games which featured physical defeat of an opponent, such as 'Cowboys and Indians', have been a feature of children's play for centuries. What has changed is the nature of the violence perpetrated. Before television and video, violence in play was physical in that the proponents touched each other. That in itself limits the type of violent moves possible. You can kill your opponent, but then he or she can get up again to fight another round. Pushing and shoving does not lead to torn limbs and final exits. However, in some computer games, graphic representations of violence are commonplace and once you have zapped the enemy, they generally cannot be reincarnated; death is final. Some may be concerned that the difference in the type of violence involved in children's play today affects children's behaviour adversely. Gunter and Harrison (1997), in a study of children and television violence, argued that it does not, because children are well aware of the fictive nature of the violence they watch. In an extensive analysis of screen violence, they suggest that 'Much of the violence found in children's programmes took place in unreal settings or circumstances, involving either animated characters or fantastic superheroes . . . Much of the violence therefore had "fairy tale" qualities about it' (Gunter and Harrison, 1997, p. 152).

Despite the lack of conclusive evidence of a direct effect, many primary teachers do find themselves concerned about the damaging potential of programmes in which violence is a strong feature. Superhero play has been banned in some nurseries and classrooms, with a general reluctance to let children engage with related discourses in the context of schooling (Sousa and Schneiderman, 1986). Anecdotal evidence suggests that many a child who has wanted to base a narrative on a popular cultural theme has been persuaded otherwise by anxious teachers, who would prefer not to read stories focused on fighting. The introduction of the Mighty Morphin Power Rangers, a superhero gang who engaged regularly in violence, resulted in widespread dissatisfaction from teachers about the level of interest in such figures from the children they taught (Levin and Carlsson-Paige, 1995).

Nevertheless, despite teacher disapproval of such texts and role models, it is clear that they hold quite a sway over the interests and emotions of a large number of young children, including girls (Marsh, 2000a). Violence is usually constructed around male discourses of power and it cannot be challenged in isolation from other constructs such as gender and 'race'. However, challenged it must be. Some have argued that it may be counterproductive to engage children in a dialogue about the violence contained in popular and media texts, as it could be seen as an attempt to impose an adult agenda on children (Grace and Tobin, 1998). Children may simply respond with answers that appear to corroborate the adult's view, leaving their own opinions relatively unchallenged (Buckingham and Sefton-Green, 1994). However, we would argue that the oppressive messages contained within children's cultural texts do need to be challenged by adults and that not all children will be able to work through these problems without some adult intervention. Children need to be offered alternative discourses, even if they do not choose to take them up. The most effective way of helping children to become more critically aware of the hegemonic discourses is to begin with children's own experiences of exclusion and oppression, and use these as a means for developing an analysis of wider concerns. The next section provides an example of how a class of 6-year-olds was helped to consider some of the issues involved.

The children were asked about their own experiences of violence. Many of the stories they told contained complaints about bullying from other children. They were asked to describe how they felt when they had been subjected to violence. The children used words such as 'hurt', 'small', 'angry', 'unfair'. This was then used as an opportunity to discuss the effects of violence in real life. The children were asked to think about the violence they saw on television and in video games. They were asked if they thought it had the same effects. The children were clearly able to distinguish between the violence in real life and that in popular culture.

JM: We talked about fighting in the playground and how you didn't like being hurt. What about when you watch fighting on television and films? How does that make you feel?
Ben: It's only pretend.
Moshmi: Yeah and they only look like there's blood but it's not.
Aaron: They get up again and go (mimics karate kick) when they dead!
Ben: It's not real, you know.

JM: Some people think that if you watch fighting on television, it makes you want to fight in the playground. What do you think about that?
Ben: Nah 'cos it's not real fighting and that.

The children were then involved in considering non-violent solutions to a problem. They were asked to think about how superheroes could defeat baddies without hurting them. These were a few of the suggestions:

- Catch the baddies and put them in jail.
- Play tricks on the baddies to catch them.
- Get the baddies in a room and lock them in.
- Give the baddies a map that takes them somewhere so far away they cannot get back.

The class were subsequently asked to write a story about a superhero in which the superhero defeated the baddies through non-violent means. Some children were able to sustain a non-aggressive narrative (see Figure 2.1). Other children were not able to maintain a non-violent stance (see Figure 2.2). These examples were discussed with the children and the difficulty of sustaining a non-violent narrative when writing about superheroes was acknowledged.

We are not suggesting that this rather superficial activity would in itself solve the difficulties surrounding violence in popular culture. That was not its intention; rather, it provided an opportunity for children to engage with an oppositional or contradictory discourse which otherwise they might not explore. Other ways in which violence could be examined by young children include the making of a documentary video in which violence in children's media is the focus, research conducted by pupils into the response to violent texts experienced by their peers, a study of violent toys and games used by their parents and grandparents, and a review of the amount and type of violence within children's television over a week. Such activities would enable children to explore the complexities of attitudes and reactions and also remind teachers that the issue of children's exposure to violence has been around for many years. Through such activities, we can provide children with tools to analyse the world around them and become more critically aware of its values.

Sexism

From their earliest years, children have been shown to hold strong opinions about their gender positionings (Whyte, 1983; Davies, 1990;

Figure 2.1 'I am Bananaman, and I will trick the baddies.' So he did, and he put a banana, and strawberries, and a green olive. And the baddies came running over to the food. And they got caught in a net. The end

Figure 2.2 Batman will trip the baddies up when they are being naughty. And Batman will head butt them. And Batman will bash them. Batman will trick them by going to his friend and saying to him go to him and tell him that you are on his side and make him go to town so I can knee him

Thorne, 1993) and their gender identities are actively constructed throughout their schooling (Davies, 1993; Mac an Ghaill, 1994; Millard, 1997). Weedon (1987) identifies three main strands of thought which seek to explain gender differences: scientific, psychoanalytical and social and historical. Millard (1997) noted that the scientific theories, which focus on biological differences, are widely disputed, along with Freudian psychoanalytical theories. The most generally accepted explanation for gendered differences locates them firmly within the theories of social construction, although with some recognition that there are specific biological differences upon which gender is built.

Many post-structuralists perceive the development of gendered positions to be a discursive battle and, as Weedon, states, at 'the centre of the struggle is the common-sense assumption that there is a natural way for girls, boys, women and men to be' (Weedon, 1987, p. 98). The social construction of gender operates in a number of ways. From birth, children are subjected to propaganda which identifies particular roles and kinds of behaviour as inherently male or female (Solsken, 1993; Millard, 1997). Sex-role stereotyping becomes cemented by habitual practices in society which serve to reinforce gender stereotypes. Weedon (1987) emphasizes how many of the daily practices associated with gender distinctions are constructed as 'common sense' by society and soon become widely accepted as true and proper. These 'gender regimes' (Kessler *et al*, 1985; Harris, Nixon and Rudduck, 1993; Millard 1997) serve to reinforce sex stereotypes: 'Actions performed in similar contexts on a daily basis have the effect of reinforcing the dominant (patriarchal) structures of society and uniformity of gendered behaviour' (Millard, 1997, p. 21).

It does not follow from the existence of these gender regimes that children will always take up conventional positions in relation to their own identities. Post-structuralism suggests that there is no unitary 'self' that stays the same, but rather that people are a mixture of various thoughts and emotions which are constantly in flux and subject to influences from without: that is, we have different 'subjectivities' which cannot be unified. It is, therefore, possible to hold beliefs, opinions and thoughts which are diametrically opposed to each other. Individuals are not entirely shaped by outside influences but, to a certain extent, are responsible for actively constructing their subjectivities. How far people are agents in their own subjective construction is a complex issue discussed by Smith (1987), Griffiths (1995), Davies (1990; 1997) and Jones (1997) amongst others. However, it is clear that individuals are more constrained in certain circumstances and their choices are determined by factors such as 'race', class, sex, sexuality, language or physical ability. In addition in some situations, children are non-agents, at times unwillingly or unknowingly positioned by events or by others.

Young children are often so determined to take up gendered identities that they engage in what Thorne (1993) terms 'borderwork' and Davies (1989) identifies as 'category-maintenance' work. These terms refer to those incidents when children are intent on emphasizing that their gendered identities as 'boys' and 'girls' are in opposition to the other category, sometimes characterized by denigration of the other group. Derrida's (1967) work is useful in analysing this phenomenon because he proposed that in any binary opposition, there is an ascendant category and a subordinate category. Thus, 'white', in Western cultures, is often used as a positive term ('white lies') and 'black' as negative ('black day'). In binary pairs such as 'males' and 'females', 'girls' and boys', males/boys are often perceived to be in the ascendant category and females/girls in the subordinate category. Davies (1997) asserts that it is often difficult for those placed in an ascendant category to understand the processes that are at work:

> They take their category membership to be normal, and normative, and those located in the other category to be marked by their difference. People inhabiting ascendant categories such as male, heterosexual, white, middle-class, able-bodied, adult or sane, often wonder what all the fuss is about, and doubt even the relevance of their own category membership in determining who they might be.
>
> (Davies, 1997, p. 13)

On the other hand, people confined to the negative, or subordinate, category are well aware of the discourses of the powerful through their experiences with education, government and society in general and are more able to see the other's position. This is a powerful theory which can be used to account for much of children's gendered behaviour. For example, girls are often willing to take on male identities and incorporate the wishes of boys in their role-play, but boys are usually unwilling to demonstrate a similar level of adaptability (Davies, 1990, 1992; Jordan, 1995; Francis, 1998; MacNaughton, 1997). Girls can thus be seen, using Davies' terms, to be 'bi-cognitive, or bi-modal' (Davies 1997, p. 27). In addition, boys are often unwilling to discuss issues of sexism and power (Davies, 1993) which suggests that, as they are in the ascendant category, they are unable to understand the experiences of the subordinate category.

Philips (1993) and Millard (1997) suggest that boys are disadvantaged to some extent by the limited range of masculinities on offer, particularly in school settings where 'being a lad' militates against seeking success in educational terms. However, this limited choice is offset by the fact that the masculine positions available to boys often provide them with greater power in a wider societal sense. Power, according to Foucault (1979), is not fixed; it can be held in different discourses at different times. So, for example, in some circumstances middle-class, white girls have more power than working-class black and white boys. In other circumstances, the female gender is a subordinate positioning whether one is white or black, working or middle class.

This brief examination of the way in which gender identities are constructed is necessary before any exploration of the sexism that is a strong feature of much of children's popular culture. The gendered discourses which are embedded so deeply within popular cultural texts have a large part to play in constructing the gender regimes we mentioned earlier. One only has to have a cursory glance at the field to note examples of the highly gendered discourses that have been offered to children: My Little Pony, Polly Pocket and Barbie were all marketed directly to girls; boys were at the same time being led towards Teenage Mutant Ninja Turtles, X Men and Batman. Young children are more than able to categorize popular cultural texts and artefacts according to perceived gendered interests (Marsh, 1998). Such texts and artefacts become markers of identity and children take great care to ensure these gender boundaries are maintained: real boys do not play with Barbie, unless it is to deface her. However, it is not clear how far these gendered toys and popular cultural icons help to define children's identity and how far they are actively taken up by children in order to reinforce that identity to others. Francis, in a study of gendered ways of being with 6- and 7-year-old children, concluded that, 'Rather than being persuaded to take up such forms of play by the forces of socialisation, children use such toys actively to demonstrate their gender' (Francis, 1998, p. 36).

It can be argued that the feminist movement did bring more awareness to the culture industries and that more powerful female role models now exist. Thus apologists point to Xena, the warrior-princess, or Lara in *Tomb Raider*, as examples of the move toward equality. However, it is clear that these icons are vacuous in terms of gender politics. Both are portrayed as physically attractive, either scantily clad as in the case of Xena, or with a tight-fitting T-shirt, as in the case of Lara. Their physical attributes are integral to the character, in a way which is more exaggerated than in male heroes. This feature is not atypical; female superhero figures are usually constructed as heterosexually desirable and inferior in status to males (Marsh, 2000a). If a female character is portrayed as brave and assertive, it is not long before more stereotypically feminine attributes are emphasized. A recent copy of *Disney's Big Time*, a comic aimed at children in the middle years, described Jessie, a female character in *Toy Story 2*, thus:

> She's a feisty little cowgirl who's not afraid to stand up to anyone – and that includes Woody! Having been outgrown by the girl who once owned her, Jessie has a big fear of being abandoned. She might come across as being tough but deep down, she's a softy at heart.
>
> (*Disney's Big Time*, issue 87, p. 7)

So it can be seen that genuinely independent, anti-sexist and challenging images of women and girls are hard to find in children's popular culture. However, Seiter (1993) suggests that rather than see girls' orientation toward such sexist and oppressive icons as Barbie and My Little Pony as reductive, we should recognize that they are positive choices for female iconography in a predominantly masculinist popular cultural universe:

> Parents should understand that for the little girl at the video or toy store to choose My Little Pony, then, is to make a quite rational choice among the limited offerings of children's consumer culture. The choice is not made out of identification with an insipid and powerless femininity but out of identification with the limited sources of power and fantasy that are available in the commercial culture of femininity.
>
> (Seiter, 1993, p. 171)

If the assertive female is othered in children's popular culture, then so too is the sensitive male. Popular culture offers only particular versions of masculinity. Connell's (1987) work has outlined how 'hegemonic masculinity' and 'emphasized femininity' are constructs which provide limits on how we define our identities. So boys are framed within heterosexual and powerful discourses which push them into roles in which violence and aggression is celebrated. Children are quick to deconstruct such images, but it is not clear if this level of analysis really challenges the boundaries of their identities. No matter how much we provide counter-hegemonic messages, children still appear to take up highly gendered discourses. However, it is also clear that children's reactions to these discourses are both accepting and resistant at the same time. For example, in a role-play area which was set up as a Batman and Batwoman Headquarters in an infant classroom, many girls demonstrated both assertive, independent characterization in role-play as Batwoman, as well as acquiescence to hegemonic masculine discourses (Marsh, 2000a).

As in the earlier discussion on violence, it is important to provide opportunities for young children to deconstruct the gendered nature of popular discourse, in order to further their understanding of the way in which our identities are shaped by cultural and societal norms. However, we need to do this from a standpoint which accepts children's own experiences and agendas if such a task is to be effective. The following examples are based on work conducted in infant classrooms in which images from popular culture were used as a means of challenging children to question hegemonic ideologies.

Barbie as superhero

The work was conducted with a class of 5- and 6-year-old children. The session began with a whole-class discussion on superheroes. The children were asked to make a list of the superheroes they knew. Not one woman appeared on this list. The children were reminded of Xena, Batgirl and Supergirl, but it was obvious that these were on the periphery of anyone's interest, including that of the girls. There followed a discussion on the gendered nature of the superhero discourse, in which it was clear that the children felt that men should be superheroes as they were stronger. The children were then asked if they wanted to write a story about a girl who was a superhero. The activity was conceived in this way because, if simply asked to write about a superhero, both boys and girls would have been likely to choose a male superhero. This was the case for an American educator, Jennifer Moon, who asked a group of children to draw themselves as a superhero. All the girls in the group drew themselves as male (Alvermann, Moon and Hagood, 1999). In the case of the class featured here, none of the boys volunteered for the task of creating a female superhero, but a number of girls did. Any hopes that this would lead to an empowered discourse in which girls were filled with visions of danger and glory, however, were soon dashed. Almost all of the girls chose Barbie as their unlikely superhero. She was most often framed within a domestic setting, as Tasheen's writing shows (Figure 2.3). Not only does her hero have a house drawn on her outfit, but Super Barbie goes

Figure 2.3 Super Barbie went to her mums house her dad said, 'You are brave.' She saved people from the witch

Figure 2.4 Once there was a Barbie and two baddies. The baddies were trying to fight. So Barbie was going to tell the police

Figure 2.5 When the Supergirl jumped on the floor she banged her head. She had blud on her head. She had a plaster on her head. Superman come to the Supergirl and then Superman and the Supergirl tidied up because it was a mess. A Spiderman come and he made a mess and then Superman and Supergirl tidied up again. A man come and sit down. He said, 'It is tidy'

straight to her mum's house and receives affirmation from her dad that she is brave when she saves people from the witch.

Lucy's Barbie-hero fared little better (Figure 2.4). In this piece, she faces two baddies but feels that her only recourse is to tell the police rather than defeat them herself, as a male superhero undoubtedly would have done.

Aisha's Supergirl would rather clean the house than save the world (Figure 2.5). This Supergirl cannot even jump about without hurting herself, but at least she gets Superman to help her tidy up!

Most of the figures produced by the girls failed to achieve the action and agency exhibited by male superheroes. This echoes other research in which girls, whilst acting out powerful discourses in role-play, positioned the female superhero as subordinate to the male in their writing (Marsh, 1999). Nevertheless, engaging the children in such tasks is important. Obviously, such work will not be sufficient for children to develop the critical skills necessary to deconstruct gendered discourses, however, it does provide a brief opportunity to engage with alternative positions.

Other activities which can be used to challenge young children's assumptions about the gendered nature of popular discourse are familiar and effective. Although advertising is improving, there are still plenty of examples of particular toys and cultural icons being targeted at boys or girls. These can be analysed, with children creating their own non-sexist adverts. Comics and magazines are an obvious source of material for studying gendered discourses. In a class of Year 5 children aged 9 and 10, children soon identified that many of the computer magazines which were popular were targeted at boys. They identified language which was used to appeal to boys, images of women as objects of desire and the almost exclusive use of male journalists.

The same class was able to suggest how video games were created to appeal to boys. Epstein (1993) has suggested that children might be asked to deconstruct gender stereotyping in printed texts by rewriting them using an oppositional discourse, or producing book reviews which analyse the level of gender discrimination. These techniques can be applied equally to televisual texts.

Racism

The gendered and violent discourse of children's popular culture has been widely analysed, the racism less so. However, it is clear that racism permeates much of the popular culture produced by large media corporations. Black characters are, if they appear at all, often marginal to the action, whether the text we examine is a film, video or computer game. Villains in many of the texts are often dark skinned. In an analysis of Disney films, Giroux (1998) outlined the racist nature of narratives such as *Lion King*, *Pocahontas* and *Aladdin*. Stereotypes abound, such as the portrayal of Native American Indians in *Pocahontas* and Arab people in *Aladdin*. Giroux notes that:

> racism in Disney's animated films does not simply appear in negative imagery or through historical misrepresentation; racist ideology also appears in racially coded language and accents. For example, *Aladdin* portrays the 'bad' Arabs with thick, foreign accents, whereas the anglicised Jasmine and *Aladdin* speak in standard, Americanized English . . . these films produce a host of representations and codes in which

children are taught that cultural differences that do not bear the imprint of white, middle-class ethnicity are deviant, inferior, ignorant, and a threat to be overcome.

(Giroux, 1998, p. 62)

However, racism in children's 'mainstream' popular culture is not confined to Disney. Films and television programmes aimed at children either exclude black characters altogether, or include tokenistic characters who remain forever on the sidelines of the narrative. In identifying the inherent racism of such texts, we are not suggesting that they should be discounted completely, or only looked at critically. A text such as Disney's *Lion King* also has confirmatory messages for some cultural groups, as one nursery teacher suggests: 'The children in my class love *Lion King*. Many of them come from Somalia and the lion represents aspects of their cultural heritage.'

An examination of toy manufacturing also leads to accusations of ethno-centricism as few toys reach the children's markets which portray black characters in a realistic manner. Mattel, after extensive criticism of its focus on producing all-white Barbies, introduced a 'Dolls of the World' range. Rogers (1999) outlines how these dolls were stereotypically designed and marketed, with hair and features modelled on the white doll and packaging which portrayed communities in reductive and offensive ways. The white Barbie thus becomes the marker for all others and is seen as the 'true' Barbie in many children's eyes. Other ranges fare little better, with black characters appearing as an afterthought, if they appear at all.

There are a number of ways in which children can engage in an analysis of the racist nature of many of the popular cultural texts they encounter. Simply cutting out black and white characters in children's comics and magazines and placing them in various categories can illuminate a number of issues. On a very simple level, children will realize that white characters are more frequently presented than black characters. An analysis of the roles that black characters have in these texts will often illustrate how they are marginalized by their positioning, almost exclusively, in the discourses of music and sport. Television programmes and films can be used for a similar analysis and children can be encouraged to produce written critiques of such products. One Year 3 class worked on a radio programme which provided an analysis of racism in children's media. Interviews were conducted with adults from a range of communities in which they were asked about their memories of their childhood cultures and how far it reflected their lives. Children can also be encouraged to produce media texts of their own in which they can be involved in the production of more positive images.

Class issues

Class issues have also been under-analysed in any work on popular culture. However, they permeate the discourses just as densely. Villains in popular cultural texts are often portrayed as working class. Kincheloe, in an analysis of the film *Home Alone*, notes how the affluent world of the boy left home alone, Kevin, is invaded by two villains, Harry and Marv:

> Harry (Pesci) and Marv (Stren) are quickly positioned as 'the other' in both screenplays: they speak in specific lower-socio-economic-class accents; obviously ethnic, Pesci exaggerates his working-class Italian accent; and just so we are not confused Stren signifies his Jewishness with a curiously gratutitous 'Happy Hanukkah' reference as he steals money from a toy store.
>
> (Kincheloe, 1998, p. 43)

Working-class children seldom feature as the central characters in children's films and television programmes and, if they do, they are often used to introduce problematic storylines such as abuse, theft and drugs. In addition, children who are brought up in single-parent families are often portrayed as having numerous attendant problems. If working-class families do appear in soap operas, they are usually living in neat housing estates with a job and a car and are obviously not families who are struggling on the edge. Although one in four children in Britain currently live in poverty, we rarely see the children of the unemployed in popular cultural texts. Again, points such as this should be raised with children in order for them to understand how some groups are excluded from mainstream discourses.

Our examination of oppressive ideologies in children's popular culture is by no means complete. Disability is another issue which is sidelined in children's popular culture. There are no disabled superheroes or disabled dolls, apart from Mattel's surprising introduction of a wheelchair-bound doll. Gay teenagers are virtually non-existent in mainstream popular culture, as are children who are brought up in gay families. In addition, Tobin (2000) points out that villains in popular cultural texts are almost always men who do not appear to have any family ties and:

in the equation of womanless and childless men with danger, I perceive the workings of homophobia. Bad guys in Disney films are often effeminate (I'm thinking, for example, of the vanity and prissiness of Captain Hook in *Peter Pan*, Gaston in *Beauty and the Beast*, Jafar in *Aladdin*, Governor Ratcliffe in *Pocahontas*, and Scar in *The Lion King*) . . . Effeminacy aside, the suggestion that men who don't live in families are dangerous to children is a pernicious fiction in the morally panicked, homophobic era in which we live . . .

(Tobin, 2000, p. 134)

These oppressive discourses should not surprise us; there is no reason why popular cultural texts should be more inclusive than other cultural forms, but it does leave teachers with the task of making the invisible visible and the visible more transparent. However, it is not only ideologies such as these which prevent many teachers from working with children's popular culture. Other aspects also deter educationalists from making good use of their narratives.

Another enduring worry for many teachers is children's penchant for the horror genre. What is it about horror that attracts children so much? The attraction is not confined to children; many adults enjoy horror stories, whether in books or film form. Twitchell (1985) argues that engaging with the horror genre helps us to overcome our fears and engage with our subliminal desires. Indeed Gaut (1993) has argued that 'monsters can serve as metaphors for our fears' (Gaut, 1993, p. 335). Horror has been a long-standing genre in literature and reached its zenith for adults at the end of the nineteenth century, with texts such as Bram Stoker's *Dracula* and Mary Shelley's *Frankenstein*. Horror series for children are usually devoid of the sexual undertones which are a feature of adult horror, but they do have a similar fascination with the fear of the unknown. In recent years, we have seen the popularity of such series as *Point Horror* and *Goosebumps* which have sold in large numbers across the world. The crazes on the *Point Horror* and *Goosebumps* series have led to a number of schools banning these texts, as they are seen to be of little educational value and thought to lead to mindless addiction. However, in Chapter 5, we examine how teachers have drawn on children's fascination with the genre to help them in motivating literacy work.

An underlying feature of the continuing antipathy towards children's popular culture is the emphasis on its apparent ability to produce zombie-like figures in children who are mindlessly in thrall to the latest craze. The role of the market in the production and maintenance of children as consumers is a continual worry (Kline, 1993).

However, this view of children is one that is predicated on a notion of the child as innocent victim. We would argue that there is a need to acknowledge the active part that children play in the construction of their own culture. Adults may develop and market specific products, but these are not always received in the ways intended. Products designed for children by adults can prove to be financially unsuccessful. Many superheroes are developed and fall from grace with barely a glance from most children. In addition, the work of Erica Rand (1998) demonstrates how Barbie dolls have been marketed by Mattel in ways which suggest that she is the all-American, archetypal female, yet decades of children have resisted these attempts to impose such a view of femininity. Thus girls have abused their dolls, cutting off protruding breasts and changing Barbie's head for Ken's, whilst others have used the dolls to explore both heterosexual and homosexual burgeoning erotic fantasies. Children will make resistant readings of cultural texts, just as adults adapt and refine cultural texts aimed at them. As Rowe states: 'To ignore or marginalize the economic and ideological dimensions of popular culture like, for example, the more anodyne, pluralistic "the-public-gets-what-the-public-wants" models or the more ecstatic forms of postmodernism would be to paint too voluntaristic and Panglossian a picture' (Rowe, 1995, p. 11).

Thus, we should not ignore the market-driven forces which provide the impetus for the production of much of children's popular culture and overemphasize children's autonomous choices in the construction of their culture. There is often enormous peer pressure to own certain cultural goods. Manufacturers are aware of children's passion for collecting and so certain brands are developed which will exploit this. For example, the Beanie Baby phenomenon has demonstrated the power of introducing artefacts that have limited distribution dates and thus are made more desirable. TY, the company that manufactures these soft toys, used clever marketing ploys to sell their products, which included limited release of some versions of the toys and normal distribution of others. Many shops insisted that customers had to buy three or four of the readily available soft toys before they could purchase the rarer versions. Queues formed outside shops as news of the arrival of a limited version spread. As a result, TY saw their profit margin of $250 million in 1996 rise to over $1 billion in 1998. Similarly, as indicated in the Introduction, a key element of the advertising campaign for the Japanese video game, Pokémon, has been to persuade children to collect all of the Pokémon characters (of which there are over 100) and so the catchphrase used in the discourse, 'Gotta catch 'em all!' is indicative of this type of marketing strategy. Such artefacts, which become collector's items and fuel childhood obsessions are nothing new, as the manufacturers who used football cards to draw customers in the early twentieth century knew very well. What has changed is the cost of these artefacts, the power of the advertising campaigns developed to encourage such obsessions and the sophisticated marketing techniques used by the producers.

There are a number of key influences on the production and marketing of children's popular culture both in Britain and internationally. The McDonaldization (Ritzer, 1998) effect can be seen to exist in relation to Americanized cultural texts which are merchandised around the world, with youngsters in many countries wanting the latest USA-derived superhero toy or video. Teenage Mutant Ninja Turtles, Power Rangers, X-Men and latterly, South Park characters, all originated from US television programming. The Disney Corporation, an American company, takes a large share of the world video market, as well as providing a range of toys and games based on the characters. However, Japan also has a strong influence on the popular culture of children in industrialized societies as they have introduced a series of electronic gadgets and toys which have caught children's imagination. For example, the introduction of the Tamagotchi in recent years was very successful. This was a small, hand-held toy with a liquid crystal display screen on which a virtual pet could be seen. Children had to feed, water and exercise this pet regularly, otherwise it died. The craze led to many schools banning the toys as children frantically tried to keep their pets alive and so were distracted from their school tasks. Some people saw the introduction of this toy as a sad reflection on the times:

> the Tamagotchi is a metaphor of our times, representing the blurring of boundaries between real and reciprocal relationships and surrogate, one-way, imaginary ones. It highlights the dominant role of technology in our lives; no longer simply a tool for use in science and industry, but now a substitute for human relationships.
>
> (Bloch and Lemish, 1999, p. 295).

The moral panic surrounding the increasingly commercial and technologized aspects of children's culture is thus not a localized fear, but global, as American and Japanese toys dominate the international market. Parents' and teachers' apprehension is fuelled by elements of the media, which tend to portray children as mindless zombies, brainwashed by the latest video game or toy and subject to the whims of manufacturers.

There is no doubt that children's popular cultural texts contain a range of transgressive and ideologically oppressive discourses, as we have seen in this chapter. We are not advocating a simplistic celebration of children's culture as we embed it into the literacy curriculum. Rather, we would argue that there is a need to engage children in productive and critical analyses of these texts, whilst not dismissing the intense pleasure they receive from them. This is a difficult balancing act that can only be achieved through a teaching approach which begins with a familiarity with, and respect for, children's experiences. In the next chapter, we move on to examine how children's engagement with a range of popular cultural texts forms a crucial part of their literacy development through play.

Note

1. Throughout the book, children's spellings will be regularized in order to facilitate reading.

3

Play and Popular Culture

Play is embedded within socio-cultural practices and so is intimately related to popular culture. However, in any discussion of play, it is difficult to get beyond the pervasive middle-class ideology presented by much of the work and we often see the experiences of a particularly privileged group of children articulated as the norm. The construction of play within an idealized and sanitized version of childhood ignores the fact that, in reality, play is as diverse as the children (and adults) who engage in it.

In any discussion of play, it is helpful to have as clear an understanding as possible of what can be a nebulous concept. Definitions of play are shaped by socio-cultural concerns and subject to political and economic constraints. There have been many attempts to produce definitive statements about what play is over the years but perhaps we should turn to Garvey's (1977) definitions which can provide a useful starting point:

1. Play is pleasurable, enjoyable. Even when not actually accompanied by signs of mirth, it is still positively valued by the player.
2. Play has no extrinsic goals. Its motivations are intrinsic and serve no other objectives. In fact, it is more an enjoyment of means than an effort devoted to some particular end. In utilitarian terms, it is inherently unproductive.
3. Play is spontaneous and voluntary. It is not obligatory but is freely chosen by the player.
4. Play involves some active engagement on the part of the player

(Garvey, 1977, p. 10).

In this definition, play is voluntary and not undertaken to pursue any specific goals. These seem to be important qualities, as play is an activity over which children have control and which they can use to meet their own agendas. Play appears to function as a means of enabling children to work out things for themselves, whether that is in social, emotional, cognitive or physical domains. However, there are differences of opinion as to the nature of play. Garvey (1977) asserts that it is always pleasurable, however, Vygotsky (1986) does suggest that play is not necessarily synonymous with pleasure, in that some play could provoke unpleasant feelings. If we accept that play can provide a means for children to explore difficult issues, then this would be a reasonable supposition to make.

There have also been widespread discussions concerning the classification of types of play. This discussion is beyond the scope of this chapter, although we will focus on specific types of play here: games, small-world and socio-dramatic role-play. Nurseries and schools promote particular versions of play through their provision. Let us take one specific type of play as an example of this phenomenon: small-world play, or microworlds. Reiber (1992), who has focused on the use of microworlds in computers, suggests that they are miniature versions of complete domains of interest. However, domains of interest are most often defined by teachers rather than children and thus we often see small-world play in classrooms replete with images of zoos, jungles and fantastical landscapes with dinosaurs and reptiles. Yet at home, children can be immersed in microworlds relating to films and television, such as *Star Wars* or *Power Rangers*. This type of microworld play is rarely sanctioned within educational settings. Although this is one small example, it is clear that it is not isolated. Socio-dramatic role-play, play with bricks, outdoor play: all are constrained by adult visions of what such play should look like.

In addition, it appears that each generation feels that it has the monopoly on the definition of play. So we often hear nostalgic cries for the days in which play which was less materialistic in nature, more socially cohesive and free from worries of violence, racism or sexism. However, it is clear that children's play in the days before television permeated their lives was not free from ideological concerns or violence and aggression. As mentioned in the previous chapter, French's (1987) survey of childhood pastimes over this century identified a strong tradition of games such as 'Cowboys and Indians', 'Cops and Robbers' and war games, all potentially violent, xenophobic and sexist. Because contemporary children's play is often bound up with popular cultural icons which are unfamiliar to many adults, suspicion is cast as to its inherent value. This has the effect of shutting nursery and classroom doors firmly against this perceived rising tide of corruption, in what becomes a mythological construction of both childhood and contemporary culture. As Walkerdine (1999) has suggested, these 'grand metanarratives of modernity elide the specificities of childhood in the present' (Walkerdine, 1999, p. 4).

The research on play and culture has been centred primarily in anthropological accounts of the nature of play in different countries and cultures (Farver, 1992; Nwokah and Ikekeonwu, 1998). From this work, it is clear that play means very different things in different societies and there is a need to avoid making generalizations about the subject which cannot be applied to all cultural groups. When research has focused on socio-economic factors associated with play, it has tended to create a deficit model, in which working-class children are perceived to engage in less symbolic role-play (Smilansky, 1968; Fein and Stork, 1981). Ramsey (1998) suggests that these findings may relate to the provision of artefacts in the role-play areas in which the research was carried out: 'role play props and books that reflect more middle-class lifestyles create for middle-class children a more familiar context than for low-income children' (Ramsey, 1998, p. 28).

Because the nature and extent of play does differ in children's lives according to their socio-cultural background, it is crucial to incorporate the cultural capital of all children into the play curriculum. This would not only enable children to feel that the classroom reflects their lives and interests, but would have benefits in relation to a range of other skills, including literacy.

There has been a range of significant work which has examined the relationship between literacy and play. One key strand of research in the area has focused on the uses children make of literacy-related material in role-play areas and the attendant benefits of these experiences. Roskos (1990), Christie (1991), Neuman and Roskos (1992, 1993), Vukelich (1991) and Hall and Robinson (1995) all demonstrate that incorporating writing and reading materials and activities into play situations can provide children with an opportunity to extend their uses of literacy and explore some of its real functions and purposes. Some studies assert that the use of literacy materials in a role-play area has a direct effect on children's literacy development. Vukelich (1994) carried out a study which examined the effects of exposure to print on 56 Reception children in a role-play area. The presence of an adult using the print in a naturalized way with the children, significantly increased the children's ability to read environmental print both in and out of context. From their review of the literature, Isenberg and Jacob (1983) assert that 'In sum, the literature suggests that engaging in symbolic play and incorporating literacy into symbolic play can have a positive influence on early literacy development' (Isenberg and Jacob, 1983, p. 274). In examining why play should have this effect on children's literacy development, there are a number of factors to consider. The first is that of play and cognitive development.

There has been a range of work which suggests that play can enhance cognitive development. Vygotsky (1978) suggested that, during play, children could achieve higher levels of cognition than at other times:

> thus, play creates a zone of proximal development of the child. In play a child always behaves beyond his average age, above his daily behaviour; in play it is as though he were a head taller than himself. As in the focus of a magnifying glass, play contains all developmental tendencies in a condensed form and is itself a major source of development.
>
> (Vygotsky, 1978, p. 102)

It would be useful here to introduce the distinction Hutt *et al.* (1989) make between epistemic and ludic play in relation to cognitive development. They suggested that the type of play which involves finding out about objects through problem-solving and investigation, epistemic play, does lead to cognitive development, to the acquisition of new knowledge. The second type of play, ludic play, involves playing with objects; not finding out about them, but finding out what can be done with them. Hutt *et al.* (1989) suggest that this type of play may only indirectly lead to learning. Incorporating literacy resources into play areas can enhance both epistemic and ludic play as children explore the materials and use them in problem-solving situations. In addition, Singer and Singer in 1990 provided a range of evidence to show that play helped children to develop oral language and improved a range of their cognitive skills. Similarly, Johnson (1990) reviewed the literature and identified a number of studies which demonstrated a positive correlation between play and cognitive development. As Wood and Attfield (1996) note, Johnson's work is important because it emphasizes that 'play serves an important cognitive consolidating function by assisting in the child's construction of meaning from experience. Intrinsic curiosity and motivation act as a spur to cognitive processes such as developing understanding, problem solving and making sense' (Wood and Attfield, 1996, p. 24). Thus it appears that there is evidence to suggest that play does have a positive effect on both cognitive and literacy development.

Second, play can allow children to experiment with a range of forms for representing the world. Meek suggests that play can introduce children 'to a wide range of symbolic systems' (Meek, 1991, p. 88). In play, children represent one form of experience through the medium of another. This ability to use symbols constitutes an important stage in children's cognitive development (Vygotsky, 1978). Symbolic representation occurs in a variety of ways: a stick becomes a wand or a pen, a stone is transformed into a jewel or a precious object. Writing and drawing become part of the symbolic representation of meaning and experience and children learn to communicate in multi-modal ways. The work of Barrs (1988), Kress (1997) and Pahl (1999) outlines how children play with notational symbols, which include drawing, letters, numbers and other symbols. In addition, their model-making becomes part of their weaving of experience and meaning as the children play with the representational tools available to them. The playfulness inherent in the fluidity of these activities is a recognition from children that literacy is not a narrowly defined set of experiences, but a broad interaction with symbols and representation which should include 'gesture, movement, dance, music, listening, talking, drawing, painting, modelling, building, storytelling, poetry sharing, scientific and mathematical investigations, rituals and religious celebrations' (Whitehead, 1997, pp. 177–8).

Children are constantly engaged in decoding the reality represented in the world around them, interpreting it according to their own sociocultural practices and experiences and then encoding it, using whatever range of materials are available to them. Play enables children to encode multi-modally, challenging prevailing notions of what constitutes literacy within the usual confines of a nursery or classroom. Play can push at well-cemented boundaries because of its very nature. Children soon learn that no one will challenge them during play on their use of a crisp packet to represent a shopping bill, whereas they can face constraints in their use of particular representational materials in other classroom activities as they are told, 'You shouldn't use felt pens for that', or given similar restrictions. As Hall (1999) has said: 'play gains its meaning not from whether it is likely to be examined, marked or even approved by adults, but by whether it works as a meaningful script for children' (Hall, 1999, p. 107). This kind of experimental play occurs not only in relation to literacy, but also to oral skills and experiences. Children play with language as they explore puns, rhymes and raps. We also discuss this aspect of play in Chapters 4 and 9.

Third, children who may not feel confident in their language and literacy skills in the nursery and classroom can develop confidence through play. In a study of a role-play area which was transformed into a Batman and Batwoman HQ (Marsh, 1999), children who had previously been described by teachers as not confident or interested in literacy were recorded taking part in reading and writing activities within the HQ. These children not only willingly engaged in literacy practices within the role-play area, they also developed a greater thirst for engaging in more formal reading and writing activities in the classroom.

Again, this confidence can inform the children's oracy development, as play offers opportunities for experimenting with language in a low-risk situation. Play can encourage children to develop confidence in their linguistic skills as they engage in activities in a much less self-conscious manner than may be the case with more formalized activities within the curriculum. Because of this, play can also be a valuable means of developing confidence in the use of an additional language:

> Bilingual children who have been introduced to concepts using English vocabulary and encouraged to engage in play which allows them to explore these concepts have been observed practising the new terminology and trying to apply it to new situations. Play is thus extending their development of English and developing confidence.
>
> (Dodwell, 1999, p. 25)

Fourth, play integrates oracy and literacy in a meaningful way. There is a strong relationship between children's talk and literacy development (Whitehead, 1997). Play can be a particularly useful means of developing the skill of storying, or relating a narrative. Enacting events through play can enable children to retell them orally, thus developing their narrative skills. This ability is central to children's language and literacy development (Meek, Warlow and Barton, 1977; Whitehead, 1997). Play can help to develop 'inner speech', a running narrative on children's actions and thoughts. This metanarrative has been seen to be particularly important in the development of cognition (Vygotsky, 1978). In addition, play can encourage other metalinguistic skills which enable children to talk about language. It provides space for children to consider what might be an appropriate form of speech in a particular circumstance: 'When Yomi tells Shakeeta, "You need to yell at me to clean, 'cause you're the mean stepsister," she is talking about the type of language that fits the role. She is demonstrating

awareness of the tone and form of the language as well as its content'
(Freeman Davidson, 1998, p. 181).

Research has demonstrated that these metalinguistic skills are an
important part of the writing process (Dyson, 1989). As young children write, the accompanying narrative can slip in and out of storying
into a commentary on the writing itself. For example, as 4-year-old
Moshie wrote her recipe for ice-cream, she said, 'This is my ice-cream
and it's nice . . . it's got chocolate . . . I get it in the park with my
nannan . . . this says 'ice cream' . . . 'm' . . . this letter's 'm', it's got a
line . . . there . . . you can't eat it.'

The fifth consideration in relation to play and the literacy curriculum is that children can explore real-life uses of literacy through play.
As Hall's (1991, 1999; Hall and Robinson, 1995) work has demonstrated, socio-dramatic play offers children opportunities to explore
how reading and writing practices interface with their everyday
world, leading them to a greater understanding of the functionality of
literacy. This knowledge can then inform children's growing competence with the acts of reading and writing.

Finally, play enables children to enter realms of fantasy and desire
in which they can explore issues of independence and agency. They
may become the key player in events of their own making and, if
literacy is incorporated into these experiences, this agency takes on a
powerful role. Children see themselves reading and writing in em-
powering contexts which may contrast with those times in the life of
the nursery and classroom when literacy is associated with some level
of coercion. So it can be seen that play, with all its attendant benefits,
can have a powerful effect on the development of literacy. There are
opportunities for even greater benefits if play is able to draw from
children's popular cultural discourses. In the next section of this chapter, we shall consider how play can be related to popular culture,
focusing on superhero role-play, toys, games and outdoor play.

Superheroes in the role-play area

Socio-dramatic role-play offers opportunities for children to engage in
the exploration of their fantasies as they take on different characters
and use a range of props to sustain narrative. Many nurseries and
schools contain role-play areas which offer opportunities for such
play. Consequently airports, hairdressers, garden centres, shops and
supermarkets, home corners and cafes have all been established in
order to engage children in play which is rooted in real life. But whose

real life? How many children living in high-rise flats in an inner-city area of poverty visit garden centres? Do all families find that they can buy the foodstuffs they need in supermarkets or do some families need to visit specialist shops to buy Halal meat or kosher foods? In an effort to ensure that role-play areas reflect a recognizable reality for children, McLeod (1991) describes how she set up a fish and chip shop in a nursery in which she worked. Because chip shops were within the realms of this group of children's everyday experience, they responded to it enthusiastically: 'The environment which we created was definitely within the children's experience and did therefore provide a positive stimulus for language growth' (McLeod, 1991, p. 43). This is a reminder of the need to take cognisance of the socio-cultural environments which form the fabric of the children's daily lives. We would argue that it is essential to incorporate children's popular culture in the socio-dramatic role play area for these reasons. As we suggested in Chapter 1, some elements of children's popular culture do cross class, racial and gender boundaries because of the 'McDonaldization' effect and so can provide a particularly useful means of offering activities which reflect the interests of all children.

Particularly appealing to young children is the superhero genre and there has been a wealth of work which has explored this phenomenon (Paley, 1984; Kostelnik, Whiren and Stein, 1986; Sousa and Schneiderman, 1986; French, 1987; Dyson, 1994). There are a number of reasons why superheroes may appeal to children. Some researchers have suggested that the discourses of power are attractive to children, who can feel powerless in the light of adults' rules and regulations (Sousa and Schneiderman, 1986; Kostelnik, Whiren and Stein, 1986). Others have pointed to the continuum which means that modern superheroes are rooted in myths and legends such as the Greek myths (French, 1987; Jordan, 1995; Coffin and Cohen, 1978; Dyson, 1996). Davies (1997) points out that children are attracted to binary discourses which offer a simple model of complex realities: good/evil, male/female, right/wrong are all bipolar concepts which permeate children's texts. Superhero play offers a perfect opportunity to explore these binary oppositions, with its proliferation of goodies and baddies, rights and wrongs.

There are also other features of the superhero which make the figure appealing to children. Superheroes are generally individualistic and alienated from the everyday society which they seek to protect. They may sometimes take part in this society, as Superman and Batman do, but are never fully involved; at any moment they may have to disappear to take on another persona. Children can struggle with the, at times conflicting, roles of being an individual and being a part of a homogenous society and so the idea that one can move seamlessly and anonymously in and out of social commitment can prove powerfully attractive.

A further attraction of superheroes for children, for whom dressing up is often an integral part of imaginative play, is their distinctive costumes. In addition to this, these heroes often have technologically advanced weaponry which is an attractive feature of toys for many boys (Sutton-Smith, 1986; Kline, 1993). However, it should not be assumed that superhero play is only attractive to boys. Girls have also been strongly drawn to the discourse (Singer and Singer, 1981; Marsh, 2000a) when its masculinist nature has been challenged.

Incorporating superhero play in the nursery and classroom can have a powerful effect on children's motivation to engage in literacy practices (Dyson, 1998; Marsh, 1999). Role-play areas can be transformed into HQs for various characters, or can become the home of a particular superhero. Once literacy materials are placed within these role-play areas, children who may not normally take part in such activities willingly may be very keen to do so (Marsh, 1999). There are obviously concerns relating to issues of violence that many teachers may have in relation to superhero play and we have already discussed many of these in Chapter 2. Whilst these fears are not easily dismissed, it is important to locate them within an ideological context in which we build *with* children the foundations for a critical analysis. As Dyson (1997) suggests, we should work towards building 'a pedagogy of responsibility that acknowledges students' pleasures whilst assisting them in an exploration of those pleasures' (Dyson, 1997, p. 179).

Superhero play's potential as a site for language development is particularly strong for bilingual children. Popular culture can provide a meeting place for culturally disparate groups and enable them to develop shared discourses. Because English is most often the language in which these superhero narratives are experienced, children may use key words and phrases in their ensuing play. Orellana (1994), in a study of three bilingual nursery-aged children whose first language was Spanish, found that the children used the English vernacular of television superheroes freely and used it to gain status within their play. Orellana states:

> The power of popular culture is suggested by the fact that the children engaged in play related to these characters on every observation out-

side of the preschool and on several within it . . . the results of this study would suggest that English can be developed by exposing children to popular culture . . .

(Orellana, 1994, pp. 188–9)

Role-play areas need not be limited to superhero play. They can reflect a whole range of children's popular cultural interests and be transformed into the Teletubby television studio, Rugrats' home, Gladiators' gym, the agents' office of the latest cult pop group and so on, all with their attendant literacy activities.

Toys

Toys have been an integral part of the iconography of childhood for centuries and cross cultural and social barriers. Cross (1997) informs us that:

> Archaeology reveals balls and dolls five thousand years old. What appear to be toy animals are found in graves from the western Indian Harappa culture of 2,800 BC. Greek children of Horace's times had hobbyhorses, toy pets, and jointed dolls of wood and clay. Hoops and knucklebones (precursors of modern ball-and-jacks sets) were common in the ancient Mediterranean. And probably the play lives of children were much richer than these remains suggest. Few of the gourds or bits of wood that doubtless served as rattles, dolls and toy animals have survived.
>
> (Cross, 1997, p. 12)

There are toys around today which have retained their popularity over a long period of time, such as dolls, marbles, hoops and yo-yos. However, there have been significant developments in the toy manufacturing industry over the course of this century. The rise of mass-manufactured toys began in the nineteenth century, as the Industrial Revolution took hold. By the beginning of the twentieth century, toy manufacturers had formed their own professional associations and were becoming a large lobbying force in industrialized societies. Department stores and toyshops catered for those who could afford mass-marketed products. At the beginning of this century, the toy industry targeted its advertising at adults and sold mainly to the wealthier, middle-class families. During the twentieth century, we saw the toy industry change its products and marketing techniques in order to appeal to the mass market and advertise directly to children. (For a detailed analysis of the history of marketing toys to children, see Kline, 1993.) It is clear that the advent of television had a significant impact on the toy industry. Television advertising created a wider audience and the toy manufacturers used the medium expertly to appeal to children's sensibilities and acquisitiveness. In addition, in the latter half of the twentieth century, we have seen a cartel of television producers, toy manufacturers and food retailers working together to package and sell toys related to television programmes. A new television show or film appears, featuring a set of characters, and soon these characters are to be seen on shop shelves, advertised widely in the media and given away free as miniature figures in McDonald's and Burger King 'happy meals'. Thus fast-food and media-related toys, two staple items in the ideological construction of a post-modern childhood, are successfully merged.

What this does is create an intertextual universe in which toys are positioned in relation to other texts and artefacts. Fleming has called this a 'narrativization' process (Fleming, 1996, p. 102) in that all these related elements form a broad narrative and relate to each other as different aspects of that narrative. The pleasure derived from playing with any one of the toys is heightened because of their relationship to the over-arching theme. However, we would suggest that when children engage with any of the artefacts in the intertextual web, they develop narratives around that artefact which may bear some relationship to the narratives produced by related texts but could also contain distinct elements. So, in fact, toys undergo not so much a 'narrativization' process as a 'metanarrativization' process.

As we saw in Chapter 2, many have criticized this commodification of the toy market, suggesting that it has made children want too many materialistic goods and bemoaning the advent of 'pester power'. However, as Fleming notes,

> In one sense, to discover that children ask Santa for more media-marketed toys when they are exposed to heavy doses of such marketing is only to say that children have to find objects of want from somewhere: asking Santa for a wooden truck rather than a Transformer is not to express some organic, inner-oriented need as distinct from the outer-directed response to TV marketing. The child will still have seen such a truck somewhere. TV, in part, just extends the size of the shop window.
>
> (Fleming, 1996, p. 29)

As seen earlier, an idealized notion of childhood is a frequent apparition in the literature concerning children and their relationship with popular culture. In particular, toys appear to receive much of the criticism, perhaps because of their connections with technology that may be unfamiliar to the adults who attempt to police their discourses. However unfamiliar the technology, it is clear that some of the less salutary features of modern toys have been unchanged for hundreds of year. Toys which promote aggressive themes have been a central part of many cultures for centuries, as children played with home-made bows and arrows and hastily constructed swords. War toys have been manufactured since the eighteenth century in many Western cultures. This is not to suggest that we celebrate such longevity but rather that we need to contextualize the issue of contemporary toys which promote violence into larger historical discourses of power, myths of warrior-heroes and the nature of hegemonic masculinity itself.

It is unarguable that toys both promote and perpetuate sexism and are an integral part of the gendered habitus (Bourdieu, 1990) of childhood. However, rather than using this fact as a means of closing the classroom doors on these artefacts, their inclusion in classroom play can form a context in which a critical analysis of these gender regimes can take place. Thus children can design and produce non-sexist toys, creating adverts which appeal to both boys and girls. Analysis of current advertisements for toys can provide a means of raising some of the key issues and this is discussed in relation to environmental print in Chapter 4. Such deconstruction need not be a means of imposing teacher ideologies on to children and denying the pleasures that popular texts offer them. It is quite possible for children to analyse the stereotypical elements of the Barbie phenomenon, for example, whilst still celebrating the pleasure received from that particular narrative. Indeed, there is evidence to suggest that children need few adult directives towards a resistant reading of a particular discourse. Formanek-Brunell (1998) has outlined how, in the nineteenth century, dolls were given to girls in the hope that they would provide a means of inculcation into the norms of domesticity. Instead, girls used the dolls in funeral play, cut off their hair, stabbed them with scissors and mutilated their bodies: 'Abuse of dolls at the hands of their owners alerts us that adult prescriptions for proper play were often not what girls had in mind' (Formanek-Brunell, 1998, p. 373). Perhaps these girls were particularly resistant to the adult agendas in the provision of such dolls because, as Fleming (1996) points out, dolls have often served to represent adults' views of what children should be like, rather than to reflect children's interests.

Nevertheless, despite the adult-imposed agendas, toys can provide a particularly gratifying source of 'narrative satisfaction' (Hilton, 1996, p. 42) for children. In their construction of play narratives, toys become symbolic representations of fears, emotions and desires, as well as enabling children to transfer issues of agency and power on to the inanimate objects. Children can use toys to construct stories that form a stage on which to play out current issues and concerns. These toy stories may be less threatening than narratives in which 'real' people show anger, feel fear, or experience abandonment and loss. Helen Bromley (1999) has used 'story boxes' successfully to stimulate both oral and written storytelling. These boxes contain various scenarios and toys with which children play before devising related narratives. Plastic figures originating from film and media texts are desirable objects for many children and, as part of a story box, provide a useful stimulus for oral and written work. For example, a group of 8-year-olds were provided with a set of figures from the *Star Wars* film. They constructed a story using these figures and, using a polaroid camera, took photographs of key events from their narrative. They then used the photographs as a basis for their written stories. This kind of work can be extremely motivating for children, particularly if they do not have access to these figures outside of school. Many children from families living in areas of poverty may not be able to afford expensive figures which are a common feature of other homes. Thus it is important that work on toys relating to popular culture does not rely on children bringing them in from home, or lead to a competitive dash to demonstrate ownership of these material goods as social markers. Although we would agree with the suggestion that toys *are* culture and are part of a process of material objectification in which identities are created and recognized (Seiter, 1998), we need to be sensitive to the fact that not all children have equal access to the same cultural artefacts.

Collections

If not all children are able to buy into the cultural ideology shaped by contemporary toys, this becomes an even more potentially divisive tool in relation to their collection of such goods. Many people appear to have a passion for collecting and children are no exception. However, crazes for the latest toy product are nothing new. Cross (1997) outlines how, in the early twentieth century, certain products provoked a buying frenzy across the United States. Most older people can remember collectors' crazes of their own childhood era, e.g. Dinky cars, trolls, gonks, Noddy figures. The only issue that has changed relates to the advertising of these products and their integration into larger narratives of film, video and television. The collectors' crazes now have global trajectories in that desire for Beanie Babies, tamagotchis and yo-yos travels across continents in an asynchronous fashion, supported by websites dedicated to their exchange and marketing. Part of the attraction must be the ephemeral nature of the products; as soon as one has built up a sufficient collection, that line is phased out and new ones appear.

How can these enthusiasms be channelled into the classroom? It is a sensitive area because, inevitably, those who collect these cultural icons will have greater resources to draw from than others. We need to avoid a situation in which classrooms become oppressive sites where cultural artefacts are exhibited in hierarchical, materialistic displays. Instead, children could be encouraged to start a whole-class collection of Beanie Babies or virtual pets, designed by themselves. Reading and writing activities could abound here as children write descriptions of their designs, make lists of features, instructions on how to care for them and so on. Narrative histories of collectors' crazes in children's living memory can be written and older members of the community interviewed about their particular toy passions. Databases containing information on particular crazes can be designed and the Internet used to research related material. Engaging children in writing letters to an imaginary critic of such crazes can provide a useful means of developing persuasive writing. In fact, one child in England actually did write to an educational newspaper in response to a research report which criticized the Beanie Baby craze for its manipulation of young children (TES, 2000b). This incensed one of the young collectors and she wrote a strong letter to the researcher, which included a number of arguments supporting the craze:

> Do you not think it is important that young minds learn value, price, variety and how scarce Beanies are? Now I have learnt not to waste money on things I shall get fed up with or trainers I use for muddy games or PE . . . So please, before abusing these harmless toys realise what you are saying and don't abuse such a great man as TY Warner and his Beanies. Also I am amazed that academics do not have better things to research.
>
> (TES, 2000c, p. 16)

Games

Games have long been identified as a means of socializing children and adults into various socio-cultural practices (Sutton-Smith, 1986).

One only has to consider the role of Monopoly in initiating children in Western societies with the ideology of capitalism. At present, there appears to be yet another moral panic about the types of games played by children in today's society. In particular, computer games have been condemned because of their location in patriarchal sites of violence and sexism. The issues related to computer games are discussed in detail in Chapter 7. Here, we outline some ways in which games rooted in children's popular culture can be used to serve the literacy curriculum.

Competitive games are one form of currency which many children share. Various versions of Snakes and Ladders and Ludo are well established in many cultures. These board games can be adapted to incorporate popular cultural icons; thus Ludo can involve the differently coloured Teletubby figures returning to their bunkers, or snakes and ladders being replaced by the rays of Pokémon monsters. Popular game shows from television can also be used to inform the literacy curriculum. Children are often great fans of *Who Wants to Be a Millionaire?* or *Family Fortunes*. After an analysis of the appeal and codes used within these shows, children can invent their own, writing rules and explanations. Some children may be extremely motivated to research questions and answers on a particular class topic, using the Encarta CD-ROM, if such research could be put to use in a well-constructed game show which has echoes of their own Saturday evening television viewing practices. In Chapter 8, we describe how one teacher used a quiz show to provide meaningful homework tasks.

Sports and games are a central feature of many children's cultural lives and a form a key part of their popular culture. Some schools have been imaginative in exploiting an interest in football and cricket, for example, in an attempt to draw on the popular currency of children. For other children, an interest in sport designer wear is as far as the interest in such matters goes, but because sport is a key focus for identity formation in contemporary life, it offers a range of potential for informing the literacy curriculum. As Anne Haas Dyson (1999) notes, it has a particular value in relation to children's writing:

> Sports media contain discourse evidencing such marked features; there are units of discourse with routine structures and predictable content, in which much emotional energy is vested by fans. These information-packed forms, like announcements and reports, are similar to the information-packed forms valued in certain kinds of school writing and, moreover, make much use of written names, a textual feature comfortable for very young writers (Clay, 1975).
>
> (Dyson, 1999, p. 381)

As Dyson suggests, literacy activities centred on sport could provide a range of opportunities for working on non-fiction genres such as reports, lists, commentaries, notices, schedules and information leaflets. Children's interests in sporting figures can be drawn upon within a classroom context in order to develop fact files, biographies, interview schedules, fanzines and websites devoted to favourite sportsmen and women. It is recognized that boys in particular are drawn to the sports genre (Livingstone and Bovill, 1999) and so this area has led to various national initiatives, such as homework clubs being located within football grounds. Nevertheless, it is important that the interests of girls in sports such as football are not overlooked and indeed the issue of gender and sport would provide a wealth of material for critical analysis of textual materials embedded within the genre.

Play in the playground

Playground culture is a phenomenon which is only familiar on the surface to many teachers. Adults supervise the outdoor area, sort out the problems, attend to cuts and bruises, but rarely have the opportunity to find out about the kinds of play in which the children are engaged. Narrative games are a key feature of playgrounds. Children work together to build shared stories based on aspects of their culture. These are usually highly gendered in nature and, inevitably, draw from the media discourses with which the children interact daily. We need to be careful to ensure that children have the space in which to act out narratives that are beyond the control of adults and so, whilst we would not advocate the wholesale colonization of children's culture for educational purposes, there are ways in which playground culture can inform the literacy curriculum. For example, children could construct a database of characters they regularly become in the playground, with accompanying notes as to the origin and features of that character. A recent survey of an inner-city class of 7-year-olds resulted in the following characters being identified as occurring regularly in the playground games:

- Cops and Robbers
- Power Rangers
- Cats and Dogs
- Tom and Jerry
- Spiderman
- Batman

- Rugrats
- Bugs
- Super Mario
- Pokémon
- Racing drivers

The rules for some of these games were identified and written down, the activity provoking much discussion as children worked out if indeed there were any underlying regulations to this play. Of course, in an increasingly regulated curriculum, this type of activity needs to be integrated with other work which is occurring. In this case, the link was to literacy hour work on poems with a playground theme.

Finally, teachers may want to consider using the play activities provided for children on holiday as a stimulus for thematic work. Many children, either through family or school visits, have enjoyed a visit to a theme park. A class's collective memories of visits which may range from a trip to Disneyland, in Orlando, to Gulliver's Kingdom in Matlock, can be drawn on in order to inform the design of a fairground ride based on a new popular attraction. In groups, children can design rides and displays around characters from a current craze such as Pokémon or Teletubbies and leaflets and posters can be created to attract visitors.

Conclusion

Throughout this chapter, we have seen that popular culture is bound up intimately with childhood experiences of play. Children, in turn, play with popular cultural texts in order to make them their own. They transform the texts they meet through television, film, video, comics and magazines and use them to create shared social discourses which work out the concerns of childhood. Thus, children become skilled in weaving narrative tapestries using whatever glittering threads attract their attention. If the medium of play can be the means of creating this synergy between popular cultural texts and children's lived realities, then the experiences become that much more pleasurable and more likely to provide the narrative satisfaction that will lead to enriched, and enriching, encounters with literacy. In the next chapter, we turn to the beginnings of reading in order to explore in more depth the opportunities for meaningful encounters with print.

4

Environmental Print

In this chapter, we intend to consider what is involved in the process of learning to read and the role played by the materials provided for early encounters with print. Once again, the focus of our discussion will be on the importance of the role of popular culture in informing the reading materials used to support children in the early stages of reading development. However, it is important to look first at the ideologies which currently influence practice in school.

Reading wars

As far back as most of the teachers currently engaged in the development of children's reading can remember, heated debates have taken place in English-speaking countries about the most effective methods of teaching young children to read. Although these debates are best known for the positioning of the arguments surrounding the prescriptions for the reading targets at Key Stage 1 of the English National Curriculum (DES, 1988), similar debates can be traced back to the nineteenth century and the development of elementary instruction (Millard, 1997, p. 33). The debate has repeatedly led to a polarization between two opposing camps of reading 'experts' who assert the superiority of one form of instruction over that of the other, with all the fervour of Swift's (1726) Lilliputian courtiers dividing on the issues of whether a boiled egg should be broken at the big or the small end. Janet Soler has described the reading debates which took place in New Zealand in the 1950s and the 1990s as 'reading wars' (Soler, 2000). She points out how technocratic solutions to a perceived 'crisis' in the teaching of reading always propose a return to formalized, direct instruction, of which phonics usually occupies a central role. The North America of the 1950s presents another perspective which seeks to locate the secret of reading instruction in a particular paradigm of learning, focusing on the smallest unit of signification – the phoneme

(Flesch, 1955). Opposed to the 'technicists' and their skills-based solutions is the work of educators, from William Godwin onwards, who emphasize the importance of story in motivating the learner (Godwin, 1793, quoted in St Clair, 1989).

Bottom up or top down?

In the United Kingdom, the bipolarities of the reading debate have been described by Pumfrey (1991) as taking the form of a top-down approach which emphasizes the priority of whole-text meaning first, in opposition to a bottom-up emphasis which proposes the prior drilling of key skills – mainly phonics. Top-down methodologies have been variously described as whole-language approaches (Goodman, 1986; Holdaway, 1979) or working with real books (Waterland, 1988; Minns, 1990). Bottom-up approaches are the ones favoured by advocates of direct phonic instruction. They suggest that in order for children to learn to read and write effectively, they should first learn the smallest parts of language in a 'part-to-whole' process, beginning with letter names, followed by the 'sounds' that letters make and only then by simple words and short sentences framed within carefully controlled texts (Chall, 1983; Lloyd, 1992; Macmillan, 1997). In the past, teachers of the youngest age groups, influenced by bottom-up approaches, were accustomed to working on skills that were thought to be the prerequisites of reading and writing, rather than on initiating reading and writing in a meaningful context.

Pumfrey argues that an exclusive adherence to either methodology imposes limitations on learning. The 'bottom-up' model underestimates the important effects of higher levels of linguistic processing of the meaning of a text and the total experiences of the reader on the lower level decoding process. The 'top-down' approach can lead to the sacrifice of accuracy and to failure in reconstructing the writer's message adequately (Pumfrey, 1991, p. 114). Pumfrey further suggests that the effective teaching of reading requires a combination of both approaches. Very few British children appear to have been subjected to either extreme of instruction (HMI, 1991). In fact in 1994, Millard reported that even during the period when a 'Real Book' approach was at its most influential, most of a group of 250 children surveyed at age 11 remembered having been taught to read by some form of decoding, that placed the word at the centre of the learning process (Millard, 1994, p. 11). At the time she commented: 'children who described learning with a whole-book method, where books were a source of pleasure in themselves, were very much in the minority' (Millard, 1994, p. 12).

Some of the children whom Millard interviewed had been taught by means of a particularly rigid school methodology, usually marked by a strict progression through a reading scheme with accompanying workbooks. They frequently reported a discontinuity between the reading that had been shared with parents at home and what had been expected of them in school. Some of them saw reading in school as rather pointless, as in the account of an 11-year-old boy describing his early experiences:

> I learned to read at home. My mum shared books with me. We read *Tex the Cowboy* and did letter jigsaws. When I started school they gave me my first reading book and all it said was "Look!"

It also appeared to create a hiatus in the real business of reading for pleasure when only a programmed approach was apparent in school. One 11-year-old girl reports on what was then the widespread practice of allowing children access to story books in school only when a reading scheme had been successfully completed:

> At home my mum and I read comics and stories together. At school I was put on a set of books. I started at stage one and two years later I was on stage six. They then let me to go back to reading story books in school, like my best book, *The Faraway Tree*.

These quotations are from children interviewed in 1992, who had experienced their earliest school reading lessons before the National Curriculum requirements had been set in place. Reading wars were raging in British newspapers at the time, with front-page banner headlines declaring 'SHAMEFUL', with a subheading: 'Seven Year Olds Failed by the System' (see Millard, 1994, p. 11). What was interesting about this débâcle was that the perceived decline in reading standards had no basis in fact (Brooks, Schagen and Nastat, 1998). However, this did not prevent excessive claims being made in the period about the failure of contemporary methods of teaching, or the superiority of one kind of reading instruction over another.

Synthetic versus analytic phonics

Although it is now widely accepted that mixed methods work best, there is a continuing debate focused on synthetic versus analytic phonics. The former involves a more programmed approach to the teaching of the phoneme–grapheme relationship. It aims to instruct children in the first stages of reading through the explicit and systematic teaching of the correspondence of the sounds to the letters that make up the 'alphabetic code' of English, that is, the segmentation and blending of sounds in words. Children are taught to read words by splitting them into individual phonemes and then building them back up into discrete units, e.g. c-a-t/cat. Words are usually learned in isolation. In fact, some synthetic phonics programmes insist that children learn all 44 phonemes before being allowed to read a book.

Analytic methods, on the other hand, embed phonics in real texts. Teachers select a text for its meaning and draw children's attention to the way individual words within the text are structured. Analytic phonics uses onset/rime where appropriate, rather than breaking words into individual phonemes. The English National Literacy Strategy has created a national resource for the explicit teaching of phonics called PiPs or Progression in Phonics. These consist of materials for whole-class teaching which claim to give structure and rigour to the teaching of phonics in the early years by incorporating both analytic and synthetic approaches to word analysis. The CD-ROM produced for teachers explains segmenting; blending; digraphs; trigraphs; phonemes in initial, medial and final positions; the principles of the phonic code; progression in phonic skills and knowledge, and provides practical guidance on correcting children's misconceptions. The activities recommended include word games which motivate participation. The emphasis, however, remains on word-level work, rather than whole language and textual meaning. It will be important for teachers to think how language work can be fitted into an appropriate context, an issue addressed later in this chapter.

An emerging harmony

An understanding of the complexity of dealing with language at phoneme, word and sentence level, at the same time as processing the whole text, has been called parallel processing (Rumelhart, 1977). Happily, as the twentieth century ended, a more balanced view of the best way of teaching reading emerged. It is now generally accepted that reading involves, as Marie Clay aptly pronounced, 'the patterning of complex behaviour' (Clay, 1979). Effective planning for reading therefore, requires children to develop a sense of meaning of whole texts, alongside an understanding of word-attack skills. Marilyn Jaeger Adams, (1990) who conducted a wide-scale study of reading research for the United States government, described the range of aspects that need to be combined in order for a reader to make sense of a text. Her model for understanding the reading process will be discussed in greater detail in Chapter 8 in relation to televisual texts. It has also been shown through inspection that children learn most effectively within a balanced provision. Fluent reading, therefore, is best seen as both dependent on children's ability to attend to the graphophonic cues of the words on the page and also on a developing knowledge of predictability based on past experiences and satisfactions of texts. A meeting of phonics and whole language occurs in methods that emphasize the need for children to learn about the structure of the words they encounter in meaningful contexts, such as a literacy-focused activity in the home, a shared story with repetitive language or the sharing of rhymes.

The importance of rhyme and phonological awareness

The latter practice is confirmed as important by research demonstrating how children develop an ability to draw analogies between the structure of familiar and unfamiliar words in order to decode print. It has been shown, in part, to be based on their ability to grasp a structure described as onset and rime (Maclean, Bryant and Bradley, 1987; Goswami, 1988; Goswami and Bryant, 1990). This refers to children's segmentions of the words they hear into the beginning (onset) and the end sound (rime). The onset is the first phoneme leading up to the vowel sound, rime is the vowel plus following phoneme(s). In Rolo, for example *r* is the onset, *olo* the rime; in *strong* (of Extra Strong Mints) *str* is the onset, *ong* the rime. This finding has allowed teachers to build up an understanding of the ways in which children can be supported to decode unfamiliar words within a familiar context, so that in a shared reading of rhymes and simple poetry, children are encouraged to make predictions and complete sentences. In hearing and predicting rhymes, children can understand speech segmentation and develop phonological awareness that will help them not only in recognizing new words when reading, but also when encoding their own spoken language in early writing activities.

Reading and relevance

Despite a new concordat found by educators, it remains important to keep in the front of our minds the learning experiences reported by the older children in Millard's study (Millard, 1994). The relevance of their accounts lies in their illustration of the key role that the medium of instruction plays in helping children to understand the purposes for reading. Persistent 'bottom-uppers' who recommend a 'phonics first' approach are still to be found recommending that children's earliest experiences of reading in school should start not with books, but with the synthesizing of sounds into words before any printed matter is introduced (Lloyd, 1992; Macmillan, 1997). We would argue that within such a teaching frame, it is children with the least experience of story in the home who would be at the greatest disadvantage. For no manner of proselytizing about the benefits of learning to blend CVC (consonant, vowel, consonant) words prior to opening a book will deter families who love stories from introducing their children to them.

Joining the literacy club

Frank Smith first employed the term 'literacy club' to describe the way in which adults model for children the advantages of the uses of literacy, based on parallels to the support they provide for oral language development (Smith, 1984). Smith signalled both the key role purpose plays in these transactions and the support adults provide in guiding each junior member's development. Margaret Clark's earlier study of young, fluent British readers showed that those who made excellent progress in school reading had been provided with a very wide range of reading materials at home, including train timetables and other forms of print available in context (Clark, 1976). Millard's research in this area (1994, 1997) has focused on the ways in which early experiences of reading have shaped older pupils' self-confidence and expectations of what reading in school involves. Boys often see less point in the reading organized by school than do girls in the same class. Girls are usually happy to do most tasks set them without questioning the purpose; boys often demand to know why they are being asked to do something. Some of the boys interviewed when they were 11 expressed a difficulty in understanding the importance of reading stories as a preparation for future employment (Millard, 1994).

No single reading scheme could possibly support the range of reading practices that are necessary to secure a firm understanding of all the nuanced uses of print in society. To motivate some of our children, it is important to make clearer links between their prior experiences of written language and reading at home and the activities presented to them in school. The print they have encountered in their early learning can range from the control buttons on a wide range of electronic devices – the television, washing machine and computer – to the signs over buses and variety of scripts used in their particular community. Therefore, as well as considering the role of schoolbooks, posters, labels and displays which have been specifically designed for learning, teachers need also to familiarize themselves with the kinds of literacy events which their pupils bring with them from home and find ways of incorporating these into their planning.

Emergent literacy

The reading wars described above were premised on a belief that most children are taught how to read in a school setting, largely through direct instruction and experiences preplanned for them by teachers. This perspective, however, has been challenged by more recent findings of researchers interested in younger children's grasp of the uses of literacy within their home environment.

Over a period of 20 years, research has redefined children's gateway into literacy, tracing literacy's starting point to the very first human exchanges between child and adult, which take place long before schooling formalizes the learning process (Hannon, 1995; Weinberger, 1996). For children in the United Kingdom, as in other developed economies, literacy awareness will be activated soon after birth by the existence of surroundings, rich in print, into which they are born. Nutbrown has described just such an early print environment in the home of one small child whose literacy development she studied in depth:

> Alex's bedroom curtains bore letters of the alphabet, as did her cot cover. Nursery rhyme tapes were played in the car – a regular accompaniment on journeys, as she travelled in her car seat, looking out on an ever-changing environment of print on advertising hoardings, in shop windows and on street signs. Some of Alex's clothes were embroidered with logos, letters and captions, such as: *Baby, ABC, I love my Daddy; Super Tot, Sweater Shop!; Good Morning Sunshine!;* and *Who loves you baby?*
>
> (Nutbrown, 2000, p. 24)

Although this vignette is rooted within a particular socio-economic context (e.g. a comfortably off, car-owning family) it does remind us of the fact that all children have some access to environmental print in the everyday world. Nutbrown's research takes its theme from earlier studies completed in the 1980s, which described in detail how very young children interact with literacy events in their environment (Goodman, 1986; Goodman, 1989; Hall, 1987). The name given to children's gradual awakening to the meanings of signs and messages embedded in the social practices of their families and wider community is 'emergent literacy'. Jo Weinberger explains that emergent literacy 'emerges from a maturing understanding about language which originates within the child' (Weinberger, 1996, p. 3). As they encounter the use of print within meaningful contexts and make attempts to replicate the activities of the adults around them, children develop an increasingly sophisticated understanding of how written language operates. This learning is not necessarily the result of taught behaviour – although many adults do directly draw children's attention to features of the print around them – but is picked up effortlessly in daily routines and when sharing ideas with others. Goodman and colleagues (1987) emphasized that the function of language was of greater importance in the first stages of learning than a mastery of form. Children need to understand how literacy works and why it is used before coming to terms with the rules and conventions of printed matter.

Prior to the impact of this research, teachers had often assumed that the process of learning to read was initiated by school and that it was teachers above all who provided the appropriate conditions in which children might develop into confident readers (except, of course, in the case of a rare 'gifted' child who arrived in school reading fluently and presented their teachers with something of a problem). Activities based on books, or other forms of writing in the home, were characterized as pre-reading behaviour, and seen as 'getting ready to read' rather than as key literacy 'events' in their own right. Today, it is considered more appropriate to see children as being literate, i.e. understanding many of the uses of print which surrounds them on school entry. Yetta Goodman has argued that children who were deemed to have 'failed' a school reading readiness test were 'doing things and had developed concepts which were part of the reading process of mature, proficient readers' (Goodman, 1980).

Hilary Minns, describing the experience brought to school by five pre-school Coventry children, comments:

> Between them the children knew about many different areas of reading: books, including holy books, food labels, notices, television labels,

notices, television titles, the names of toys and the instructions on how to assemble them, advertisements, newspapers (in more than one language), shopping catalogues, calendars, cards for celebrations (birthday, Diwali, and so on, letters, bills, crosswords, the writing on coins and bank notes, story-books, novels and the telephone directory. Reading was modelled for them by parents and other family members, the priest, people on television and shop assistants.

(Minns, 1993, p. 27)

Nutbrown and Hannon (1997) summarized the importance of the emergent literacy perspective in this way: 'Emergent or developmental literacy supposes that children, before they go to school, are active in their pursuit of literacy skills, knowledge and understanding, and that, in so doing, they have generated a positive view of literacy. They see literacy as exciting, interesting, a "good thing" to get involved in' (Nutbrown and Hannon, 1997, p. 5).

There has been a tendency amongst educationalists to privilege interactions with story books above other types of literacy practices. This has led to work which has identified those families who do not regularly share picture books with their young children as deficient or deprived in some way, despite Heath's (1983) ground-breaking work which showed that children living in poor families had a range of other rich interactions with the adults who surrounded them. We would not disagree that there are many pleasures to be gained from sharing a picture book with children and there are certainly a range of skills that children develop as we do so. However, as Yetta Goodman reminds us, 'There is no single road to becoming literate' (Goodman *et al.*, 1997, p. 56) and there are certainly many children who travel along highways which are not crowded with bookshops and libraries. This does not mean that these families are any less loving and nurturing than those who do create opportunities for book-sharing, yet one would be forgiven for arriving at that conclusion at times, given the evangelical nature of some family literacy programmes. As Carol Taylor (1999) has suggested, when discussing family literacy programmes that are based on a deficit model:

At the heart of this model is the premise that only the 'schooled' model of literacy is relevant and that disadvantaged adults pass on illiteracy (like a disease) to their children. These programmes focus on transmitting mainstream school literacy practices into the home without recognising the validity, or even presence, of home literacy practices.

(Taylor, 1999, p. 176)

There have been studies which have detailed the wide range of literacy practices undertaken by families with different socio-economic status (Heath, 1983; Taylor and Dorsey-Gaines, 1988; Purcell-Gates, 1996). These studies have revealed the rich range of literacy events that occur within working-class homes, many of which do not involve book reading. Instead, Purcell-Gates reports in her year-long study of 20 low-income families that, 'the majority of the print used in the homes involved, for example, reading container text (e.g. cereal boxes, milk cartons), flyers, coupons, advertisements, movie or TV notices, writing grocery and to-do lists, and signing names' (Purcell-Gates, 1996, p. 425). Given that many children do encounter this wide range of print, rather than experiencing extensive story-book reading, it would seem imperative to draw on their experience once they attend nursery or school.

One of the richest sources of print for small children is the neighbourhood. A local environment is replete with semiotic messages consisting of house names and numbers, road signs, bus stops, billboards and hoardings, shop fronts, advertising displays and posters, as well as all the richness of print situated inside doctors' waiting rooms, the hairdresser, the local play group and the newsagent. From their first months of life, children become very familiar with their own neighbourhood. They have particularly well-travelled routes, first to friends' homes, the local park and the shops, next on journeys to playgroup and nursery and eventually to primary school. Weinberger's study found that half of the 40 parents of nursery children whom she interviewed had been accustomed to pointing out print in their environment to their children before they reached nursery age (Weinberger, 1996, p. 18). Family rituals play an important part in developing this awareness, so that many young children can be seen pointing out favourite food items from the child seat of a supermarket trolley, picking up sweets and a comic when the weekly papers are being paid for, exchanging library books alongside a parent, posting a letter and checking the time of collection on the post-box, or reading the destinations and times when making a journey, for example on Sheffield's Supertram.

Figure 4.1 is a piece of writing completed by a son of one of the authors when he was in a Reception class, over 20 years ago. The proud parent saved it because of its philanthropic message. However, years later when unearthing it from an extensive collection of his early writing kept as mementos of childhood, the young man explained it was, in fact, a depiction of a hoarding seen every morning

Figure 4.1 Give mony to the poor

on his way to a nursery school in Leeds. It recorded the family car passing the site of a large Oxfam poster. At the time of its production, only the words held meaning for his mother, but the boy was drawing on visual, as well as print, literacy to record his impressions of his environment. The words are a gloss on the kinds of posters that were usually displayed. The important point to note here is that children are very aware of their surroundings and can draw on a wide range of such experiences when making sense of their daily routine. It is knowledge that can also be used to good purpose by the teachers.

Using the local environment

In 1999, Hannon and Nutbrown completed research on an 18-month early literacy education programme they had devised for parents and their young children, prior to school entry. They worked with an experimental group of over 80 families to encourage recognition of emergent literacy and to help parents support their children's early learning. The programme addressed several strands of literacy for which parental support was readily available. One strand was based on print in the environment and the activities centred on this theme included a literacy walk, in which parents and children carrying clipboards spotted and recorded aspects of the print in the streets surrounding the nursery, the housing estate and local shopping area. They were asked to match their observations to a printed set of signs and notices. Another activity arranged for parents of nursery children was an environmental print open day, involving a wide variety of games made by staff using the familiar print from packages, brought from the children's homes (Nutbrown and Hannon, 1997, pp. 210–12).

For those wishing to introduce this activity, the information looked for might include the following:

- the name of the area
- street names – looking for particular patterns such as the 'Flower Estate' in Sheffield, which uses the names of well-known flowers, and Nottingham, where roads are often given names from the turn of the century, e.g. Albert, Lily, Ethel
- traffic directions – noting the shape of the sign as well as the message
- advertisements on hoardings, buses and bus-stop messages
- shop signs and promotional material (i.e. SALE, BARGAINS, FINAL REDUCTIONS, SPECIAL OFFER, CLOSING DOWN)
- signs round the school grounds.

In creating school work based on environmental print, it is important to remind ourselves that, because literacy is embedded in social relations, it is likely to vary between cultures. Teachers need an awareness of variations created in terms of region, ethnicity and social class. More particularly, it is important to recognize that children's understanding of literacy will depend upon the literacy 'culture' or 'cultures' they experience (Nutbrown and Hannon, 1997, p. 19). When introducing any work based on environmental activity, care should therefore be taken to include the wide variety of scripts appropriate to local communities, which may include Urdu, Chinese and Arabic, amongst other languages. When taking children on an environmental print walk, signs on mosques or community shops should be given the same attention as the signs on post offices or bus stops. Similarly, packaging and sources of print used in other activities should be representative of the products used in all the children's homes. As an alternative to a clipboard, a camera could be used to record language spotted en route, to be pasted later into a scrapbook or album. These could then be used by older pupils to create a local guide to the area or an Eye-Spy book of local amenities. A class might also enjoy compiling its own address book, using a notebook with a letter of the alphabet on each page under which the addresses of families, friends and school visitors can be recorded.

Work on environmental print can be extended with older pupils and developed into a school research project on many different aspects of the local environment. Pupils may be asked to map the local area, making plans of their own streets and labelling their own and their friends' houses, the site of any parks, local amenities and shops. One school undertook a survey of the litter found in the area in order to determine from the packages and labels they found, where the main source of litter might come from. They then wrote letters to the local council, advising where litter bins might be located and ran an anti-litter campaign for parents and children, focusing on the area outside the school gates.

Working at a word level: the logographic stage

It has been shown that children recognize words as whole units before they begin to identify individual letters (Frith, 1985). That is, they recognize the shape of the word rather than perceiving it is made up of specific elements. Logos are designed to be instantly identifiable by shape and colour, as well through the letters which spell a product's name. Young children's ability to identify well-known logos prior to letters, can be used to draw their attention to the way the sign is constructed. Pupils can learn syllabification from breaking up the names of familiar products whilst clapping them out. A new range of products could be used on different occasions, breakfast cereals one day: Weet-a-bix, Co-Co-Pops, Corn-flakes; sweets the next: Smar-ties, Po-los, Mal-tes-ers. Awareness of onset and rime can be enhanced by looking at the names of popular products to find sound patterning. Of particular use are words with repetitious sounds. Words such as KitKat, Co-Co (Pops) and Coca-Cola use a shared onset, whereas Rolo and Polo have the same rime. Such words can be used to develop phonological awareness alongside the more familiar forms of nursery rhymes and jingles (Maclean, Bryant and Bradley, 1987).

Young children will enjoy the easy identification of key letter shapes – M for McDonald's and K for Kellogg being the two most universally recognized, followed closely by Wall's and Disney. A collection of logos, slogans and labels may be used in the production of games which encourage the matching of a label and the image of the product; the same principle can be applied to car names and badges. Large print can be scoured to produce the elements of a particular child's name. Each child could be helped to search for a product that shares an initial letter with his or her name and be asked to link them, e.g. Darren and Disney, Wahid and Wall's, Katie and Kelloggs, Paul and Pringles, Rehana and Reebok. With older pupils, a group alliterative poem might be shaped from similar work, with the support of the teacher who gives forethought in providing appropriate labels or packaging for each child:

> Food We Like
> Kerry likes Kelloggs – rice crispies and cornflakes
> Siobhan likes Snickers but doesn't eat Smarties
> Tabijah likes Tizer and also likes Treets
> Wayne likes Wispas and Wall's ice-cream
> James likes Jaffa cakes but does not like Juicy Fruits
> Ansa likes Alpen and also eats apples
> Dale likes Dairylea, his favourites are Dunkers
> Laika likes Lucozade but not lemonade.

The body is a key site for the popular cultural interests of many children. Apart from jewellery, hair accessories and stick-on tattoos, children are attracted to particular styles of clothing according to their friendship and cultural groups. This fascination for clothing has, in recent years, merged with an equally strong attraction for sport. Sports clothing manufacturers have targeted children in their advertising campaigns and now clothes with particular logos, such as Nike's 'swoosh', are extremely popular. Teachers are, understandably, wary of incorporating work on such fashion items in the classroom, as many families cannot afford designer labels. However, if approached with sensitivity, children's knowledge of such logos from television advertising can be drawn upon to engage them in word-level work as pupils clap out Ad-i-das and Ree-bok and debate whether the pronunciation of a rival product is Nike or Ni-ke.

Other word-level activities for young children based on environmental print might include the following:

- making an alphabet frieze for the nursery children based on the cut out names of well-known products: A for Alpen, B for Bounce, C for Coco Pops, etc. See also Ann Ketch's account of using her 'Delicious Alphabet' book to support emergent writing (Ketch, 1991)

- allowing children to devise their own labels, signs and posters when developing a creative play areas
- helping children to use their prior knowledge of context plus initial consonants to predict what a word will be from its first letters, then revealing the rest of the word to confirm or correct the prediction. This can be done on an overhead projector or by displaying enlarged brand names on cards.

Work on environmental print is usually confined to the early years, yet older children still engage with the range of print around them and this interest could be drawn upon in the classroom. Many shops now use alliteration, word play, tongue-twisters or puns in their signs in order to attract attention. Here are some taken from the local shopping area of one class: Cost Cutters; Toys R Us; Hair We Go, Hair Razors, Snippers, Wok Wok, The Cod Father, Going Places. Pupils can be asked to list the names they have particularly noticed, perhaps having previously been set the task as homework to be shared with parents and then discuss in groups what makes particular names memorable, or how they work. Children will particularly enjoy being asked to invent new shop signs, especially if they focus on stores they would like to visit such as sports, toys, computer and music shops. At sentence level, pupils' attention can be drawn to the kinds of sentences used to attract shoppers, in particular, the use of imperatives and questions to engage the reader in dialogue. Grammar 'experts' can look for 'errors' in the print employed in the environment: deliberate misspellings for example, misplaced or 'grocers' apostrophes and imaginatively formed plurals. Access to computers and a growing confidence in their use should enable pupils to make their own signs and labels by using a variety of fonts and colouring, and sizing their letters for impact. More adventurous and skilled computer users can design letters that have shadowed images, words that shiver to signify cold, melt to show heat or bounce on the line to express energy.

Visual literacy

In Chapters 7 and 8, we will be exploring the concept of visual literacy in more detail. Here, however, it is perhaps useful to consider the notion of visual literacy in relation to children's encounters with signs, posters and advertisements in the environment. Considine (1986) has

Figure 4.2 Example of packaging analysis

defined visual literacy in relation to children's books, but the definition is useful here. Visual literacy refers to the ability: 'to comprehend and create images in a variety of media in order to communicate effectively . . . Visually literate students should be able to produce and interpret visual images' (Considine, 1986, pp. 38). Signs, posters and advertising provide some of culture's most potent combinations of text and image and so pupils can be asked to consider the interplay of image and text, as well as identify specific features of the language used. Packaging can be analysed and key features identified (Figure 4.2).

Children can collect advertisements for a particular range of products (for example chocolate bars, pet food or sports kit) and ask what colours are most often used for these products, or whether cartoons or real people endorse them. For example, it is currently possible to buy pasta in tomato sauce shaped as Teletubbies, Barbie, Mr Men and other media characters. Questions can be asked about the signification of these choices. Pupils could investigate what other kinds of food are sold with such iconography and explore the marketing devices employed to attract the young child when out shopping through 'pester

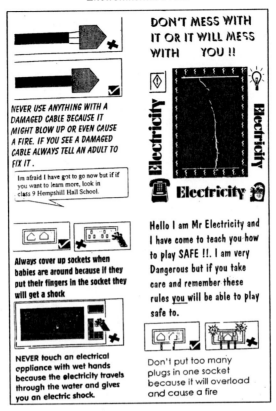

NEVER USE ANYTHING WITH A DAMAGED CABLE BECAUSE IT MIGHT BLOW UP OR EVEN CAUSE A FIRE. IF YOU SEE A DAMAGED CABLE ALWAYS TELL AN ADULT TO FIX IT.

Im afraid I have got to go now but if if you want to learn more, look in class 9 Hempshill Hall School.

DON'T MESS WITH IT OR IT WILL MESS WITH YOU !!

Electricity

Electricity

Electricity

Always cover up sockets when babies are around because if they put their fingers in the socket they will get a shock

Hello I am Mr Electricity and I have come to teach you how to play SAFE !!. I am very Dangerous but if you take care and remember these rules you will be able to play safe to.

NEVER touch an electrical appliance with wet hands because the electricity travels through the water and gives you an electric shock.

Don't put too many plugs in one socket because it will overload and cause a fire

Figure 4.3 Example of a safety leaflet

factor'. Issues of cultural inclusion or exclusion can be raised by asking who is shown using particular products and whether the families in advertising are represented stereotypically as Caucasian. Older pupils may draw on their accumulated knowledge of how the media works to create posters and pamphlets for products or projects of their own devising – as in the example of a safety leaflet produced for younger pupils by a Year 6 boy (Figure 4.3). He has employed a wide range of appropriate fonts and symbols in order to make his work stand out.

Developing an understanding of semiotics

Work on advertising, posters, labels and packaging design involves an implicit awareness of the place of signs in society and can lead to the beginnings of an understanding of semiotics. Semiotics is the study of signs. In fact, the word semiosis comes from the Greek word for signs, and the study of signs depends on an understanding of the way a sign can be broken down into two parts: the 'signifier' and the 'signified'. The 'signifier' is the physical form of the sign in words, images or sounds. The 'signified' is the mental concept referred to, its meaning. The signifier and the signified together form the sign. For example, the red rose (the sign) is the archetypal sign for true love and what is signified by the act of presenting a rose to a woman is romance (Figure 4.4).

To understand what is being 'said', semioticians look for connotations – the meanings which accrue to a signifier by its history of use. For example, white cowboy hats signify the good guys in Westerns, deep throated whispering (as performed by Don Corleone, the Godfather, or Darth Vader in *Star Wars*) signify villains. Signs do not mirror reality, but echo the received ideas of a particular culture (Barthes, 1973). A focus on the way that meaning is made up of fragments of codes can draw children's attention to the aspects of old stories, myths, cultural values and conventions used to promote commodities and their production, distribution and consumption in their lives (Godzich, 1985). They can begin to see how ideas are manipulated and controlled to create desire. Semiotics will also allow them to begin to understand some of the building blocks of media texts and how they are positioned as readers and consumers. In relation to environmental print, a teacher's know-ledge of semiotics can inform children's explorations of the way in which images and text are positioned in posters and advertisements in order to address the viewer/reader and evoke particular responses.

Pupils can begin to investigate how advertisers target specific consumers by surveying where posters are sited in the locality, or where

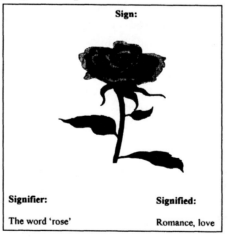

Figure 4.4 Sign, signifier, signified

advertisements are placed in comics, newspapers and magazines. Older pupils can be helped to understand how advertisers manipulate the form of print to influence the reader, or how colour and design are used to direct specific toys at particular age groups or towards a particular gender. What, for example, is signified by the choice of pale pink and turquoise for vanity sets and black and red for replica cars and bikes? This close analysis of visual and printed texts at the levels of both denotation and connotation will develop the kinds of critical reading skills which will become increasingly important for an 'information-age'.

Developing critical literacy

A semiotic approach is necessary in order to develop habits of reading that stress the importance of understanding more than the words as they appear on the page. Critical literacy is the term most widely used to describe textual analysis which looks to an understanding of how particular discourses shape human interaction (Lankshear and Mc-Claren, 1993). Its foundations lie in the work of literacy theorists such as Freire (1972) and Giroux (1981) who have promoted the need for literacy to focus on emancipatory ends. The Australian theorists, Freebody and Luke (Freebody and Luke, 1990; Freebody, 1992), building on these ideas, have constructed a model to describe four 'roles' for the reader in a postmodern, text-based culture which is helpful in guiding planning for reading development. Environmental print is appropriate to each of the four roles of the reader, which they describe as:

- code breaker (coding competence, recognizing signs)
- meaning-maker (semantic competence, understanding what items are being promoted)
- text user (pragmatic competence, able to produce appropriate texts)
- text critic (critical competence, understanding the commercial or manipulative purpose of the texts and their power to manipulate) (Freebody and Luke, 1990; Freebody, 1992).

The area most neglected in early reading development is the last of these roles. The old adage that children learn to read and then read to learn makes some teachers in the early stages focus on skill acquisition related to decoding and understanding the content, rather than more analytical and critical work. Further, most reading schemes are anodyne productions which do not mirror the reality of many children's worlds. An emphasis on story can frequently seem like an emphasis on escapism, no matter what the 'emotional' truths of the texts. Chris Searle has described how British schools distance the acquisition of literacy from community life, 'for reasons of spurious neutrality' and by a focus on individual creativity, act to further exclude working-class children (Searle, 1993, p. 172). Searle invokes the example of Paulo Freire in Brazil and the work of other mass literacy campaigns to argue that 'people and children learn best when they read their own worlds as well as their own words' (ibid.) and he continues to argue that children are never too young 'to confront, criticize, or question, as well as to form their own rational attitudes to issues arising from their own worlds' (ibid.).

Very young children can also begin to discuss important issues related to print in their environment, the effect of graffiti in the street, methods of sales promotion, the exaggerations of the advertiser and the addictions and disappointments of consumerism. While developing an awareness of the range of linguistic techniques used to promote the products which they themselves desire, they can be encouraged to become critically aware of the advertising techniques they encounter and be allowed to discuss issues such as designer branding, product placement and commercial tie-ins of toys and garments to popular forms of entertainment. As we suggested in Chapter 2, there is a tendency by those who disapprove of the use in school of aspects of popular culture, such as advertising and marketing, to assume that children are simply passive receivers of consumer culture, rather than critical participants in a consumer society. The acquisition of critical literacy needs to be seen as more than an ability to 'understand' what is read, but also needs to include the ability to read the 'world' behind the text (Freire, 1972) as well as the words on the page. Interpreting the messages that lie behind the advertisers' slogans is therefore an important part of the reading process and should be incorporated in schemes of work for pupils.

Shopping catalogues are a cheap and useful resource for helping children to consider the 'hidden' messages implicit in the use of photographs to illustrate specific items ranging from do-it-yourself to wedding promotions. They are frequently given away free in supermarkets and retail outlets, and can be the source of critical reading. For example, an Argos catalogue can be used to examine which items are directed at boys and which at girls, what claims are made for the playthings and any language used to describe them. In this way, pupils can begin to unpick the stereotypical choices that are presented.

Using print in play settings

We discussed the importance of incorporating print materials into early play in Chapter 3, however, it is important to note here that the reading matter discussed above can play an important part in role-play settings in the later stages of primary school. Too often, creative and imaginative play is seen as appropriate only to the first years of schooling (and even here it is under pressure from more formalized and routine literacy events such as the literacy hour). However, role-play, based on work in offices, the local cinema, or television studio settings is useful for stimulating a wide range of literacy activities in older children. Boys in particular, relish any opportunity to take part in literacy events in role (Frater, 1997). So, for example, pupils may role-play a busy newspaper office using computer simulations to generate national stories, or concentrate on the everyday events of school life to provide copy for their papers. Computers facilitate the simulation of newsprint.

Writing brought from the home

Children should be encouraged to bring in a wide range of writing from their homes, including handwritten texts in a variety of scripts. They may include shopping lists, postcards, greeting cards, invitations, short notes and Post-its, pieces that have been word-processed including small ads and, where appropriate, household bills. Pupils may use them for a sorting task which emphasizes the different purposes of the writing; to inform, to send greetings, to invite to a meeting or party, to persuade, to buy, to help memory, to record important information and so on. Greeting cards are readily available and a rich source of images and text for semiotic analysis. Collections of cards brought from home can be used for sorting activities in the early years. For example, cards can be sorted in terms of the likely age of the recipient, or whether the words and images have a particular cultural message. Birthday cards can be analysed, leading to discussions on what language or images are presented as appropriate for boys, compared with those appropriate for girls. Similarly, pupils might ask what images or language are chosen for granddad, which for a grandma. Verses too can be read to look for key words and messages. Both Christmas and birthday cards carry culturally specific messages and it is important to show children who is included or excluded by certain texts. Displays of greetings from a range of cultures would be an important aspect of any semiotic work on these texts. Again, these activities can be undertaken on a more complex level with older pupils. Junk mail can also be the start of a critical reading session, raising awareness of how language can be used to make offers and promises that are not necessarily meant to be fulfilled. The trick is in finding 'the get-out clause'. Pupils can ask who is the author of what first appear to be anonymous texts. Adapting a simple communication model they can ask: Who? says what? to whom? with what purpose? Pupils in the role of language 'detectives', they can identify the small 'weasel' words that make a huge difference to meaning, such as 'could' and 'may'. They could also use these skills in looking at the claims of campaigners for particular environmental issues such as fox-hunting, where leaflets stating different sides of a case are readily available.

The society we inhabit is rich in print resources, indeed many would argue that our homes and institutions are awash with far too much print information. Every one of us is a consumer and advertising knows just how to focus on the young, long before they can read fluently. However, the very ubiquity of environmental print can sometimes prevent teachers from realizing its full potential as the basis for reading and writing activities in school. It is frequently confined to the early stages of learning in the primary school and is often not revisited until encountered as part of media studies in the upper part of the secondary school. This is a pity, for the texts discussed in detail above are perfect vehicles for all three levels of work in literacy required by the current National Literacy Framework. They enable an approach that focuses on word, sentence and whole-text levels, as a part of the development of knowledge about language in context. They also lend themselves to the development of a more politically critical approach to the texts that bombard us. Further, the necessary texts are freely available and can be brought in from home at little extra cost in terms of time or effort. Brochures and catalogues can be obtained in bulk from co-operative businesses and agencies. With care in the selection of appropriate packaging, newspapers, posters and leaflets, the teacher can create an environment in which all pupils feel empowered by their prior knowledge; for in analysing name brands, logos and other advertising copy, pupils draw on their own formulation of the world; a knowledge that is readily available to all community members, whatever their age or ethnicity. In contrast, the next chapter compares the nature of children's home and personal reading in relation to those texts most frequently offered to them by their teachers.

5

Encouraging the Reading Habit

'Extraordinary how potent cheap music is', remarks a character in Noel Coward's *Private Lives*. As with music, so with fiction; it is not always the greatest works that exercise the most powerful pull on the imagination of young readers. This chapter considers the nature of children's personal choice of reading in relation to that presented to them by their teachers in school. It argues that many children are placed at a disadvantage by a curriculum that limits reading to a series of set texts, or great works, and approved children's fiction. It suggests that teachers need to become more familiar with the books that children are encountering outside school. First, however, we would like to consider the experience of one English graduate, written on an in-service course when she was asked to reflect on her experience of reading in school.

A Prologue to Reading
The English teacher's look of disdain could not be missed as she picked up the book I was reading in the school library at lunchtime and found it was a family saga, not a great work of literary merit. I was seventeen, in the sixth form, and seeking a place to read English Literature at University. Nevertheless, in more private moments, I enjoyed immersing myself in the books of Agatha Christie, Mazo de la Roche and Dorothy L Sayers, all of which my teacher considered cheap and undemanding fictions. At the time, I was mortified at 'letting myself down' and incapable of offering any word in my self-defence. If only I had been aware then of the intertextual nature of my reading, I would have explained that at fourteen, my curiosity as to why one of the characters in Mazo de la Roche's *Jalna* had disciplined his son for taking a young girl to see *Othello* had motivated me to read the whole play, looking for the controversial sections. Further, that the popular press furore over the publication of *Lady Chatterley's Lover* had introduced me to Lawrence's prose. Perhaps it would not have helped to explain that I interspersed the avid reading of what I have now come to know, through Barthes'(1974) categorisation as 'lisible' (readerly) texts, such as

romances, detective stories and horror, with collections of beat poetry and the novels of Thomas Hardy – 'scriptible', or more literary texts, all of which I borrowed regularly from my local library.

Nor would a short history of my earliest reading tastes have impressed her. My first thrills were from the pen of Enid Blyton and the writers of the Toytown stories, which featured Larry the Lamb and Dennis Daschund, later from Susan Coolidge, Richmal Crompton and Captain Johns, authors of a 'second rank' who were not usually found in the recommendations of English specialists. My parents had begun to feed my insatiable appetite for print from my earliest years, with anything they could lay their hands on. My regular reading matter included the children's corner from *Woman's Own*, the Salvation Army's *Young Warrior*, Enid Blyton's *Sunny Stories* and a series of missionary stories recounting the lives of such worthies as Elizabeth Frye, David Livingstone and Gladys Aylwood. As I grew older, they bought me the Collin's Classics, *Little Women*, *Heidi* and *Black Beauty*. As for the widely acknowledged early children's classics such as *The Tale of Peter Rabbit*, *The House at Pooh Corner*, *The Wind in the Willows* and *Alice's Adventures in Wonderland*, these I encountered for the first time much later, on the bookshelves of my university contemporaries from more middle class backgrounds who had brought them to University alongside their copies of *Vanity Fair*, *Middlemarch* and *Wuthering Heights*.

We have begun this chapter with one individual's recollection of reading experiences because it is important, when considering what has been previously written about the influence of literature on children's development, to note that the all commentators carry with them what James Britton, echoing Harding, called a memory of their 'past satisfactions'. Britton described these satisfactions as gradually evolving into an appreciation of more 'literary' values:

> Our sense of literary form increases as we find satisfaction in works which, by their complexity or the subtlety of their distinctions, make greater and greater demands upon us. Our sense of form increases as our frame of reference of reality grows with experience, primary and secondary of the world we live in. A sense of literary form must grow thus from within; it is the legacy of past satisfactions.
>
> (Britton, 1997, p. 108)

Advocates of the importance of quality in children's encounters with books predicate many of their arguments on privileged childhood experiences of access to 'great' literature from 'a golden age' and are often shut out from any knowledge of the cheaper and, arguably, more thrilling reading matter of working-class homes; the kind of reading Alan Bennett recalls as marking his own initiation into reading (Bennett, 1994).

Reading, as with every other aspect of our culture, is deeply riven by class and its matter both signals and encourages a divergence of experience and interest along class, 'race' and gender lines. The most virulent attacks on popular culture are often mounted by those members of the middle and working classes whose literary and privileged education has successfully lifted them above what they come to see as the debased, exploitative, commercial texts of their origins.

In Chapter 1, we described Matthew Arnold's claims for the importance of literature in education as a way of holding on to humanistic values in a world where he perceived mass culture created an indiscriminating populace, bent on easy pleasures. Richard Hoggart similarly rails against 'the trivialisation, the fragmentation and the opinionation encouraged by popular providers' (Hoggart, 1958, p. 321). But perhaps the most acerbic criticism of the commercialization of publishing is to be found in the work of F. R. Leavis and his followers, Frank Kermode, David Holbrook and Denys Thompson, all of whom have had a profound effect on the teaching of English in schools in the post-war years. Their emphasis on choosing works of literature as the repository of the best values of the times in which they were created can still be traced in the choice of texts for the secondary English curriculum. In defence of a cultured society, Arnold, Hoggart and Leavis all selected literary works to act as their touchstones of moral values, representing, as Arnold put it, 'the best that has been thought and known in the world everywhere' (Arnold, 1963, p. 70). For Arnold, the selection includes works from the Hellenic world, Sophocles and Empedocles being particular favourites; for Hoggart, it is the great works of Englishmen like Shakespeare, Shaw and Wells, whom he records as having featured in the choice of earlier, more serious working class readers (Hoggart, 1958, pp. 319–20). Leavis created his particular version of English Studies in *The Great Tradition* (Leavis, 1962) consisting of major novelists, outside of whom few others were considered worthy of close reading. The emphasis of these thinkers is on critical literary analysis and represents a view of education that promotes a search for value in creative works in order to promote discrimination, taste and an appreciation of literary quality. Only those books that can be studied in terms of their handling of powerful moral issues are valued. As Eagleton suggests, through publication in the journal *Scrutiny*, Leavis and his acolytes established a map of English literature which named only two and a half women, Emily Dickinson being included as a marginal case (Eagleton, 1983, p. 33). When Leavisites like Denys Thompson did turn their attention to 'cultural studies', it was usually to decry the debasement of the English language and the commercialism of the advertisers' craft (Thompson, 1970). The role of the English specialist was seen to involve defending the language against encroachments, as Terry Eagleton wryly comments: 'Their task was to safeguard English from the *Daily Herald,* and from ill-starred languages such as French where words were not able concretely to enact their own meanings' (Eagleton, 1996, p. 32). For Leavis and his followers, only those who were able to discern quality in literature were to be considered fully literate.

The emphasis on quality in children's reading

That to some extent this view prevails in English teaching today is reflected in the prescription of the current National Curriculum Orders for English of specific kinds of reading for secondary school, most notably in the requirement to teach both the works of Shakespeare and pre-twentieth century texts. In the primary school, the pressure for literary value may appear less obvious and the recommendations for reading less prescriptive, nevertheless, a view prevails that the reading curriculum should have, at its heart, encounters with 'quality' literature. It is why the development of independence in reading at Key Stage 2 is often equated with being led to read more complex and demanding fiction from a recognized group of children's authors and books. Indeed, the general requirement to read established texts is part of the National Curriculum orders which state:

> The range should include:
> - a range of modern fiction by significant children's authors
> - long-established children's fiction
> - a range of good-quality modern poetry
> - classic poetry
> - texts drawn from a variety of cultures and traditions
> - myths, legends and traditional stories
> - playscripts.
>
> (DfEE, 2000, p. 54)

The first category, 'significant children's authors', is often selected from fiction which has been awarded literary prizes such as *River Boy,* by Tom Bowler, the 1998 winner of the Carnegie Medal. Prize-winning books are usually selected by well-educated adults with a love of literature, coupled with an altruistic desire to enrich young minds. Just as critics of adult works like Arnold, Hoggart and Leavis held clearly stated views about the value of the great works they chose, so writers on children's literature present us with a 'golden age' to which it is assumed all children need to be given access. Perhaps the Leavisite tradition can be said to live on longest amongst the critics of children's books. For example, Victor Watson, who has written about and edited many collections of essays on children's fiction, chooses *Tom's Midnight Garden*, written by Philippa Pearce, as a model of good writing for children (Watson, 1992 p. 21). Further, the National Literacy Framework, which contains recommendations for achieving targets for every term of every year, recommends the following texts for text level work with Year 5 (10-year-old children) in term 3: Dickens's *David Copperfield*, Faulkner's *Moonfleet*, Kingsley's *The Water Babies*, Defoe's *Gulliver's Travels* and *Robinson Crusoe* (albeit mostly in truncated forms) and Keats's *La Belle Dame Sans Merci*. Those who work closely with this age group know that this kind of book represents a very small percentage of the narrative encounters reported by young readers and that there is an element of nostalgia in an adult desire to prolong the relationship of child with 'classic' text, privileging the printed word as the one sure route to literacy.

Nevertheless, the argument that children deserve to be given access to writing which will nourish their intellectual growth is persuasive and one that we would not want to discount. There remains a place for sharing 'quality' books with classes of all ages. Their effects can be readily supported by invoking examples of a literary use of language that challenges and extends the linguistic understanding of its young readers. Helping pupils to encounter the best literary language should certainly be part of any school's curriculum, for an encounter with new language, wherever it presents itself, is a pleasure. We have been told of a very young child remarking, as images of waves appeared on the television, 'An ocean tumbled by' – a phrase echoed from her bedtime reading of Sendack's *Where the Wild Things Are* – and of another who, while puzzling over Hare in Alison Uttley's *Little Grey Rabbit's Christmas* eating a snowflake 'with relish', asked, 'Could it be Henderson's?' But a stimulus through a delight in language is not confined to the idiom of books; children's comics, and boys' comics in particular, offer a teeming source of new language, as we will explore further in Chapter 6.

It is often on the grounds of limited language that critics reject popular fiction. Margery Fisher (1964) disdainfully dismisses the linguistic simplicity of Enid Blyton texts ('Enid Blyton and others think that children are taxed too much if they are confronted by so much as a polysyllable') by comparing them unfavourably with the complexities of the language found in Beatrix Potter's stories:

> "My friends will arrive in a minute and you are not to be seen; I am affronted," said Mrs Tabitha Twitchit; or Jemima Puddleduck's search for a 'convenient dry nesting place' or Sally Henny Penny's 'remarkable assortment of bargains'. It is learning without tears, if you like. It is also an enormous pleasure, the sharp shock of a new, exciting word; a pleasure for the listening child and a pleasure for the adventurous reader getting at it phonetically and making a guess at its meaning.
>
> (Fisher, 1964, p. 28)

This single dismissive comparison is all Fisher has to say of Enid Blyton's books, though in 1961, when her guide to children's literature, *Intent Upon Reading* was first published, Blyton was the most widely read children's author. It was the kind of reading that counted for nothing in the book world Fisher inhabited, where adults recommended books for other adults to buy for children. Yet Blyton's books remain almost as popular 40 years on and are often a source of shared pleasure between the generations.

On an unofficial Blyton Internet website, dedicated to her own and her daughter's favourite children's author, a mother explains how she experienced this hostility:

> Enid Blyton's books have received much literary criticism, indeed the attitudes displayed in many of the books can be considered as sexist and outdated. Indeed at the end of the fifties many librarians refused to stock books by Enid Blyton on the grounds that children would not read the great works of literature, this had the result that Enid Blyton sold even more books. I can remember that one of my teachers at school told the class that he did not wish to see any pupil bring Enid Blyton books into the class. All I can say is that as a child I really enjoyed her books, reading late into the night under torchlight. It was Enid Blyton who started off my love of books and reading. This is what I wrote in April 98:
>
> 'My oldest daughter is now ten and my eldest son is nine. Both are reading Enid Blyton. After reading the *Island of Adventure*, my daughter told me it was very exciting, since then she has read the Adventure series and the Mystery series.'
>
> (Blyton website, accessed 6 January 2000)

Both mother and daughter have written extensively about their favourite writer and her books and the content of this website is a testimony to the rich story experiences that have been shared between the generations, with their continuing power to stimulate creative work.

Roald Dahl's books have frequently met with similar hostility from teachers, partly because of their gross depiction of adults (particularly older female relatives and single women) and partly because of the irreverent language. However, the language could hardly be dismissed as unadventurous in its delineation of glutinous bodily functions, bad eating habits and lively backchat, usually targeted at children's elders and betters. Currently, every survey, whether conducted locally or nationally, records Dahl as the outright winner of the children's popularity stakes (Bardsley, 1991; Millard, 1997; Hall and Coles, 1999), so much so that one might argue that any child who has not had the opportunity to read these stories may be thought to have missed out on a shared childhood pleasure. Dahl also inspires a wide range of his readers to construct sites about his work, as one webmaster explains:

> Roald Dahl has been my favorite author since Mrs. Jordan read 'The BFG' to my 3rd-grade class, and I've now read just about everything he ever wrote. I got the idea for this site four years ago (in 1996) when I did a web search for 'Roald Dahl' and found about 3 measly pages. I knew that I could offer information and resources on Dahl that no one else could, and I'm interested in web designing and publishing. Pretty soon I had my site up and running.
>
> (Dahl website, accessed 6 January 2000)

Popular fiction captures many children's imaginations over long periods of time, as testified by the large number of other individual web pages that contain reviews and comments on authors such as Dahl, Stine and Blyton and series such as Goosebumps, Chillers and Sweet Valley High. Many of these publications also have official sites where users can find information and track new publications. Teachers need to be alert to pupils' interests, however, new cults in reading occur at surprisingly short intervals. No sooner has the dominance of one new series been documented than another emerges (Benton, 1995), from Point Horror to Chillers, from Chillers to Goosebumps and now on to Animorphs and Megamorphs and, of course, Pokémon.

It is with both exuberance and personal authority that children of all ages will approach an invitation to discuss the texts they know well.

Millard has reported how, when researching the different tendencies in boys' and girls' reading interests, one boy had become particularly animated when discussing his huge collection of *Beano* annuals, in contrast with a previous desultory conversation held about the 'reading book' he was obliged to carry with him by the school (Millard, 1997, p. 85). Yet, when adults turn their attention to children's favourite cult fictional characters, it is usually to invoke apocalyptic visions of a cultural decline, so grave as to end all hope of protecting childhood innocence. The fact, however, is that cult characters create a shared bond between the members of their young audiences and mark out particular stages in childhood development, which progress from Thomas the Tank Engine to Dennis the Menace and on to the Simpsons; from My Little Pony to *The Faraway Tree* and Betty Boop. Newsagents are currently stocking both comics and story books which feature: Rugrats, Action Men, Barbie, Pokémon, Noddy, Scooby Doo, Teletubbies, Spiderman and the Simpsons. They also usually stock cheap book versions of popular films such as *Star Wars, ET, Men In Black*, all the Disney retellings of fairy and popular tales and the Roger Hargreaves's Mr Men and Little Miss series.

There are, of course, as we noted in Chapter 2, many things to question in the promulgation and marketing of popular fictions. On one side, the defenders of the Leavisite cultural heritage model suggest that these fictions trivialize the intellect and debase the national language. At the other end of the political spectrum, socialist analysts balk at the commercial exploitation of children through cheaply produced products, which they point out not only include oppressively stereotypical representation of gender and 'race', but also a willingness to indulge in violence in the name of action. Anxiety about the effect of the culture industry and its process of commodification (see Adorno, 1991) is at the heart of much teacher opposition to products which are carefully designed to work subtly on children's desires.

Yet, however simplistic and manipulative both the stated and covert messages of popular culture, however vigilant the teacher in trying to ban them from the classroom, it is impossible for teachers to exclude the excited discourse which surrounds the arrival of a new comic character, television programme, Disney film or their related products, from the classroom. First, they are carried in materially as images on book-bags, carriers, pencil cases and even on pens, pencils and rubbers, as well as in small replicas and thin comic supplements which are easily smuggled in pockets. Second, they invade the imagination and become the staple of playground fantasy play and conversation. Even those who have no ready access at home to primary sources of information are quickly drawn into their imaginative worlds by this reading community, as we show in relation to pop songs in Chapter 9. We deny children the opportunity to reflect on these sources of interest and pleasure at our peril, for not only are they are able to motivate both reading and writing, but also they can outplay the teacher's best endeavours to promote her own well-loved texts.

Popular culture allows the personal to sneak into the predictability of school routine, through the symbols created by the child's inner world. A glimpse of the power of children's private reading exercises is sometimes casually revealed to us in the work we ask them to do as part of a school routine. In a book review, following from the shared reading of *Owl Babies* as a big book in the literacy hour, one 6-year-old girl had written:

> I like Bill best because he's cute and sweet. You should read it. I think it is the best story we have ever read. It is like *The Far Away Tree*. It's very exciting because things happen and you don't know what other exciting things are going to happen. They cuddle up together 'cos they're scared. It reminds me of my baby black and white kitten what died.

Here, her home reading of fantasy and suspense fuse to inform her response to the school text, as does her empathy with the vulnerability of the small creatures, remembered in the death of her kitten. If we are to benefit from children's prior understanding and develop their interest in other aspects of reading and learning in school, there needs to be clarity about the ways in which their early experiences are used and the pedagogical purposes that can be derived from popular fictions.

Popular fiction in the early years

What then are the practical implications of attending to children's interests and personal choices when developing reading in the first years of schooling? Many researchers have described the disadvantage 'less well-read' children experience in accommodating to a schooled literacy in which fictional narrative plays the major part in promoting reading (Heath, 1983, Wells, 1987; Millard, 1994, 1997). The task now is not to elaborate the differences found, the inequity is only too clear, but to find ways to contest it. The discontinuities that currently exist between school-based literacy events and those in the home need to be narrowed more effectively if children are to be allowed to join a community of well-informed readers.

First, it is important for teachers themselves to find out about and understand the effect of children's response to popular culture. Working against this at present is a national discourse which wishes to reinstate the teaching of reading as a professional concern with a preferred methodology, supported by materials which carry the endorsement of specific academic authority. When looking at the history of reading, it is possible to identify a repeated desire in those who govern education to control and formalize methods of instruction (Millard, 1994, 1997). Even the methodology that appears most to build from the child's interests, 'reading with real books' or 'a whole language' approach, has been given a professional label which may baffle ordinary parents and, just like reading schemes, suggests that instruction was a 'specialist' task. Indeed, many advocates of a 'real book' methodology had very definite ideas of exactly what a real book was and this rarely included books brought in from home that had been bought in the local newsagents.

Learning to read with Postman Pat and Sooty

In the early stages of reading then, inclusion of story books about characters with whom the class are already familiar will help them have confidence in following a story. A new character appearing in the conversations of the playground can be the cue for the teacher and class to write a shared story together in the form of a big book, incorporating the language brought from the screen. Illustrations can be provided by the children, or cut out of popular comics and magazines. A word of warning, however: these activities should grow from the characters the children choose, not ones that are familiar only to the teacher. There is little more 'sad' in the eyes of a school child than a teacher who is trying to be trendy and getting it wrong. Catchphrases can be written to be placed in speech bubbles and given to the appropriate characters: Sooty says, 'Let's get busy', the Teletubbies call, 'Again, again'. Popular story characters can be used to emphasize letter sounds:

- Laa-laa likes laughing a lot
- Noddy needs new neighbours
- Postman Pat picks up parcels
- Sooty sees Sweep skating by

Children can be encouraged to add their own words as the phrases are constructed. An early reading tree, used to record the most popular stories of all members of a class by writing their titles and characters on the leaves of wide-spreading branches, should include favourite story characters and titles from video, as well as the books that have been read. As children settle into school, interviews will enable a picture of home reading practices to be built up. Figure 5.1 is a sample schedule designed to be used when working with children and parents. It is quite detailed and individual teachers may wish to concentrate on only one or two aspects.

ABOUT READING
Do you like the stories we read in school?
What kind of stories do you like best?
Tell me about the people who read with you.
Who reads most in your home?
Who reads most to you at home?
How often do you read to someone at home ? Who do you read to most?
Where do you get most of the stories you like ? What is its name?
Are you sharing a book at home which you have chosen for yourself?
Do you have any specially favourite stories or books? What are their names?
Do you have any favourite stories on video or tape ? What are their names?

Which of these would you prefer to do if you could choose?
a) read a story   ☐
b) read a comic   ☐
c) use a computer   ☐
d) watch a video   ☐

How do you usually spend your time after school? (choose as many as you like)
e) playing outside   ☐
f) reading books   ☐
g) reading comics   ☐
h) watching television   ☐
i) on the computer   ☐
j) other (tell me which)   ☐

Can you finish the following sentence?
I think stories are . . . .

Figure 5.1 Reading questionnaire

For older children, an interesting way of finding out about their interests is to ask them to write a story of their reading, using a form they like best (Figure 5.2).

In a Year 6 class, which took part in an earlier research project (Millard, 1994), the pupils read the prepared list with their teachers and made suggestions about ways in which they might make their individual stories of reading more interesting for an outside reader. On their own initiative, one class chose to present their work in the style of one of their favourite books, magazines or comics. They

---

STORIES OF READING

Write the story of how you learned to read. It will help your teacher find out more about the kinds of books you enjoy reading and the sort of reading you did there. Here are some of the things you could include.
Write about as many of them as you like.

a) Learning to read.
   Who taught you? Did you find it easy or hard?
   Can you remember any of your first books?
b) Reading in school.
   Things you liked reading and things you didn't enjoy.
   Opinions on the books teachers have read to you.
c) Favourite books you've read more than once.
   What are they about? Why do you like them?
   Do you share these books with anyone else?
d) Where do you get your books and how do you choose them?
e) Do you buy any comics or magazines? Which ones?
   Write about your favourite characters or features.
f) Do you like reading information books?
   What do you read about in particular?
g) Where and when do you enjoy reading?
h) Do you like reading to other people or reading out loud?
i) What do other people say about your reading? (e.g. parents, teachers, friends)

Figure 5.2 Stories of reading

described a wide range of reading interests as well as those we know to be popular, like Goosebumps, Roald Dahl and Judy Blume. These ranged from books considered classic texts like *Black Beauty*, to popular adult fiction such as the horror stories of Stephen King, as well as a wide selection of comics and magazines that reflected a variety of hobbies. Just as interesting as the titles of the books they recorded in their reading stories was the variety of formats and genres they introduced into the task. By drawing on their knowledge of comics and adventure books in structuring their accounts, they revealed far more about their reading interests than are usually accounted for in reading diaries. Two boys presented their narratives in the style of fantasy adventure books, because these were their favourite reading material. They both set out their writing using the convention of asking the reader to choose from one or two optional follow-on pages, in the manner of these publications. Comics also featured as a preferred model for some children writing about their favourite reading. Such stories of reading collected from pupils can alert teachers to the importance that experience of particular forms of narrative has had, by shaping pupils' responses in a deliberate way (Figure 5.3).

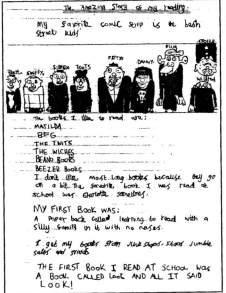

Figure 5.3   Example of a story of reading

Once teachers have become familiar with their own pupils' interests, it is usually the case that there will be a need to widen the choice of reading matter which is brought into school. This should include some books which are the spin-offs of current television and film narratives for individual reading, as well as the topical crazes in series fiction. Their interest in a particular genre can lead on to other texts. From Goosebumps to David Almond's *Skellig*, for example or from Sweet Valley High to Judy Blume and Jacqueline Wilson; the secret is to start from a known interest.

One of the earliest ways of helping children to become more discriminating in their reading is to help them express a preference about the stories they have encountered, through the use of book reviews. Another way of monitoring children's reading interests is to allow them to photocopy a passage from a favourite book and mark it up before reading it aloud to the class. They could also be asked to add a few lines to explain what they particularly liked about their chosen piece. Of course, such work needs to be done selectively; nothing has deterred children from reading more, than the knowledge that they will always have to produce a review once they have finished reading each new book.

Exploiting children's interest in series fiction

Children's unquestionable delight in the cults surrounding series fiction can be the focus of work in school to encourage both reading and writing. The repetitive nature of the formulae to which series fiction is written lends itself to genre analysis and discussion of how to create appropriate atmospheres, or what characters to include. Children can be asked to analyse a particularly suspenseful section of a Goosebumps book and then attempt to replicate some of the linguistic and stylistic features they find (Figure 5.4). One student teacher, for example, asked a class of 9-year-olds to write to R. L. Stine with ideas for a new story (Figure 5.5). These kinds of activities draw on children's fascination with the horror genre and enable them to demonstrate the extensive expertise many of them have in the area.

Further, the inclusion of popular culture in classroom literature can be particularly useful in motivating reluctant boy readers who are widely reported to engage in less voluntary reading, both at home and school (Millard, 1997; Hall and Coles, 1999). Such texts can be used to inform oral storytelling activities, as well as reading and writing. Michael Wilson (2000) analysed the contemporary legends in stories commonly exchanged amongst teenagers and found that many of them related to tales in the Point Horror series. He concludes that:

> These are not books to be kept pristine on the bookshelf, but ones to be stuffed into coat pockets, swapped, read quickly and talked about. Like oral stories, Point Horror novels are used as items of social currency and perhaps these verbal exchanges are the first steps in the assimilation of literature into folklore.
>
> (Wilson, 2000, pp. 3–4)

Children can trace the mythic elements in such horror series and see how authors draw from contemporary and traditional oral folklore.

Imaginative approaches to genre tasks can also be devised from popular culture, as in this Goosebump recipe which can be used for the shared reading of a procedural text:

MONSTER BLOOD: THE REAL RECIPE

A Goosebumps fans' favourite and a timeless classic, to be handed down through the generations from mother to daughter and from phantom to son.

Here's what to do:

1. Place 3 tablespoons of cornstarch in a bowl.
2. Slowly add 3 tablespoons of water, stirring constantly.

Figure 5.4 Analysis of a section of a Goosebumps book

Figure 5.5 New ideas letter to R. L. Stine

3. Add food colouring one drop at a time until desired colour is achieved.

As most people know, the blood of a healthy monster is green. However, you may wish to experiment with other creepy colour combinations.

(Goosebumps website, 6 January 2000, and adapted to English spelling)

Children could invent their own recipes for a Goosebumps tale, e.g. Ingredients: one scary setting, a few creepy characters and so on. Children could produce their own frames for use when writing a short, scary story, which would involve them in the analysis of structure and other features of the genre.

Series fiction is particularly appealing because of its predictability; readers become familiar with aspects of the genre and this provides a measure of comfort and reassurance. This, of course, is an aspect of the genre that critics despise, yet it is this very feature which creates communities of readers in young children. Their familiarity provides a sense of satisfaction when reading in that our expectations are met and the world is, after all, a safe and predictable place. In addition, such texts become a part of the social discourse, the 'lingua franca' of the playground (Seiter, 1993, p. 7) and to engage in the discourse, children need to read any books within the series. The fact that they contain familiar and repeatable patterns means that children can exchange views on the texts without reading exactly the same stories as their friends, although of course that is usually one of their aims.

Using picture books with older pupils

There should be provision for the continuation of pleasure in picture narratives throughout primary years, including suitable graphic novels from the accepted *Tin Tin* and *Asterix* strips, to those which draw on comic book formats such as those of *Spiderman* or Japanese *Manga*. Comic-style versions of famous stories or poems such as *Oliver Twist*, *Hiawatha* and *The Rhyme of the Ancient Mariner* can also provide images to compare with the written descriptions from the novel or poem, with visual depictions of settings, characters and events.

Young writers should be allowed to incorporate drawings in their writing about the characters from the comics, films and picture stories in vogue. Drawings help them to develop ideas which can be extended into writing. Using their illustrations, children can be helped to develop written descriptions and extend their ideas beyond the exchange of dialogue. They can also be encouraged to use comic as well as book formats for their own work, in order to develop plot structure.

Reading beyond the narrative text

The greater part of this chapter has concentrated largely on the satisfactions to be derived from a narrative text, yet those who work with children also know that the book and its reader represent a very small percentage of the literacy events now possible. In their home reading or computer use, children are often presented with information, facts and figures which have as much currency in their shared conversations as the plots of stories or characters in films. As they enter school, children can be helped most by coming into contact with the familiar. Reading should not be presented as something that happens only in school, for it is those children whose homes are not reflective of given school practice who will be most alienated. The privileging of print may be seen as being out of step with much of the rapid changes taking place in the world. Gunther Kress, for example, argues that 'literacy is turning out to be highly unstable', referring to the rapid changes in the communication of information by means of technology

(Kress, 1997, p. 2). He further suggests that current anxieties about a decline in literacy are misplaced and that popular culture, with its multi-modal forms of communication, may better prepare the young for the 'information explosion' of the workplace than conventional print media are able to do. Kress proposes that it is the very pace of the programmes blamed for our children's diminishing attention span which create the potential for responding effectively to new sources of information (Kress, 1997). Not all children's first textual encounters come through story book fiction, as Doris Lessing records in her auto-biography: 'I learned to read and triumphantly entered the world of information through print on cigarette packets, grocery packaging, the big words on top of newspapers, the Army & Navy catalogue, words written under pictures and then books themselves' (Lessing, 1994, p. 82).

Linking home and school

As children progress through the education system, it is important that teachers continue to address the gap between home and school by becoming aware of what motivates children to read outside their classrooms and understanding how this can be channelled into pro-ductive learning. This does not mean that we are advocating the end of the study of English or literature as we have come to know them. It is not, as some would have us think, a simple choice between soap operas and Shakespeare or comics and Dickens or between books which re-create a vividly imagined experience and those which form part of a commercial operation. The categories of popular and can-onized culture are not mutually exclusive; indeed, a moment's reflec-tion will show this to be the case. Dickens and Shakespeare both catered for the tastes of popular 'markets' and incorporated aspects of popular culture in their work. We would argue that a knowledge of one type of text helps to increase the understanding of another. Small children who know about comic-book villains can, when it is appro-priate, also see how Dickens's descriptions of corrupt characters are created, both on the page and on the screen. The important point is that the purpose for the presence of *any* text in the class needs to be understood and the objectives of learning thought through. There is a habit of thought which believes a book can teach lessons of itself through simple exposure to it; the teacher needs only to ensure the quality of the text and pupils will automatically benefit. It is what Hall and Coles describe as the tendency of' 'leap-frogging from one quality assured text to another' (Hall and Coles, 1999, p. 150). Such planning can lead to undirected and profitless work, which is at its worst in an approach to Shakespeare that takes the resistant, desk-bound pupil through the speeches line for line, or a complex story by Dickens, word for word, at too early an age.

It is the quality of the encounter between child and text which should be the teacher's main concern and which should guide both the choice of reading matter and purpose. Popular texts can also provide complex and intricate plots; characters in such books may be colourful and engaging, the language demanding and imaginative. In their analysis of the language of both Dahl's *The BFG* and Alcott's *Little Women*, Hall and Coles demonstrate the linguistic richness of two commercially produced texts, arguing persuasively 'that high quality reading experiences can arise from an interaction between a reader and virtually any text . . . It is unhelpful to adopt a negative, deficit model of children's reading choices' (Hall and Coles, 1999, p. 144).

It is a clear focus on the purpose set for reading that teachers will find most helpful when deciding what books to purchase for their classes and the narratives, whether print or media based, from which they can create more extended work. Finally, there is, of course, much more to reading than becoming familiar with the works of 'great writers', or engaging with fictional narratives. This chapter has only glanced at the importance of other forms of narrative pleasures in developing literacy. The next chapter looks at a far more controversial form of popular culture, the comic, and examines how this medium can also support children in joining the 'literacy club' (Smith, 1988).

6

Comics

Comics have never been popular with educationalists. There is something about the combination of cartoon images and racy colloquial language that distresses a significant proportion of adults who concern themselves with the reading habits of children and worry about the consequences of the genre for academic and social learning. Indeed, some go so far as to suggest that reading comics may have even worse consequences. Elizabeth Stutz, in an essay on electronic entertainment, asks if the makers of nuclear bombs and the technology of mass warfare 'have been inspired by the enjoyment of comics and cartoons in their childhood?' (Stutz, 1996, p. 69). The most concerted attacks in the past have been reserved for the American comic book, which is often presented as competing for adolescents' interest in more 'wholesome' and 'educational' forms of reading. Of particular concern is the attraction of the superhero discourse for children of a very young age (see Chapter 3 for a fuller discussion of this). Critics' anxieties are frequently based on a deficit model, whereby those who choose to read books in graphic forms are seen as denying themselves encounters with more 'nourishing' material, just as children who eat beefburgers and chips are imagined *en masse* as rejecting green vegetables and citrus fruit. This view found its most extreme expression in the writing of Dr Frederick Wertham, Senior Psychiatrist to New York City Hospitals, who in 1954 published a book with the emotive title *Seduction of the Innocent*. In it, he propounded the thesis that comic books could be held accountable for the growth in juvenile delinquency. He illustrated his argument with graphic accounts of visual horrors and acts of violence that he had found in comic-book texts. Wertham warned a 10-year-old girl of the dangers of Wonder Woman in these emotive terms:

> Supposing . . . you get used to eating sandwiches made with very strong seasonings, with onions and peppers and highly spiced mustard. You will lose your taste for simple bread and butter and for finer

food. The same is true for reading strong comic books. If later you want to read a good novel it may describe how a young boy and girl sit together and watch the rain falling. They talk about themselves and the pages of the book describe what their innermost little thoughts are. This is what is called literature. But you will never be able to appreciate that if in comic book fashion you expect that any minute someone will appear and pitch both of them out of the window.

(Quoted in Richler, 1977, p. 300)

Similar criticisms have been repeatedly levelled at the homegrown British comic. Almost as soon as the first comic papers appeared at the beginning of the twentieth century, they were stigmatized by the use of the term 'penny dreadfuls' and associated with other sensational publications. As Rose (1984) reminds us, they were denounced in the newspapers as

rubbish, (What Boys Do Read – the Need for Stemming a River of Yellow Rubbish, *The Book Monthly*, September 1910 p. 883–5) and were leading to a decay of the infantile mind: 'when our books are bought as rubbish, sold as rubbish and received as rubbish, it is perhaps natural for anyone to suppose that they are read and written in the same spirit (Guardian, 2 May, 1900).

(Rose, 1984, p. 108)

Reading comics was seen as an unwholesome addiction that distracted delivery boys from their work and encouraged idleness. In the 1950s, Richard Hoggart chronicled aspects of working-class culture, including popular reading habits, in *The Uses of Literacy*. He depicted the proliferation of comic strips in the popular press as a 'rash' and described young servicemen's reading of comics as 'a passive visual taking-on of bad mass-art geared to a very low mental age' (Hoggart 1958, p. 201). Frank Whitehead, in the 1970s, while noting that teachers need to be aware of the popularity of comic-reading, saw this genre as 'deplorable' in its gross commercial exploitation of children's interests and considered that teachers should try their best to counteract their influence. In advising on how to respond to children who read only comics, he suggested that:

The most teachers can do is to take note of the preoccupations this culture testifies to in his pupils' make-up and then try to find and make available as many books as he can (the more recent in publication date the better) which engage with these preoccupations in a mode which is both more sensitive and constructive.

(Whitehead *et al.* 1977, p. 185)

Comic book productions for boys were described as 'uncouth publications', their language 'feebly emasculated and exclamatory', able to 'contribute virtually nothing to the development of reading ability' (ibid.). On the other hand, little girls' comics such as *Twinkle* and *My Little Pony* have also been the object of much criticism with Mary Hilton, for example, whose work has been important in developing our understanding of the significance of children's popular culture, dismissing *My Little Pony* as containing 'saccharine inanities' (Hilton, 1996, p. 12). Boys' comics have been thought to promote violence, girls' to induce a soppy passivity based on a preoccupation with domesticity, appearance and dress, which denies girls agency in the adult world.

A debased and inferior medium?

The argument of many educators is that children simply deserve better. Many teachers, who themselves have been educated within a system that emphasizes the value of enrichment through reading, are therefore more inclined to exclude comics from consideration altogether; some confine them for use on wet lunch times. Often, arguments against comics coincide with the criticism levelled against the material available on film, computer games and video. The images of some comic books appear lurid and sensational. They seem both over-sexualized, as in the representation of well-developed female characters, such as *Cat Woman*, *Halo Jones* and *Xena the Warror Princess*, and excessively violent, as represented in the stories of *Judge Dredd* and *The Incredible Hulk*. In addition, the language and humour may seem offensive in their coarseness and lack of respect for authority, as in Bart Simpson's catchphrase 'eat my shorts' or the deliberate play on 'bad' language in *South Park*, emphasized even more in the cartoon comic strip spin-offs. We do not wish to downplay genuine concerns about the stereotypical nature of much comic material and its gendered biases, however, as we have argued in Chapter 2, these issues are best discussed in context and as we demonstrate below, in using comics in class, a teacher will be able to raise important questions of commercial exploitation, violent resolutions and sex-stereotypical behaviours.

There is more to teachers' dismissal of the genre than a concern for the story content, however. Although comics are created from an interaction of image and text, it is the drawings which predominate and define the genre (Lewis, 1996, p. 16). The whole skill of a comic depends on the artist being able to unfold a plot in the space of 8–12 picture frames, using relatively few words. In many people's minds, there remains a rather simplistic correlation between 'looking at pictures' and a deficient literacy, as it is thought that it is only those who are unable to read the words who have a need for illustration. Visual literacy, except in its highest manifestations in the work of designers and classical artists, is rarely granted status within our education system. Within the realms of aesthetic criticism, it is only John Ruskin whose work emphasizes the importance of the visual as an aspect of the intellectual (Ruskin, 1985). Readers and lovers of images are, therefore, thought of as inherently inferior to those who read books. Teachers have been taught to consider the movement from pictures to words largely as an intellectual progression. In such a schema, babies start by being shown pictures in texts of all kinds and move on to sharing picture books with adults. Gradually, as they learn to read, more and more words are included in their texts until the young reader arrives at a stage when illustrations can be dispensed with altogether. The same principle is applied to their writing, in that an assumption is made about the developmental stages to move through, in which drawing is given less status than writing. Thus, it is assumed that when first given writing tools, young children will make marks randomly, proceed to drawing recognizable forms, next form letters and eventually manage words and then sentences, drawing featuring only as a dispensable embellishment. Teachers can find themselves criticized when using drawing and colouring as outcomes of learning. This is despite the move to new forms of literacy in which the visual is a significant part of communication (Kress, 1997).

The role of the image

In the later stages of primary schooling, children often measure their reading ability by the density of print and length of the texts that they can manage. Books for older children that combine a challenging text with illustrations, as in *Alice's Adventures in Wonderland* or Kipling's *Just So Stories*, are rarer. The dismissal of visual imagery embedded within a text has not always been the case, as testified by the combination of illustration and poetry found in Blake, the contribution of Tenniel's drawings to Lewis Carroll's fantasies and the work of a number of artists who illustrated Dickens's novels. However, current school versions of classic texts usually exclude the original illustrations and even if these are present, as in Blake's *Songs of Innocence*, they are likely to be given only a passing glance and not read as integral to the meaning. Indeed, despite the very rich resource of picture stories available to younger children, it is nearly always the words that fix the attention of their teachers. As Marriott comments:

> These two ideas, that picture books are an age-related phenomenon and that the ability to understand pictures is an unambiguous skill which young children automatically develop, often lead to a third, that picture books provide a kind of prop which sustains and supports the initially incompetent beginning reader ... And often implicit is the belief that the sooner the children's behaviour resembles that of the adult reader, seen as routinely and skilfully absorbing pages of unbroken and unillustrated print – the better.
>
> (Marriott, 1998, p. 2)

In reading research, boys' pleasure in visual texts is often classified as a limitation, as revealed in the following comment from Gemma Moss when reporting some preliminary findings of her Fact and Fiction Project. Moss suggests that 'it is the potential for equal social status that seems to draw weaker boy readers towards visually-based non-fiction' and that their interest in cards and stickers is 'boys doing friendship' (Moss, 1999, p. 19). There is, in her report, a strongly implied criticism of a form of shared text which requires a minimum of interaction with printed words for a complete understanding or shared significance. However, it is doubtful whether the quips and jokes Moss describes as taking place during the sharing process are independent of the text which surrounds these images.

Teachers' prejudice against introducing all kinds of children's narrative pleasures into the classroom that bypass the written word is not surprising, given the heavy reliance on textbooks in most school subjects. We all want children to become fluent and competent readers in their primary years and those who look at pictures (mainly boys) in reading time appear to be limiting their ability to develop both fluency and critical reading skills. However, it is a stance which can work against the earliest literacy experiences and reading pleasures of a large number of children and lead to the neglect of a resource that, when used well, can bring real benefits to the development of critical textual awareness. In the next part of this chapter, therefore, drawing evidence largely from our own research, we intend to consider some of the positive aspects of children's delight in their comics and suggest ways in which they may be let into the classroom. For many children, the reading of comics remains an essential part of the experience of childhood. It is a weekly ritual, with the prospect of pleasures that can be shared with others, both adults and peers, along with the sweets that might accompany the purchase. Further, for most young readers, comics are a pleasure restricted to early childhood, readily given up to more demanding reading matter, only to be renewed again when they themselves become parents (Rosen, 1996).

Comics as an aspect of children's reading choices

Who, then, buys and reads comics? In the United Kingdom, there has been little systematic surveying of primary school children's choices in popular culture. Davies and Brember (1993) asked 611 Year 2, Year 4 and Year 6 children about their reading habits. When asked to choose between stories, comics and non-fiction as their favourite reading material, stories were the first choice of both boys and girls, followed by comics as a second choice. This survey thus suggested that comics were a significant factor in the home reading diet of both boys and girls in primary schools, but no further details of what kinds of comics were reported except that there was a growing interest in magazine reading which replaced comic reading by both boys and girls in Year 6. Davies and Brember did, however, show that more boys than expected chose comics as their favourite reading material, with comics being as popular as stories in Years 4 and 6.

In the United States, a more recent survey of 419 sixth-grade middle-school children's reading (Worthy, Moorman and Turner, 1999) found that comics and cartoons ranked third in children's stated reading preferences. Although the numbers of comics nominated as preferences trailed well behind the scary stories of horror series such as Goosebumps, the researchers nevertheless reported that 'light materials, including scary series books, comics and magazines topped the lists for every sub-group of students'. They also concluded that a 'limited availability of preferred reading in schools leaves pupils with three choices: reading something outside their interests, obtaining preferred materials themselves or not reading at all' (Worthy, Moorman and Turner, 1999, p. 3). They suggested that students who cannot afford to purchase their own resources are more dependent on school sources and therefore have more limited choice of reading matter.

We know more from research about the older age group and their tastes may therefore be used as some kind of indicator of the popularity of comics in the community as a whole. In their 1994–95 study of the reading interests of almost 8,000 children, Hall and Coles (1999) reported that comics were less popular than books in the sample of

10–14-year-olds as a whole and that the purchase of comics decreased as children grew older. However in the 10+ age group, comics accounted for over a third (34.2 per cent) of children's reading matter, which was roughly equivalent to the numbers who bought books (35.9 per cent). Moreover, 6 per cent of the pupils buying comics reported purchasing two or more titles. Boys in particular bought more comics and sustained their reading interest in them over a longer period. In the older age groups, this interest was mostly displaced by an expansion into newspaper and magazine reading, something that Davies and Brember's study had noted beginning in Year 6. It may therefore be concluded that an early familiarity with weekly publications prepares children for later reading of periodical non-fiction and information texts. Girls' choice of periodicals has marked socio-economic stratification, whereas for boys, tastes in comics and periodicals cross social barriers and therefore can be seen as a widely shared experience and source of cultural knowledge (Hall and Coles, 1999, p. 58).

In a much smaller sample of 255 11-year-old readers, who were surveyed during their first term of secondary school, Millard (1997) also found a gendered pattern of interest in comics and magazines which was more marked than the differences found in boys' and girls' book reading. This was possibly because their book reading was heavily influenced by the texts and authors promoted in school. By the age of 11, fewer of the children reported reading a comic regularly, but those who did were overwhelmingly boys. Just under a third of the 134 11-year-old boys read a comic regularly, whereas less than a tenth of the 121 girls reported that they still read one. Instead, apart from the few who read *The Beano* and *The Dandy*, girls overwhelmingly opted for a wide range of teenage magazines, which mixed information about pop stars, fashion and personal relationships with picture stories and make-up tips. The fact remains, however, that comics provide a stepping stone to other kinds of reading and their acceptance as part of the reading matter of school can serve to support those who are reluctant to read books for pleasure, whether fiction or non-fiction.

The interactive reader

Comic readership should be seen as contributing to the development of young readers through its connectedness to other literacy practices. Most comics encourage interaction through a page devoted to readers' letters and the swapping of information and jokes. Moreover, in recent years, the most popular comics like the *The Beano* have created interactive websites on the Internet which allow children to write news items, play games and complete puzzles. *The Beano* site also provides information about the publication's history, dating back to 1938, and documents the introduction of the various characters and storylines. This historical focus appeals to a small number of boys who identifed themselves as comic collectors in Millard's (1997) interviews.

David was one such boy, a good reader, both by his own account and in the estimation of his teacher. He had become a connoisseur of the comic genre, explaining in an interview that he had been collecting comics from 1989 and owned some that went back to 1980:

David: I've still got them, 'cos I wanted to see what they were like a bit ago, what the drawings were like, and colour and stuff like that.

Interviewer: So is it the drawings in comics you really like, rather than the story?

David: No. It's the story that I like. It's just that I like to see how it changes. 'Cos like now I've changed from *Beano* an' all 'cos Dennis the Menace is changed, and he looks like a five year old now.

The existence of a website providing facts and figures about dates and characters, changes and traditions can allow pupils like David to pursue a research project into a favourite genre that will involve him in more complex reading.

A powerful shared childhood memory

For some children then, comics provide an early introduction to reading which can be shared and discussed with friends as well as parents and siblings. Alan Bennett is one of a number of successful 'literary' writers who have described an early interest in the comic genre. Bennett, talking of his avid reading of popular fiction as a young boy, comments: 'I had read quite a few story-books by this time, as I had learned to read quite early by dint, it seemed to me, of staring over my brother's shoulder at the comic he was reading until suddenly it made sense' (Bennett, 1994, p. 4)

North American writer, Mordecai Richler, is included as an outsider's voice in *The Cool Web* (1977), a collection of essays celebrating the role of narrative in education. His essay tackles the criticism of the genre's 'cheapness', opposing to this judgement the deeply felt boyhood pleasures which had made comic books irresistible to his generation. Michael Rosen, the poet and broadcaster, has described his experience of sharing *The Beano* with Isaac, his 6-year-old son, detailing the complex range of skills the publication encourages in the young reader (Rosen, 1996, p. 123). Some fellow women academics have described their early comic reading as an 'alternative reading scheme' which moved from early picture comics like *Twinkle* to more robust comics such as *The Beano* in mid-childhood and on to older girl comics like *Girl, Jackie, Bunty* or *School Friend* during the pre-adolescent stage.

All the experiences recounted above relate to home rather than school encounters with texts, and the implication is that this alternative form of reading is taking place beyond the teacher's gaze in order to avoid disapproval. However, we should encounter less difficulty in making a case for the inclusion of comics in today's classrooms. A shift has taken place in the readers' interest from books perceived as great works, dependent on the genius of the writer for their power, to a concentration on writing as text in its multiplicity of forms. This view, which was first signalled by Barthes in 'The Death of the Author' (1977), has gradually worked its way into schools, allowing a more developed understanding of text-based work with children. A number of teachers who have developed a wider interest in textuality have included comics as part of their repertoire. Such a teacher is Helen Bromley, who starts from a recollection of personal childhood pleasures in the comic text which she later shared with her own daughter. She identifies several key areas in which comics can assist in developing a critical knowledge of how texts work. These are:

- the use of jokes, puns and alliteration
- a range of voices, such as those of the narrator, the editor and the inclusion of sound effects which employ visual puns and differentiated type faces to convey meaning
- a multi-layering of meaning
- intertextuality – bringing in references to other texts and cultural forms of knowledge (Bromley, 2000, p. 34).

We may conclude, therefore, both from the professional writers' autobiographical reminiscences, along with a small range of classroom studies, that comics have always been an important part of reading experience for a sizeable portion of children in the primary school years, particularly boys. Not only that, but comics and periodicals are a shared reading pleasure and that for many children whose families cannot afford to buy a wide range of books, comics provide reading material that can be readily shared or swapped. The use of comics in school can provide a link to the reading experience of children for whom books may be associated predominantly with school work.

Most primary schools already operate a home-school lending library which enables children to take books home on a regular basis. In addition, primary schools encourage children to take home their reading books as a means of involving parents in their children's literacy development. The texts which enter the home from school, therefore, are either part of an established canon of children's literature, or are embedded within a published reading scheme. In either case, these are texts which are part of the 'cultural capital' (Bourdieu, 1990) of schooled literacy and which reflect, for the most part, the norms, beliefs and values of the dominant classes (Lankshear *et al.*, 1997; Luke, 1993b). Some evidence of the positive role of the incorporation of comics into school reading practices in the early years is provided by the results of Marsh's project which developed home-school comic libraries in two Sheffield schools (Millard and Marsh, 2000). Two Reception/Year 1 classes and one Year 3 class were involved in the project. Sixty-nine children took part: 34 girls and 35 boys. The children came from diverse ethnic and linguistic communities, including African-Caribbean, Bangladeshi, Chinese, English, Irish, Pakistani and Somali communities. Marsh found that although only 23 per cent of the total number of children in the study had been bought a comic in the two-week period prior to the project, the majority of children in the study (94 per cent) did report that they looked at the comics of siblings, relatives, neighbours and friends at home on a regular basis. A home-school comic lending library was set up in each classroom. The children were allowed to borrow one comic a week over half a term and during the project children, parents and teachers were interviewed.

Taking it all back home

The children responded enthusiastically to the project and all began by taking the comics home on a weekly basis. The three teachers involved felt generally that the children had been very motivated as a result of the project: 'The children loved it . . . it was really motivating for them and they talked a lot about it to each other during the week' (Jane, Reception/Year 1 teacher); 'at reading time, I was getting requests like, "Can I go to the comic box?" ' (Harry, Year 3 teacher).

Interviews with the children revealed that most of them preferred to borrow comics rather than books, although the project was not set up in ways which made these two choices oppositional. During the project, the children still took books home on the usual basis. The children were overwhelmingly of the opinion that taking comics home should be a regular occurrence in school: 'We should take comics home because the children get happy' (Ansa, aged 5).

Children often appropriated adult preoccupations with educational development to argue their case: 'It's a good idea to take comics home 'cos children like comics and we read 'em lots of times and it's good for your reading' (Viola, aged 7); 'They're good for your writings and spelling and you might learn something' (Dale, aged 5); 'I like taking the comics home 'cos they're good to read and you can do lots of things . . . like quizzes and that. It makes you want to read more times 'cos you want to read all the comics and . . . then you do all the games and that lot. They're better than books' (Marcus, aged 8).

The interactive nature of the comics was their most popular aspect. Eighty-five per cent of children stated that the fact that they could complete games and puzzles in the comics was their favourite feature and was what made the comics more attractive to them than books. This was true of both Reception/Year 1 and the Year 3 classes: 'I like to read the comics . . . you can play some games' (Malik, aged 5); 'I like doing the quizzes and games. And you can do word searches and that' (Alia, aged 8).

In today's media-saturated age, some children may find interactions with conventional story books too static in comparison with the vividly imaged, interactive stories of their computer games, in which they can become the protagonist and create their own destinies. This interactive element of comics was very appealing to those interviewed. Some children also liked the fact that there were pictures to support their reading:

> I like comics because they have lots of little cartoons like you don't have to read them in one go and you can do them in sections. It looks like there's chapters. They're easier to read than books . . . there's too many lines so sometimes I jump lines and comics are in speech bubbles.
>
> (Sam, aged 6)

On the surface, this may appear to characterize the reading of boys who, it has been suggested, may use visual texts as a means of escaping the hard work involved in reading continuous prose (Moss, 1999).

However, the complexities of the layout of comics and the reading skills they demand are by no means unchallenging. Most of the children perceived comics to be easier to read than books, many stating that books contained 'harder words'. Yet a quick comparison of their reading books and comics proved that this was not the case and that both kinds of texts contained unknown words, demanding different reading skills dependent on level. In a previous study, Millard had similarly found that the comic reading of older boys (10–13) involved decoding complex language, particularly those comics that encouraged the use of technical vocabulary (Millard, 1994, pp. 103–50).

Not only boys, but families too

One of the teachers in Marsh's study worried that children would pressurize parents to buy comics and that parents would become dissatisfied with the project. In fact, this did not happen. Most children reported that parents felt happy about them taking comics home from school. The five parents interviewed expressed positive views: 'The thing is with comics he picks the stories out and we have to have them over and over again . . . he loves them. I don't mind comics, I always think it is better to read anything than nothing at all . . . to me, reading is reading' (Carlos's dad); 'It's been really good. He loves bringing them home and I read them with him. *Beano* and *Dandy* have been about years and they have always been good fun' (Joe's dad); 'I think the comic library is a good idea . . . it gets them interested in different things' (Saira's mum). It is of note that two of these positive comments are from dads, a group who figure less frequently in children's accounts of support for home reading and whose reading is often seen as different and more work-oriented by their children (Millard, 1997; Pidgeon, 1993, pp. 30–2). It is useful to find a genre for which male family members demonstrate a natural enthusiasm.

Some children talked about the communal reading experiences which the comics promoted within and beyond the immediate family: 'I like comics 'cos it's got loads of pages. I readed it with my dad. He said, "Well done". My big brother and sister reads it with me' (Amjid, aged 5); 'My brother likes to read comics and he likes to look at the pictures. My baby likes the teddy bear one comics. Comics are hard to read. I like hard words to read in the comics. My brother said the "caterpillar" one' (Umar, aged 6); 'My name is Ayesha and I like reading comics 'cos there's lots of cartoons . . . I play teacher games and my next-door-neighbour comes and reads it to me' (Ayesha, aged 5). When asked about these instances, children said that their families did not share reading books in the same way. It would appear that taking comics home increased the opportunities for some families to engage in reading activities which were a more familiar part of their cultural 'habitus' (Bourdieu, 1990). Four of the five parents interviewed insisted on telling the researcher about the comics they had enjoyed as a child.

The teachers involved in this project were equally convinced of the learning opportunities presented by comics. One of the teachers suggested that the work on the genre was beneficial because it had helped children to read both print and visual elements, a requirement that was replicated in school textbooks:

> There is concern at the moment to get children reading different types of texts rather than just plain straight narrative and aside from the comic stories, the number of other types of texts they've managed to find their way around is just . . . they read tables, they read quizzes, they knew the little bubbles were separate to the rest of the text. While this was going on, I was doing a piece of work on maths textbooks where similar skills are required because you are given a table and asked to interpret it. There's a little bubble there with a piece of information in, stuff like that . . . children find it much harder to do that. I felt I was seeing exactly the same stuff going on with comics as I was with maths textbooks but that they were finding it harder with maths textbooks.
>
> (Harry)

The involvement with the comic-lending project encouraged the infant teachers involved to introduce work based on comic characters and the linguistic features of these texts into their literacy curriculum (Ineson and Marsh, 2000).

Work on comics in the classroom

The following examples arose from the work on the comics undertaken in the classrooms during the project. Because of the short nature of comic texts, they were integrated into shared reading and writing sessions as part of the literacy hour. Activities included work on story structure where children were asked to sequence cut up versions of a comic strips. They progressed to identifying the 'complication' in the stories, that is those points which precipitate the events that follow (Thomas, 1998, calls these 'hinge points'). This is an activity

Figure 6.1   Child's additions to a comic strip

that can be tackled at any level, depending on the complexity of the comic or graphic novel chosen. Children can be given the beginning and end of a comic strip and asked to work out what would have happened in the middle of the story (Figure 6.1).

Other activities can include familiar work on character, stereotyping and setting. These are as applicable to the superhero narratives of Batman and Superman as they are to the characters created for younger readers such as Barbie and Bob the Builder. The nature of periodicals means that an understanding of character can be developed. Character databases can be constructed and added to on a weekly basis, as a new issue appears. The children can thus track character changes over time. Comics lend themselves to rich word level work with their use of puns, alliteration, assonance and onomatopoeia. One class was asked to devise glossaries to provide definitions of onomatopoeic words they found in comics (see Ineson and Marsh, 2000).

Work can also be undertaken on other genres associated with the comic. Letters, competitions, puzzles and advertisements, all provide excellent material for analysis. Pupils of all levels can undertake a survey of their classes' periodical reading, entering their results on a database and producing their own school-based comic from the interests they identified. At word level, comics are replete in 'specialist' vocabulary. Reading a Dennis the Menace story, which used the word 'menacemobile' could lead to a discussion of morphology ('menacemobile', 'popemobile', mobile phone, mobile classroom and so on). Contractions are another familiar feature of comics which children can study and can be a pleasurable means of introducing work on cataphoric and anaphoric references. There are also puns, alliteration and plentiful use of excessive punctuation – especially exclamations and specialist signs to indicate bad language or ranting: !**?! **? !!.

Information and communications technology, literacy and comics

Computer access provides a further stimulus to reading and writing. As discussed previously, the websites of the *The Beano* and the *The Dandy* offer many opportunities for interactive work. On the *The Beano* site for example, readers are encouraged to become a cub reporter for Gnasher the Gnewshound. Examples are given of established stories, such as the one entitled 'Bananaman and the Banana Bandit!' which begins: '*Dandy* star shaken and stirred! That well-known weedy individual and alter-ego of supergoon, Bananaman, Little Eric, was on his way to get his daily supply of bananas, when he was knocked over by what he later described as a "Masked bedsheet" ' (*Beano* website, accessed 6 May 2000). The site's invitation into this activity reads: 'Gnasher the Gnewshound Gneeds cub reporters, with the further question 'Have **YOU** got a grrreat item of gnews? Then let us gnow, er, know".' This can provide a focus for understanding where a silent 'g' is used both appropriately and inappropriately in the text. The writing resembles the playful use of language often favoured by boys in their own narratives (Millard, 1997) and would provide a stimulus to other pupils' written work.

Problematic stories: sex, stereotyping and savagery

However, there remain the concerns of ideology, outlined in Chapter 2, which found expression in the comments of one of the teachers in the comic lending project, who was concerned about the stereotypical aspects of the material provided: 'We've worked very hard to make sure the books we have are multi-cultural but the comics . . . er, they have mostly white characters and that does worry me' (Amy, Reception/Year 1 teacher).

The children, when asked if they thought that most teachers would agree with them taking comics home to read, generally thought that they would not because of the violence contained within the genre: 'Teachers wouldn't like all the fighting and kicking in comics, that's why they won't let you take them home' (Asia, aged 7); 'Cos there's too much kicking and that's why' (Mohammed, aged 5).

The teachers and children raise important issues here. They include not only our concern for all of those who are excluded from the stories of comic strip texts, but also about marketing strategies that provide technological mastery and physical prowess for boys and offer girls a focus on personal appearance and domestic harmony. Women teachers in particular, frequently experience real discomfort when confronted with the violent and war-like narratives found in comics aimed at older boys, such as *Judge Dredd* and *Batman* and replicated in the play and story writing of much younger children. But as Urquhart reminds us:

> We need therefore to be mindful that children reading popular fictions may find within them something more subtle than a simple taking in of cultural indoctrination. With boys, simply deploring fighting fan-atasies as 'social conditioning' into a masculinity that celebrates vio-lence as a solution to conflict might similarly miss the complexity of boys' involvements with these popular fictions. Pre-adolescent chil-dren are notably subversive of and resistant to authoritative and so-cially sanctioned roles and values.
>
> (Urquhart, 1996, p. 159)

Dyson has also discussed children's use of superheroes in dramatic role-play, similarly suggesting that 'commercial culture becomes semio-tic material for making sense of social experience' (Dyson, 1997, p. 15). She argues that because this culture is not 'reified and set apart for study in schools or museums', it is able to be reworked for purposes of 'social affiliation' and 'social play' and this 'unofficial' knowledge used to negotiate public meanings. The commercially produced characters have established meanings that can be played with or reworked in the context of our pupils' changing sense of identities and social roles. The 'unofficial' comic characters do not have fixed meanings and once allowed into the official space of the classroom, emergent meanings can be more readily analysed and where necessary challenged and interrogated. Because children's cult figures are used to cement peer affiliations, children from middle-class homes whose parents seek to prevent them engaging with popular culture still manage to acquire sufficient background knowledge about characters, plots and structures in order to relate to their classmates (Dyson, 1997, p. 114). Further, Dyson's work shows the importance of the role played by teachers 'willing to engage with the issues of children's lives that we as adults may not choose to see' (ibid., p. 164). Dyson makes the point that such teachers both understand and engage with the interplay of children's emerging cultural texts in the official curriculum.

It would be wrong to conclude from our study that comics fit neatly into every pupil's literacy practices, for in some families comics may be as alien a concept as books. Nevertheless, comics can offer a valuable alternative link to the reading that many children engage in at home and in the community. This form of popular culture has a particular appeal in that it is also able to draw in non-traditional support for literacy development, including the engagement of dads and older male siblings in the pleasures of a well-loved text. As we have shown earlier, critics of the use of reading material which is more deeply embedded within children's daily cultural and social lives, as opposed to more canonical texts, argue as if an interest in one denies the importance of the other. There is no evidence to show that children who have taken real pleasure in light fictions in their childhood are less likely to engage with more powerful texts in their adult lives. Indeed, the collective testimonies of Alan Bennett, Mordecai Richler, Michael Rosen and Helen Bromley referred to in this chapter and the experience of both authors of this book provide anecdotal evidence to the contrary.

Of more concern, as Worthy, Moorman and Turner (1999) reported in the study cited earlier, is the fact that 'there is an ever-increasing gap between student preferences and materials that schools provide and recommend' (ibid., p. 23), which works to disadvantage the poorer members of communities. As teachers and researchers, we need to do more to explore that gap and find ways of building more secure bridges between school and home literacy practices. Comics provide one cheap and effective way of supporting this link. In the next chapter, we move on to explore how computer games also provide many children with opportunities to develop narrative pleasures that are often overlooked within school.

7

Computer Games

'Video games are better than books 'cos you can be a player in games and you just have to read books.' Jahed, the child who proffered this comment when asked about books and computer games,[1] is typical of his generation. In a major study of children's interests in the new media, Sonia Livingstone and Moira Bovill, from the London School of Economics and Political Science, found, in their interviews and surveys with over 1,500 6–17-year-olds, that:

> Books are widely seen as old-fashioned, boring, frustrating, and on their way out . . . There are of course a few children and young people for whom reading books was pleasurable. Those who read for pleasure are usually middle-class children, girls or younger children for whom being able to read is a novel accomplishment . . . But with these notable exceptions, there seemed to be a general consensus particularly amongst older children that books are on their way out.
>
> (Livingstone and Bovill, 1999, pp. 17–19)

Livingstone and Bovill's data suggests that children are spending more of their leisure time watching television and playing computer games than reading books. This chapter explores some of the attractions that computer games have for young children and discusses the features much criticized by adults. The relationship between the skills needed to play these games and more traditional literacy skills are then outlined, before the chapter moves on to explore how the games can be used to inform the literacy curriculum in schools. We close with a brief look at popular culture in relation to other forms of new media.

Which computer games?

The 'nintendo generation' (Green, Reid and Bigum, 1998; Luke, 2000) we teach in primary schools today has grown up surrounded by a range of computer games and related products. Most children have some access to computer games, whether or not they have them at home (Sanger *et al.*, 1997; Millard, 1997). Livingstone and Bovill report in *Young People, New Media* that very few children and young people in their survey (6 per cent of boys and 14 per cent of girls) had no access to computer games at home (Livingstone and Bovill, 1999, p. 21). These figures, of course, mask large class differences in the ownership and use of computer games. Working-class children are much more likely to own a games console than a personal computer (PC) (Gailey, 1993; Sefton-Green, 1999; Millard, 2000). Games consoles are the machines which are more widely known as Nintendo and Sony Playstations or Dreamcast. They are potent computers that are orientated solely towards the playing of games, to the extent that the more powerful aspects of the computers inside them are disguised (Fleming, 1996). Of course, these are not the types of computers favoured by schools.

Computers with advanced word-processing facilities are more often found in the homes of middle-class children and classrooms. These machines are also capable of providing a platform for games and many children do use them for this purpose. However, the types of games that can be used with PCs can also be educational in nature, more so than those designed for games consoles. In addition, many middle-class parents exert more control over the choices their children can make in relation to computer games. In a study in New York and Boston, Gailey (1993) found that middle-class parents avoided purchasing games which had paramilitary overtones or focused on gang-fighting. The working-class parents 'were more likely to buy the sports, ninja and paramilitary adventure series and had not purchased the spatial relations games, except Pinball and Paper Boy' (Gailey, 1993, p. 85).

This has clear implications for schools. Once again, we find the 'cultural capital' (Bourdieu, 1977) of middle-class children reflected in school discourses, a process which inevitably leads to inequality of access and educational outcomes (Giroux, 1988; Lankshear *et al.*, 1997). Many teachers are more likely to be familiar with the software to which middle-class children have access and the study by Sanger *et al.* (1998) demonstrated that most teachers disapprove of the kinds of games likely to be used by working-class children: 'teachers were disinclined to embrace anything related to commercial, as opposed to educational, hardware and software . . . Games magazines were unknown territory to many teachers (and parents) with whom we talked, although teachers admitted to banishing them from schools without any knowledge of the contents' (Sanger *et al.*, 1998, p. 39). Disapproval of these games is usually founded on misgivings about the level of violence and fears of addiction. We will explore these concerns later in the chapter.

The computer games industry has grown enormously since its humble beginnings in the 1980s. From the early days of the ZF Spectrum, Atari machines and the 8-bit hand-held consoles made by Sega and Nintendo, in the 1990s we saw the development of more powerful games machines. The new 16-bit consoles enabled graphics and sound effects to become richer and sharper in detail. The computer games industry has become a multibillion dollar business as the favourite leisure pursuit of children. It is also clear that is a market which is highly gendered in nature. Cassell and Jenkins (1998) report that 'approximately 75 to 85 percent of the sales and revenues generated by the $10 billion game industry are derived from male consumers' (Cassell and Jenkins, 1998, p. 11). There is a growing market for computer games for girls, but it is clear that most games are developed with boys in mind. The following section of the chapter examines issues of gender in relation to the computer games market and explores how far an involvement 'in children's and youth culture almost always involves participation as a gendered, classed and ethnic subject' (Alloway and Gilbert, 1998, p. 96).

Gender and games

The Livingstone and Bovill report (1999) found that 79 per cent of boys in their survey played computer games, as opposed to 49 per cent of girls. This would appear to support the claims of other researchers who suggest that boys are much heavier users of the genre than girls (Millard, 1997, 2000; Sanger *et al.*, 1998; Cassell and Jenkins, 1998; Alloway and Gilbert, 1998). One of the reasons for this disparity in use is undoubtedly the way in which the games are marketed. A quick survey of the shelves in any games shop will confirm that many covers feature images of boys and men. In addition, the games magazines aimed at children are usually positioned at the male reader. Here is an example of the type of text which is common in these magazines:

> If you're quietly cruising down the high street in your flash motor, you
> can be sure that you're not gonna look too hot. To make an impression

on your mates (hey, and the ladies, of course . . .), laying down loads of rubber is definitely the way to play. So in *Metropolis Street Racer* you can pull off some amazing power slides, swing the tail of your motor around the city streets.

(Field, 2000, p. 17)

The construction of the reader as male is overt enough to suggest that the magazine publishers have little real interest in reaching a female market. In addition, they appear to be keen to develop an image of the male market which reflects only hegemonic masculinities. Alloway and Gilbert (1998) offer a comprehensive review of the misogynistic and machismo language of many computer games magazines and advertisements and suggest that: 'our overall impression of gaming texts is that they produce and market hegemonic masculinity that is predicated on fierce individualism, competition and rivalry, domination and control of others, violent action, and a disregard for all forms of life other than for the self' (Alloway and Gilbert, 1998, p. 107).

In addition to the marketing of the games, there are other features which may not be appealing to girls. In the popular market, games tend to feature a preponderance of male characters. Players are often invited to choose a specific character, which they use to navigate the game. A number of games are now offering one or more female characters which a player can choose, but female characters are still in the minority. The extent to which this can have a major effect on the subject identities of children playing the games is open to question. In cultural studies, there has been a range of work which has sought to address how far a viewer identifies with characters in a film or television narrative, with the notion of identification open to question (Barker and Brooks, 1998). Although some might argue that game players are not invited to identify as the characters, merely to use them as a tool, nevertheless the creation of a virtual world, populated mainly by men, is hardly appealing to girls.

In addition, the representation of women in many of the games is questionable. Often, women appear as characters to be rescued or killed. Gailey (1993) argues that class issues are bound up in this: 'Gender and class are intimately linked in the games. "Good" women are hierarchically organized and function as motivations and rewards for bravery – handmaidens will do at lower levels, but the higher status princess awaits only the most skilful and successful hero' (Gailey, 1993, p. 87). Because of the level of criticism of the sexism inherent within the games, some manufacturers have responded by extending the number of female characters and making them stronger protagonists of action, rather than as villains to be zapped or heroines to be rescued. However, these concessions have been framed within a masculinist discourse in which female characters are still defined by stereotypes: 'As one twelve-year-old girl said after switching from the single female character in the game "Odyssey" to one of the male characters, "I don't like the way she dies. The male characters scream when they're slaughtered. The female character whimpers" ' (Cassell and Jenkins, 1998, p. 10). There may now be more female characters as active players in games, but they are usually skimpily dressed with Barbie-like figures and an emphasis on feminized sexuality. Thus Lara Croft, the protagonist in the popular *Tomb Raider* series, is celebrated more widely for her physical attributes than fighting skills and is to be featured in a full-length film, such is her popularity with many boys and young men. These retrogressively patriarchal ideologies do little to attract girls to the genre.

Nevertheless, many girls are attracted to computer games and enjoy playing them, although few spend as long on them as do their male counterparts. Inevitably, the types of games girls enjoy do differ from those played most often by boys (Millard, 1997, p. 71). There are a number of different types of games within the range offered to children. In the fantasy/adventure/odyssey games, players have to pursue a quest in which they encounter a variety of challenges and utilize their problem-solving skills. Players are aided in their journey by their success in acquiring various tools to help them in their task. This genre often appears in the form of platform games in which players move from easy to progressively more difficult levels with the same basic interface. 'Shoot 'em ups' or 'Beat 'em ups' are terms used generally to refer to games in which players have to defeat enemies through fighting, either individually or in gangs. Racing games involve vehicles or objects which navigate tracks that can become increasingly complex according to the level played. Sports games feature boxing, football, skateboarding, wrestling and so on. Some games are related to films, television and Disney cartoons and the latter are particular favourites of young children, e.g. *A Bug's Life, 101 Dalmatians*. Other games are overtly educational in nature and are usually designed to promote literacy and numeracy skills. These latter games are aimed primarily at the PC user market. Some research suggests that girls prefer adventure games which involve problem-solving skills (Sanger *et al.*, 1998), whilst other research identifies that boys enjoy fighting and sports games (Gailey, 1993). In a previous study of the narrative interests of 255 11-year-olds, Millard reported that:

Girls prefer the less violent, more quest forms of the platform games in which the goal is to get to a particular area of a building to retrieve treasure or to rescue a person. Interestingly, the game most frequently named as a favourite by the girls in this survey was *Lemmings* – a game in which the player gains points and moves to higher levels, not by zapping the small mammals, but by saving them from destruction. Boys, on the whole, prefer the quicker-paced, more violent 'beat 'em ups', with the sub-set 'shoot 'em ups' being especially popular.

(Millard, 1997, p. 71)

However, if the oppressive nature of the way in which men and women are constructed within the games discourse is clear, it can also be argued that the hegemonic masculinity celebrated within these games is limiting to boys. The games present only one version of masculinity, one which celebrates aggression, violence, power and individualism. In addition, the well-built, muscled men who appear in the games bear little resemblance to the pre-pubescent boys who play them.

Issues of 'race' are also not sufficiently addressed in the gaming world. Some newer games, such as *Theme Park World*, feature black and ethnic minority characters, but these are still outnumbered by white characters. In addition, some games position the black and ethnic minority characters as villains to be defeated or captured (Gailey, 1993). Stereotyped images abound and such games do little to challenge hegemonic discourses of white privilege and power. The world of children's books has made progress towards equality in terms of representation in the last decades and most teachers strive to include a balance of cultures in the books they choose for their classes. It appears as if entering the world of computer games means taking a retrogressive step and that it will be many more years before the pressure on games manufacturers to address issues of representation has any meaningful effect.

However, despite the insidiousness of these retrogressive stereotypes, the most vocal concern of many parents, teachers and journalists appears to be the violence inherent within the games discourse. Most of the popular games involve some level of violence, whether that is fighting, kicking, zapping or killing opponents. Perhaps such fears are fuelled by the fact that, rather than being passive, game players are positioned as participants in the violence. However, as was suggested in Chapter 2, this attempt to find direct causal effects between media consumption and violence has been criticized by those who question the research methods used to prove this (Barker and

Petley, 1997). It would appear that we need much more detailed research which maps out the ways in which children respond to the violent scenarios offered in computer games.

Another concern which many have is that the games are addictive (Griffiths, 1993). However, there is little real evidence of this. Some studies suggest that there is a wide range of level of involvement with the games, with a very small percentage of children playing for over two hours a day and others for less than two hours a week (Funk, Behmann and Buchman, 1997; Hall and Coles, 1999). Livingstone and Bovill (1999) state that the average is 45 minutes of computer game playing per day. There is no evidence to suggest that children play computer games more often than they watch television, therefore, and so the suggestion that children are becoming zombies because of overexposure to the genre is ill-founded. A further concern is that of isolation; many people fear that children are becoming lonely creatures, locked in their own bedrooms playing games on their own and, therefore, less likely to socialize with others. Again, it appears that these fears have little grounding in reality. The study carried out by Sanger *et al.* (1998) suggests that very few children spend most of their time playing solitary games. In fact, the games appear to offer a range of opportunities for interaction as children swop experiences, exchange news on games and trade information relating to the navigation of the programs. Millard (1997, p. 73) also found that boys in particular used access to computers to cement friendships

So far, we have focused on the pervasive criticisms made of computer games and attempted to map out the complex terrain of the genre. In the next section, we want to move on to explore some of the benefits that may be accrued by playing such games, in particular the literacy skills which may be developed in their use.

The skills that game-playing can develop

There are a number of studies which suggest that hand/eye coordination is developed as children manipulate the figures on screen around tracks and paths (Loftus and Loftus, 1983; Greenfield, 1984; Gagnon, 1985). Gagnon (1985) argues that games also improve spatial skills when children have to navigate objects in relation to other features on the screen. Certainly, the ability to process visual information from a number of sources and work out their relationship to each other appears to be a key skill required by most of the games. A number of games also develop problem-solving skills (Greenfield, 1984) as children have to work out rules, plan ways of achieving a goal and solve difficulties presented to them along the way. Greenfield (1984) also argues that computer games develop children's skills in parallel processing, that is their ability to absorb information from a number of sources at once. Rumelhart (1977) suggests that this skill is central to the reading process. Greenfield outlines how games enable children to 'induce the relations among multiple interacting variables' (Greenfield, 1984, p. 103), with the emphasis on induction rather than children being told explicitly how things work. In addition, the need to induce the relationships between multiple variables is often combined with the requirement to do so at high speed, as the games move quickly through their settings. This is a complex skill which often leaves adult spectators of children playing computer games in awe. Greenfield (1984) also argues that the multiple levels of difficulty presented in most games are important for scaffolding children's learning as they move from easier levels to more difficult ones. Children can choose to attempt a more difficult level which contains many features of the previous level. This provides them with a certain degree of confidence and recognition of prior learning, at the same time as presenting new challenges. These factors make the games very motivating for children and provide ideal learning opportunities, features which the producers of more educationally orientated games are beginning to emulate. It would certainly seem that computer games enhance children's ability to concentrate for long periods of time and this can impact on other areas of learning. Playing games also develops children's aptitude for independent work.

Computer games and literacy

Computer games demand that children are able to read visual images as well as print. Kress and van Leeuwin (1996) outline how visual literacy skills are needed to read the multi-modal texts of a technological age, in which linear texts are disrupted by the use of hyperlinks, with print and image juxtaposed in challenging ways. They also argue that the language of the screen is replacing that of the page as the primary code of representation. Visual imagery is paramount in computer games and presents particular challenges to children as they are required to decipher the meaning of specific signs, symbols and images, which are integral to each game.

The games themselves sometimes feature written instructions within their narrative and so also demand print-reading skills. In addition, games are often accompanied by written instructions. However, some research suggests that children are more likely to try to work out the rules of a game whilst playing it than read instructions first (Al-Eidan, 1999). Nevertheless, there exists a wide range of supporting texts and reference materials on both page and screen to provide gamesters of all ages with 'cheats' for popular games. These are widely accessed by older boys in particular.

It is the case that there are indirect benefits for literacy development to be accrued from playing video games. For example, Robinson (1997) has explored the similarities that exist between reading print and televisual narratives and suggests that: 'it is their understandings of and familiarity with narrative on which the children are drawing, rather than any similarities inherent in the media. They are learning about narrative from their encounters with narrative in whichever medium, rather than being taught by television how to read print or vice versa' (Robinson, 1997, p. 180). We would suggest that children are also learning much about the narrative genre as they play many of the popular computer games. In the next section, we explore the connections between more traditional storytelling and the narratives of computer games.

Narrative and computer games

Tzetan Todorov (1977) has suggested that narratives contain a 'causal transformation'. As he explains:

> An *ideal* narrative begins with a stable situation which is disturbed by some power or force. There results a state of disequilibrium: by the action of a force directed in the opposite direction, the equilibrium is re-established; the second equilibrium is similar to the first but the two are never identical.
>
> (Todorov, 1977, p. 111)

In this sense, computer games can be said to be narratives in that they involve some sort of transformation. The problem-resolution factor, which Todorov suggests is a part of narrative structure, is embedded within them. Games usually involve characters in a specific setting and the interaction between characters and setting becomes a central part of the narrative, as it is in traditional forms. In addition, if we consider game structure in the light of the work of Vladimir Propp

Table 7.1 Propp's character analysis

Villain	Causes harm; needs defeating
Donor	Provides hero with magical agent which helps in quest
Helper	Aids in quest – can take hero to right place etc.
Victim	Needs to be saved from villain
Dispatcher	Sends hero off on quest
Hero	Character who performs key role; defeats the villain and rescues the victim
False hero	Can present unfounded claims

Table 7.2 Key differences between print and computer narratives

Print narratives	Electronic narratives
Linear and multilinear	Non-linear/multidirectional
Author tells, reader 'listens'	Reader/player is part of the story
Low in participation	High in participation
Words basic	Images and sound basic
Reader guided through territory	Reader/player explores territory
Interior world basic	Exterior world basic
Imagination	Immersion
Strong characterization	Weak characterization
Endings strong	Endings weak or problematical
Reader external to events	Reader/player is internal to events
Participation by identification	Actual participation in narrative
Illustrations relatively simple	Graphics, music and sound powerful
Construction of story hidden	Construction of story to be discovered

Source: Berger (2000).

(1968), we can see that some of what he has to say about narrative structure can also be applied to computer games. Propp analysed a large number of Russian folktales in terms of their structure and the role of characters within them. He suggested that different characters performed different functions in stories. Table 7.1 is a summary of the characters identified and their key functions.

This is not to suggest that all stories contain the characters in Table 7.1; however, many contain a range of them. An array of these characters can also be found in many computer games. Most have a hero who needs to undertake a quest in order to defeat one or more enemies. During this quest, the hero must collect a range of magical agents from various donors in order to increase his or her powers. There is sometimes a victim, often a princess or weak female, who needs to be rescued. So children learn much about the structures and conventional features of narratives as they play computer games. However, there are key differences between print and computer narratives. Arthur Asa Berger (2000) has detailed a number of these (Table 7.2).

The key difference that Berger identifies is the way in which computer games enable the player to enter the narrative and become part of the story. This provides the player with only an illusion of power; in reality, players can do little to change the fundamental structure of the story. Berger argues that this experience may be less satisfying for children because 'Interactivity prevents children from escaping from prison of selves the way books do' (Berger, 2000, p. 40). However, it is this immersion in the world of computer games which children love, as the absorption appears to enable them to escape from everyday concerns. It may be this ability to be a more active player in the narrative which causes older children to become less interested in books. The popularity of interactive puzzle and adventure books, in which children can choose which direction the narrative takes, may in part result from the success of computer games.

Ultimately, perhaps, it is the location of computer games within a 'transmedia intertextuality' (Kinder, 1991, p. 3) that promotes literacy skills. There is evidence which suggests that some children who play computer games read related books or comics (Al-Eidan, 1999). Roe and Muijs (1998) studied children who were 'heavy users' of computer games, that is, they played for more than two hours a day. They found that the heavy users reported reading more than other children in the study: 'They also report reading more comics and books, although the latter should be set in the context of the fact that they tend to prefer less demanding material such as picture books' (Roe and Muijs, 1998, p. 190). This reminds us of the dismissive attitude towards the use of visual literacy skills discussed in relation to children's reading of comics in Chapter 6. These researchers do not explore the nature of the reading material with which the children engaged. It is possible that they were reading magazines and comics related to the computer games they were playing, as Millard found in an earlier project (Millard, 1997, pp. 65–6). In addition, one study suggests that children who enjoy computer games read the magazines for the 'cheats' which enable them to acquire specific skills in order to be more successful players (Al-Eidan, 1999).

There have been concerns that the playing of computer games will lead to the demise of reading, as there is research which suggests that children spend more time playing computer games than they do reading books (Livingstone and Bovill, 1999). However, there is no evidence to suggest that it is computer games which are causing this reduction in book reading. In fact, one could argue that the studies cited above are all indicative of the motivational effect that computer games playing can have on reading. Certainly, our recent findings in relation to Pokémon suggest that the related books have been very popular in schools.

It is this location of computer games within the intertextual world of related products such as books, comics, magazines and films which provides rich opportunities for reading experiences in the widest sense of the term. The most successful games have exploited this self-referential world and develop in children a desire to acquire the artefacts as a means of becoming a member of a particular cultural club. The hugely popular computer game, Pokémon has embedded itself within children's cultural spaces by exploiting an intertextual web: 'the game is only part of the rapidly proliferating phenomenon. Pokémon is also a cartoon series, a movie and a collection of miniature figurines; and a plethora of merchandising tie-ins, magazines, books, comics and fast-food sponsorship deals' (Burkeman, 2000, p. 2). Many children we have worked with in primary schools have been avid collectors of Pokémon cards and stickers without ever having played the game. Rather, they have watched the television series or seen the movie and thus entered the narrative at a level which matches their traditional patterns of media consumption.

A recent survey of 6- and 7-year-olds in a multicultural, inner-city school suggested that the games which were cited as most frequently played were:

- Pokémon
- Super Mario Brothers
- Sonic the Hedgehog
- Rugrats
- South Park
- Superman
- The Simpsons.

Most of these games are related to other aspects of children's culture. As outlined in Chapter 3, this constitutes a 'narrativisation' process (Fleming, 1996, p. 102), in which artefacts are collectively linked to an overriding theme to form a metanarrative. The pleasure derived from playing with any one of the commodities is heightened because of associated meanings derived from others. Thus children can join in the Pokémon narrative at any level; they need not own the computer game or have watched the television programme on satellite channels. There are therefore, we would argue, greater opportunities than ever before for promoting reading and writing activities framed within the intertextual universe of children's cultural lives.

Computer games in the classroom

There is a range of rich opportunities for utilizing children's interest in computer games in order to develop literacy skills in the classroom. These need not involve playing the games in school, although this can be the means of developing children's oracy skills as they discuss ways of problem-solving grouped around a shared screen, or give each other instructions in relation to favourite games. In addition, as Beavis (1998) suggests:

> The inclusion of computer games has much to offer to the study of text in the curriculum. Viewing electronic games as text raises questions of textuality and engagement, interestingly collapses reader/writer boundaries in the act of playing, teases out notions of readings as both multiple and constrained, reshapes and works within existing notions of narrative, and gives reading positions quite physical as well as prescriptive new dimensions.
>
> (Beavis, 1998, p. 247)

However, if teachers feel uneasy about children using the games themselves in the classroom, there are other ways in which reading and writing activities could be linked to them. Computer games provide another useful source of material for classroom surveys. Databases can be constructed and the types of games, reasons for liking them and a quality rating recorded. The data can lead to analysis and a discussion of the gendered nature of the games chosen by the class members. Reviews of computer games are another means of provoking discussion over controversial issues such as racism, sexism and violence in the games and the children can be asked to analyse these aspects, along with other features such as graphics and visual and sound effects. Collecting reviews from magazines and comparing opinions written about the same game by different writers can provoke much discussion and facilitate the development of critical literacy skills.

my pok'emon is
called Digyround.
he's atack is
called mud atack
he blows mud at
people.

Figure 7.1 A 6-year-old's own Pokémon character

Children can be provided with opportunities to design their own computer game. This may involve actual work on a computer if the relevant software is available, but need not do so. A paper-based version of the task proved to be a means of developing motivation for writing with a class of 6-year-old children. They were asked first to develop their own Pokémon character (Figure 7.1). They were then invited to design a computer game which incorporated this character (Figure 7.2).

Activities suggested for use with comics in Chapter 6, which developed understanding of narrative structure, can also be used in relation to computer games. These include making comic strips of computer game stories, or sequencing them through images and captions. Similarly, writing about characters in the games and developing profiles for them provide opportunities for children to transfer their skills in analysing characters in stories to the games genre. Transporting a favourite character from a game and making him or her the hero of a written story can stimulate children to write about cultural worlds which are more familiar to them than those usually offered within the literacy classroom. Characters in computer games can be analysed in terms of the stereotypical images they present. Once children realize that the protagonists are usually represented as aggressors, they can be

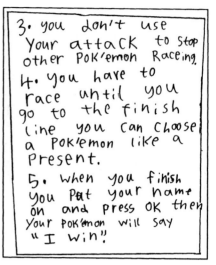

Figure 7.2 A computer game incorporating the 6-year-old's Pokémon character

asked to challenge the conventional discourse and asked to design a game like *Lemmings* in which the aim is to save the characters rather than zap them.

There have been many scare stories in the press in relation to computer games (TES, 2000a). Pokémon has been singled out recently, particularly in relation to skirmishes about the possession of rare cards. These minor incidents, which would not normally attract press interest, have been splashed in major broadsheets because of their relationship to the Pokémon phenomenon (*Guardian*, 2000). Children can be asked to analyse these articles, identifying those features of the text which position the reader e.g. use of inflammatory language and stereotyping of participants. Following these reports, many schools have elected to ban Pokémon cards from the premises. In response to this, children could be asked to debate whether this is a wise course of action. A class of 6-year-olds were sent the following letter by one of the authors as a means of stimulating a response which would develop their skills in persuasive writing, and provide them with an opportunity to consider the arguments for and against such crazes:

Dear Class 2,

I am not very happy with this Pokémon craze, which is all the rage in schools at the moment. I think children think and talk about Pokémon too much when they should be thinking about other things. I can't see what is so good about Pokémon – isn't there a lot of fighting in it? I am going to write to Mr Blair and ask him to ban it altogether unless you can give me ten good reasons why I shouldn't. I look forward to hearing from you,

Yours sincerely,
Mr Grey.

The children responded with passion:

Dear Mr Grey,

We don't think that you should ask Mr Blair to ban Pokémon. Here are ten reasons why not:

1. The Pokémon have special powers.
2. They battle together but they don't kill anybody.
3. The Pokémon listen to their master and help their trainers.
4. There's lots of Pokémon to choose from.
5. The trainers care about their Pokémon.
6. Pokémon have shiny stickers.
7. Sometimes, our mums might like them.
8. The trainers train the Pokémon.
9. The Pokémon song is good.
10. Everybody likes Pokémon.

Please can you not ban Pokémon?

Yours sincerely,
Class 2.

This has now developed into a continuing exchange of letters, with children eager to justify their interest in the narrative. Older children could work on building up reasoned, persuasive arguments, using evidence to support their points.

Dyson (1996) outlines how a class of children steeped in the worlds of superheroes were introduced to Greek gods who shared some of the superheroes' transcendental powers. Popular culture provides a range of opportunities for moving children between texts which operate in parallel cultural worlds. Characters in the Pokémon series all have special powers and characteristics, which are carefully documented on cards and in handbooks. Children could use these profiles as a model for constructing outlines of mythological characters such as Hercules, Odysseus and Circe. This activity would provide much valuable opportunity for research.

There is a range of other opportunities which will promote children's computer literacy skills, building on their interest in computer games. There are many websites devoted to particular games which could be reviewed by children and, indeed, they could create their own sites based on favourite games. Children can use specific software to develop promotional literature, posters and leaflets, relating to games they have devised. Computer games' glossaries are also a useful means of getting children to work on definitions of terms specific to the genre, e.g. power-ups, turn-based, RPG gem. In addition, these activities all contribute to children's development in ICT, as they can be asked to use word-processors, desktop publishing software, web-authoring tools, multimedia packages, digital cameras and scanners when available.

New media

There are other forms of new media with which children engage. These include the Internet, digital television and communications technology. Television is the focus of Chapter 8, so here we want to consider briefly the role that the Internet and communications technology play in children's cultural lives.

The Internet is becoming a major part of the fabric of our social, economic and cultural lives in these first years of the third millennium. The effects on the structure of social life have yet to be fully unravelled, but the web is having an impact on the forms of children's popular culture. There are many websites devoted to children's favourite interests and pastimes, including computer games, television shows, pop stars, comics and books. These are frequently visited and extend the narrative satisfaction children receive from the discourses with which they engage. Older children and young people frequent chat rooms and are developing acronyms, signs and symbols to aid their communication (Abbott, 1998). The Internet is fast becoming a primary medium for film-makers and animators. However, as yet, most children who do have access to PCs in the home appear to be using them to play games rather than use the Internet. In addition, class plays a major role in access to this technology:

> We find that both access and use of IT at home are much higher amongst middle-class children. Almost twice as many middle-class

compared with working-class children use a PC at home, three times as many use a multi-media computer and eight times as many have personally used the Internet.

(Livingstone and Bovill, 1999, p. 31)

However, as digital technology progresses at an extremely fast rate, it will not be long before more children have access to the Internet from television screens in the home. This will have a major impact on children's consumption of web sites devoted to their interests. Inevitably, it will have further repercussions for children's literacy skills as they navigate text on screen, read text juxtaposed with images and follow hyperlinks. The nature of the reading act is changing irrevocably and schools need to equip children with the skills they require to navigate this complex terrain. Training children in information retrieval skills using the Internet is essential, particularly for those children who as yet have no home access and can be made a very motivating task if related in some way to aspects of popular culture. In one school, children were asked to find ten sites devoted to Pokémon which provided information about the complex naming system used. This activity developed a range of literacy skills which included work on etymology.

Communications technology is playing an increasing part in children's cultural lives as they use e-mail and mobile phones. Again, access to these artefacts is related to class, but as the technology becomes cheaper, more children will become familiar with them. Many schools are now using e-mail and children are using the medium to communicate with other classes. The use of attachment tools is a useful means of developing collaborative projects as children can send lengthy documents to each other. This could be developed into a writing project, where children send each other compositions, which can then be reviewed and returned to the author. Children can take part in tandem writing using e-mail. Communicating in pairs and focusing on a joint writing task such as a report, children add a paragraph each time to their partner's writing. They have to ensure that they are writing in the same style as their partner so that the writing demonstrates cohesion. Children could also be asked to review linguistic aspects of e-mail communication and identify ways in which language changes when people use the medium e.g. use of abbreviations, acronyms and less formal use of punctuation marks.

Mobile phones are fast becoming a ubiquitous form of communication, with the use of text-messages increasingly popular in the last year. Mobile phone companies and academics alike are interested in the phenomenon and journalists speculate on the impact they are having on writing culture:

> The earth's population as a whole sent three billion text messages in December 1999 alone . . . and industry observers expect that figure to reach ten billion by the end of this year . . . It's impossible to know what effect emails and text messages will have on us, but it is clear that they have instigated the biggest boom in 'letter' writing for 200 years; and while we don't, yet, have a text-message novel, the tight, subject-less sentences and the reproduced emails in *Bridget Jones' Diary* have at least a touch of the digital missives.
>
> (Benson, 2000, pp. 25–7)

Children's interest in mobile phones can be utilized within the class-room by asking them to devise rules for their use in society (e.g. 'No talking in a loud voice into mobile phones on buses and trains and annoying other passengers!'), or write stories in which mysterious text messages appear on someone's mobile phone. Like users of e-mail, mobile phone enthusiasts are fast inventing a range of abbreviations, signs and symbols to facilitate communication. Children will enjoy inventing new ones, or compiling a dictionary of those in use.

All the activities suggest in this chapter are designed to develop children's confidence in and familiarity with a range of technology. It is important that schools do not ignore the arrival of various aspects of new media into children's lives, as what may happen is that those who have access to such technology at home will become more expert in the use of tools that will be central to both work and leisure in the future. As Sefton-Green and Buckingham (1998) warn:

> Access to home computers is possibly as important a part of cultural capital as access to books; yet without support and development it can easily lead to a reinforcement of the status quo . . . Without suitable software, without teaching, without opportunities to make and circu-late products, young people may end up merely replicating existing social inequalities – and at the same time feeding the profits of the big computer multinationals.
>
> (Sefton-Green and Buckingham, 1998, p. 82)

Conclusion

As children become increasingly sophisticated users of media and new technology, we need to be aware of how this discourse informs their cultural lives outside of school. It is clear that some of the prob-lems which many adults found in the old media (violence, addiction, corruption) are still felt to be an integral aspect of new media technologies. Perhaps these fears will never go away and will arise in relation to any new cultural form for children with which adults are unfamiliar. Some may suggest that these fears are a necessary aid to keeping the producers of such technologies aware of parental concerns and so help restrict the development of the most oppressive discourses. Yet despite all the worries expressed by parents, children are still attracted to texts which evoke adult disapproval. This is nowhere more apparent than in relation to television and film and it is to the moving image we now turn in the next chapter.

Note

1. 'Computer games' has been used to describe games played on a PC, whilst 'video games' is a term which has been applied to games on hand-held consoles. In this chapter, 'computer games' is used as a term for both types of games.

8

Television and Film

It is television, more than any other medium, perhaps, that has attracted the fiercest criticism, with the tone of some critics becoming near hysterical:

> Perhaps the increase in the crime rate, the violence in society, the boredom suffered by children and teenagers, the lack of creativity in people's lives, the alarming suicide numbers, are connected to the thousands of not just wasted, but detrimental hours, young people have spent glued to the television.

> (Brooky, 1998, pp. 3–4)

This chapter provides an overview of research on children and television in order to provide a more reasoned and measured response. In addition, it explores ways in which children's overwhelming attraction to the medium can be incorporated into the classroom in order to develop a range of literacy skills. First, however, we map out the full extent of children's engagement with television, video and film and discuss the implications of their fascination with the moving image.

Children's television consumption

The Livingstone and Bovill report (1999) found that 99 per cent of children and young people aged between 6 and 17 years watch television and that they watch it for, on average, two and a half hours per day. There was no significant difference in gender in terms of the amount of television consumption. The programmes they reported as their favourites contained no surprises: soap opera was the first choice, with cartoons second and sport third. However, when gender was brought into the equation, the picture changed. Girls liked soap operas best, followed by other serials (such as *Animal Hospital*) and then cartoons. Boys' first choice was sport, followed by cartoons and then soap operas. As with their computer games, girls appeared to be attracted primarily to narrative genres and boys to competitive sports (Millard, 1997). Livingstone and Bovill (1999) found that younger children enjoyed watching videos and generally children did not distinguish between videos and television.

One issue that has been of concern since the advent of television is that of displacement. The question for educationalists has been, if children spend more of their time watching television, what have they given up? The major worry, of course, is that children have stopped reading. However, it would appear that this fear is ill-founded. Neuman (1995) suggests that television-watching displaced listening to the radio, or going to the cinema, rather than reading and that as new media arrive they displace interaction with other media which offer equivalent experiences. In addition, she suggests that in some cases, the reading of books is *stimulated* by television-watching, a point we will return to later in the chapter. It would also appear that television viewing is seen by the children in the Livingstone and Bovill (1999) study as something to do when they are bored, thus suggesting that it displaces doing nothing. In addition, Neuman (1995) draws our attention to the fact that studies on the amount of reading children undertake each day have indicated that there has been no reduction in the amount of time spent reading. In the 1940s, 1950s and 1960s, children reported reading for 15 minutes each day (Lyness, 1952; Witty, 1967). This was also found to be the case in the 1980s (Neuman, 1988). Interestingly enough, Livingstone and Bovill (1999) reported that children in the 1990s also reported reading for 15 minutes each day. It appears that there is little evidence that watching television is displacing reading.

However, there have been other suggestions that television-watching does affect reading, in that children who watch more television are less fluent readers. Neuman (1995), in a thorough review of the literature, outlines many studies which found no significant relationship between the watching of television and cognitive development and some which found small but significant relationships. She suggests that, 'At the very minimum . . . a negative, though modest, relationship exists between television and reading achievement' (Neuman, 1995, p. 42). However, it is clear that this is evidence is not strong enough to warrant making any significant claims with regard to the relationship between television viewing and reading. It may be that children who are less confident readers spend more time watching television because it is less demanding for them. This does not mean that television is a cause of their lack of skills and confidence in reading. In addition, Gunter and McAleer (1997) suggest that there is evidence that watching television can enhance children's cognitive skills. We would suggest that, as there is no strong evidence of a positive or negative effect on reading from the amount of television children watch, we should focus instead on ways it might be used to promote reading in the classroom. We will return to this issue later in the chapter.

Another fear voiced in relation to children's interaction with television is that of addiction. As with computer games, there have been many media scares that children are becoming 'TV zombies' (Storkey, 1999). Again, there is little concrete evidence to support this. Most children appear to watch television for about 18 hours a week on average (Livingstone and Bovill, 1999) and very few children report watching television as their sole pastime for hours on end. Rather, children appear to be mixing their use of media in that they watch television, read, play computer games and listen to music as leisure activities and are not particularly dependent upon any one of them. In addition, it is clear that children are not the passive viewers that many assume them to be. It has been noted that adults are far from being 'couch potatoes' when they watch television. Willis (1990) records studies in which adults have been watched as they sit in front of the screen. He notes that:

> when they are watching, they are far from passive. They shout back at the screen, make sarcastic comments about people's hair-styles and dress sense, sing along with the advertising jingles, talk about the programmes while they are still on. Far from being the passive watchers of political mythology, they actively collaborate with the screen to create and recreate a web of meanings that are relevant to them and anchored in their own lives.
>
> (Willis, 1990, p. 32)

It is no different with children. Palmer (1986), in an Australian study, found that children rarely sat for long periods of time watching television. Rather, they danced and sang in front of it, ate, slept, did their homework, played games and engaged in a range of other activities. When children do sit down to focus on a programme, like adults, they interact with the screen. Buckingham's (1993b) work has been central to the development of our understanding of how children make sense of the symbolic material with which they are presented and link their viewing with other aspects of experience. They are often, in fact, as active in their meaning-making in relation to television as they are when reading books or magazines.

However, there have been other criticisms related to violence similar to those examined elsewhere in this book and the conclusions reached are the same. For example, there is no strong evidence that violence on television and film has an effect on children (Barker and Petley, 1997). In fact, as Buckingham (1993b) points out in a study of 6–11-year-olds' television-viewing, it is very difficult to predict what children will find frightening, with some children reporting that sequences of *Mary Poppins* and Fairy Liquid advertisements had scared them.

From the evidence presented so far, it is clear that the moving image plays a central part in children's cultural lives, whether the medium in question is television, film or video. There are many differences between television and film which we do not have space to explore here. Throughout the chapter, we will refer to a focus on both as work on the 'moving image'. We now consider what similarities there may be in the processes involved in reading moving images and printed text.

Reading print and televisual narratives

It is important that the links between the reading processes used in decoding and understanding print and other forms of text are compared and contrasted in order to inform our understanding of the relationships between them. The work of Neuman (1995) and Robinson (1997) has been instrumental in illuminating the processes involved. Both have argued that children are active meaning-makers in relation to both print and televisual texts, rather than passive consumers of either. In a study of her son's responses to a book and television programme of the same narrative, Neuman concluded that:

> David's processing approach appears strikingly similar for both print and televised stories. In each, he is actively engaged in searching for meaning. As an experienced reader and viewer, he tends to be drawn to creating an interpretive framework for each story; individual symbolic elements of each medium are not mentioned. While the means of conveying information are different, the skills and knowledge needed to interpret each medium appear to be the same.
>
> (Neuman, 1995, p. 80)

In addition, Robinson (1997) asserts that it is in children's understanding of narrative where similarities are to be found. Television and print texts share a number of features. Narratives, whatever the medium used to construct them, draw on sets of conventions known and shared by their audiences. These conventions structure signs into chains of signification which are reinforced by repetition. A view of a row of wet slate roofs can signify a working-class district, or a close-up shot lit from below will signify menace, for instance. When children are encouraged to talk about television, they are learning to make sense of these storytelling conventions, some of which are shared with other forms of text. For example, character can be constructed through binary opposition. In Westerns, whether the medium is a comic-book cartoon or blockbuster film, a white hat represents the goody and a black hat, stereotypically, the baddy. However, although televisual and print narratives share some of the same characteristics, they are also very different. For example, the moving image can provide details about character and setting which cannot be achieved without the interaction of sound and images. Similarly, written narratives can use intradiegetic and extradiegetic narrative techniques to reveal thoughts and feelings in a very different way from films and television. Children need to learn how the language of moving images and printed texts can both differ and offer the same ways of signifying meaning.

If we move from a consideration of the *forms* of the different media to the *processes* involved in reading each, we see that there is also overlap. We would suggest that the similarities between reading processes, needed in order to make sense of printed and televisual narratives, differ in the extent to which each medium draws upon aural or visual perception. In order to compare the processes involved in reading both print and televisual texts, we have drawn on a widely accepted model of the reading process produced by Marilyn Jager-Adams (Adams, 1990). Adams uses the diagram in Figure 8.1 to explain the relationship between phonic, syntactic and semantic cues.

We have added the italicized categories to Figure 8.1 in order to explain the different strands which can affect contextual understanding. We have learned from reader response criticism that the reader brings a set of prior expectations to any decoding of a new text (Iser, 1978; Fish, 1980). The socio-cultural context in which we read a text, as well as prior experience of that genre, affects the meanings we derive from it. A practising Moslem would derive much more meaning from a passage of the Koran, for example, than an atheist, having no knowledge of the Moslem religion. As Robinson (1997) points out, children reading the Ahlbergs' popular book, *Each Peach Pear Plum*, need a familiarity with Western nursery rhymes in order to understand fully the text and its intertextual references. Figure 8.1 shows how these

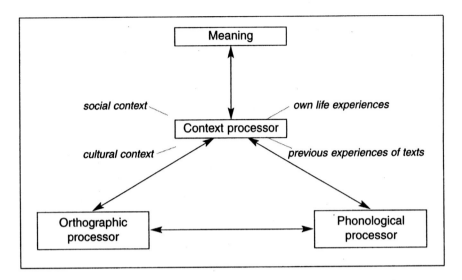

Figure 8.1 Reading print texts   *Source*: adapted from Adams (1990)

factors impinge on contextual processing. Adams (1990) suggests that the reading process demands the interplay of these different elements. The reader assigns meaning to a printed text through decoding phoneme–grapheme relationships, while at the same time making sense of any inter-textual relationships that exist. We would argue that this complex interplay between signifier and signified also enables the construction of meaning from televisual texts; it is only the nature of the decoding system which differs. Instead of depending on orthographic and phonological processing systems, the reader of tele-visual texts uses aural and visual processing skills to read the narrative (Figure 8.2).

The arrow between the visual and aural processors here is dotted. When reading printed text, there is a clear relationship between phonemes and graphemes. When reading televisual texts, some aural elements may relate to visual (as in characters' dialogue), others will not.

We know that children draw on semantic cues when reading both print and televisual texts. It has also been argued that they draw on syntactic cues and that both film and televisual texts have an underlying grammar, just as language does (Metz, 1974; Salomon, 1979; Turner, 1994; Messenger-Davies, 1997). Children absorb this grammar and use it when interpreting televisual texts. Messenger-Davies (1997) argues that parallels can even be seen in relation to active and passive

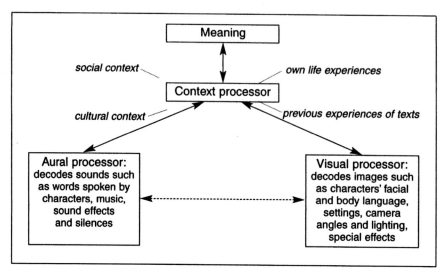

Figure 8.2   Reading televisual texts
Source: adapted from Adams (1990, p. 158)

sentences. As part of her doctoral research, Messenger-Davies showed people two versions of the same action on film. One was a medium-shot of a woman lifting a toy chair, which she suggested was analogous to the active sentence: 'The woman lifts the chair', as the most important aspect of the shot was the woman. The second shot included a close-up of the chair being lifted by the woman. This, the author argued, was equivalent to the passive sentence 'The chair is lifted by the woman'. Messenger-Davis commented:

> Normally, people recall the agents of actions better than the objects they are acting upon. However, this is not the case with passive sentences, which put the object in the foreground and make it more memorable. As with recall of passive sentences, the people taking part in my research who saw the cut-to-close-up version were more likely to remember the chair than the woman. The opposite was the case with the uncut version . . . The structure of the visual sequence thus seemed to parallel grammatical linguistic structures in viewers' minds.
>
> (Messenger-Davies, 1995, p. 38)

Similarly, other theorists have created a grammar of film that analyses the framing of film narrative through camera angle, close-ups and long shots, camera movement and lighting (Turner,1994). However, we feel that caution needs to be used here. The precise nature of grammar in relation to spoken and written language has been contested over the years (Halliday, 1973; Carter, 1990) and there are key differences between grammatical models used, for example, in relation to descriptive or prescriptive systems. Similarly, the grammatical systems created by the structural conventions of television and film are not fixed. As Buckingham (1993b) has argued in relation to Salomon's (1979) attempt to define the characteristics of television's symbolic system:

> There is a danger here of defining this symbolic system as a kind of rigid 'grammar', in which discrete units are sent to possess a fixed, objective meaning. Yet a zoom, for example, may 'mean' very different things at different times; and it may on occasions 'mean' effectively the same thing as a tracking shot or an 'irising' movement or a cut to a close-up.
>
> (Buckingham, 1993b, pp. 30–1)

Interestingly, this may also be applied to the grammar of spoken and written language; a word can function as an adverb in one sentence and a noun in another. The complexity and instability of both systems means that comparison between different modes of communication is, at best, precarious. Nevertheless, it is clear that both televisual and printed texts are subject to structural systems which can be recognized and analysed and which help readers to make sense.

There are other ways in which the reading processes involved in both modes can be compared. Table 8.1 summarizes the key similarities and differences involved in reading printed and televisual texts. The two columns are not interrelated.

As Table 8.1 demonstrates, we feel that children draw on some of the same skills when making sense of both print and televisual texts. Both involve a recognition of the nature of literacy as a set of practices which are embedded within our social and cultural lives (Street, 1984; Barton, 1994). It follows that teachers who are aware of the semiotic processes needed to decode both televisual and print texts are in a better position to draw attention to the parallels between them. In this way, each medium can be used to support the reading of the other.

Comparing book and film

Working with film and text versions of the same text is a valuable means of developing understanding of plot, setting, character and themes. The rich interplay possible between the media means that children can transfer their understanding from one form to the other.

Table 8.1 Similarities and differences in reading print and televisual texts

Similarities in reading print and televisual texts	Differences in reading print and televisual texts
Readers form 'interpretive communities' (Fish, 1980)	Printed texts make meaning through printed words and symbols, televisual texts use images, symbols, sounds, spoken and written words
Reading develops social, cognitive and emotional skills	
Reading involves orchestration of a range of skills – either phonic, graphic, syntactic and semantic (print) or aural, visual and semantic (televisual)	Televisual texts can be more ephemeral if not taped and stored; printed texts can be revisited over time
Prediction is an important part of the reading process	Printed texts are more accessible to non-linear reading. Pages are easier to manage than screens for rereading (although the advent of new technology through digital versatile disc [DVD] is changing this)
Readers are active meaning-makers, drawing from their own life experiences and encounters with texts	
Readers are socially, historically, politically, economically and culturally situated	Fictional printed texts are more likely to use a narrator; inference is not demanded in the same way as in some televisual texts
Readers fill the gaps in the text	
Linear narratives occur in each medium (stories) as well as non-linear texts (some non-fiction, documentaries)	Printed texts can give more direct access to characters' thoughts and feelings and can develop more complex psychological frames
Readers draw on their understanding of the particular genres they encounter	
Readers identify with or feel alienated from characters	
Readers willingly suspend disbelief	
Readers can reread texts	

Browne (1999), in a study of her young daughter's juxtaposing of visual and printed versions of the same texts, reported that watching videos helped her daughter to gain confidence and enjoyment in the books. Children can become familiar with the language of books as they watch and re-watch videos. In addition, film narratives can help children's oral and written responses to a text. David Parker, working with Key Stage 2 children on a film version of Roald Dahl's *Fantastic Mr Fox*, suggested that the children's implicit understanding of film narrative enhanced their comprehension skills and written responses to the text (Parker, 1999).

One junior class worked on the similarities and differences between the print and film versions of *The Lion, the Witch and the Wardrobe*. They were then asked to focus on a particular section of the book. The children read the section in shared reading sessions, then watched the film version of the same episode. The class were then asked to develop their own storyboard for that section of the book. Figure 8.3 is one girl's attempt at the task. From this, the children worked on a script for the characters in the scene (Figure 8.4). Finally, the children wrote a narrative version of the scene (Figure 8.5). The teacher felt that the children's writing had improved because of this work and that they had a greater insight into characters' actions, feelings and thoughts.

Children's work on characterization can be enhanced through opportunities to compare book and film. Films can provide us with a more concrete picture of characters and make visible characteristics which were implicit within the printed narrative, enabling the viewer to reach new insights. So, as one child said after watching the first few scenes of the film version of *Matilda*: 'I knew more about the mum after seeing the film and all she cared about was how she looked and she dropped the baby in the sink, going "Uh!Uh!"'. She only cared about herself.' On the other hand, some may feel that watching characters on film, when one has built up a private picture through reading, is too restrictive and channels interpretation into limited directions. Children could conduct a survey on people's reactions to this dilemma and explore how far expectations are met in relation to particular texts.

Genre is a theoretical construct which crosses many media and so can be drawn upon in any analysis of film and television. Generic conventions can be analysed, compared and contrasted across media. For example, detective stories in books and television share many features, e.g. setting, types of characters. However, there are certain features of the genre which appear in film and television that are obviously not contained in books, e.g. scary music, music which builds suspense, shot/reverse-shot cuts which show the reactions of suspects and so on. Such direct comparisons of the way in which genre is treated in each media are useful (Table 8.2).

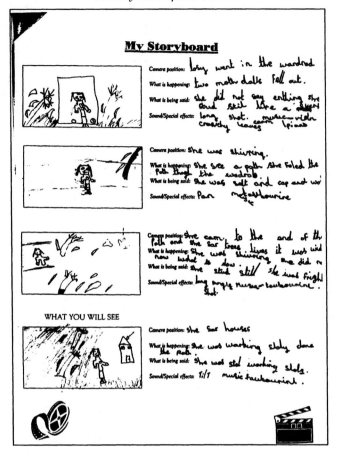

Figure 8.3 Storyboard

Script

Lucy: WoW! this Werdrobe is big. (amazed)
She Walked throw the warm cots.
To the end of the Wardrobe lucy Was
shivring. (puzzled)
Lucy: lucy did not know wich way
to go. (Spriced)
Edmin: I Wonder were Lucy has got to.
(puzzled)
Lucy: lucy went done the path she
the midle path. (puzzled)
lucy Went warking down the path saying
hello hello. (amazed)

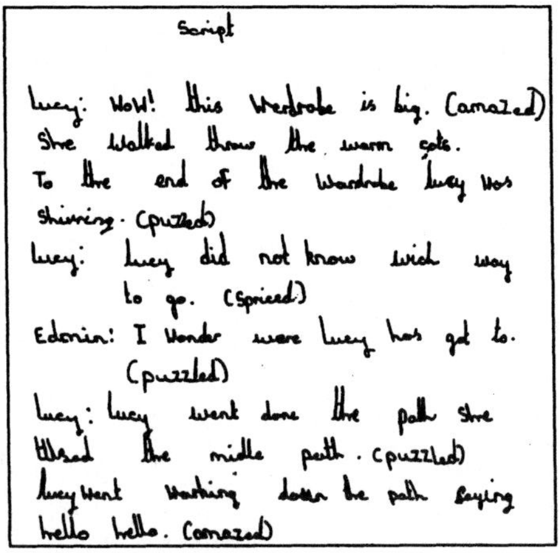

Figure 8.4 Script for characters in the scene

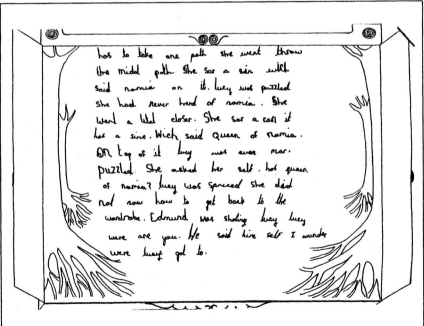

Figure 8.5 Narrative version of the scene

Table 8.2 Comparison of horror genre

Horror books	Horror films
Short sentences	Scary music
Cliffhangers at the end of each chapter	Dark lighting
Scary words, e.g. shriek, creep	Gruesome make-up

Children's favourite genres can be identified and comparisons made with national surveys. Programmes which cross genres can be analysed, as they provide particularly rich sources of generic conventions and are usually popular with children. For example, a recent favourite is the American series *Buffy the Vampire Slayer* which mixes conventions from horror movies and mystery stories as well as incorporating humour and parody.

These are just a few suggestions for work which compares books with their filmed versions; there are many more valuable texts in the area which focus in much more depth on this topic (Craggs, 1992; Film Education, 1999a, 1999b). It would appear that this movement between media is essential, as televisual texts have a central place within the narrative system of children's cultural universe. Children are motivated to read those texts which relate to their television, film and video consumption. So Robinson (1997) notes that *Thomas the Tank Engine* books were around long before the television series appeared, but their popularity increased because of children's exposure to the narrative on television. Book sales increase whenever their narratives are released on film. Many children's shelves at home are filled with books and comics which relate to their television and film interests, whether that is cartoons, television series or Disney videos. Once again, we can see that intertextuality promotes, rather than inhibits, reading. This pattern emerges in a survey of the favourite books of a group of Reception children. The subjects of the books included:

- Pokémon
- Lion King
- Cinderella
- Little Mermaid
- Winnie the Pooh
- Pingu
- Toy Story
- Star Wars.

All these books relate to children's film, television and video consumption. This was a pattern found by Neuman (1995) in her study of three American families' literacy activities in the home. She reported that children moved from printed texts to television and back to printed texts again in their quest for pleasure and concluded that:

> Rather than displace one activity for another, the children often engaged in what appeared to be a spirited interplay between the media. As interests were established, children alternated between video-based and print-related experiences on the basis of its accessibility, and their capacity to make optimal uses of the particular medium. These activities seemed to be guided by children's rather consistent patterns of interest, instead of the specific medium presentation.
>
> (Neuman, 1995, p. 180)

This movement between media has become even more complex with the introduction of computer games, stickers, collectors' cards, toys and other artefacts which are all related to particular television programmes and/or films. The opportunities for reading are extensive and include the blurb on videos, as Bromley (1996) outlined in her description of a group of children who read the cover of a video and demonstrated a number of critical literacy skills. These included an ability to decode typographical features and to understand the marketing motives of the producers. However, we would not want to emphasize work in the classroom on comparison of printed text and film at the expense of a focus on the moving image itself. In the next section, we move on to examine the notion of 'media literacy'.

Media literacy

As with all labels, the term 'media literacy' has been open to debate and challenge. It is concerned primarily with literacy practices which enable children to access, analyse and produce media texts. Media education is the primary means by which children can develop skills in media literacy, but much work is also done through the subject of English. This does create difficulties, as Balzagette (2000) points out, in that the process of analysing the moving image is often made synonymous with that of analysing printed text, when in fact they are different kinds of texts and often (but, we would argue, not always) need different kinds of deconstructive and productive techniques. However, it is worth remembering that media education is much wider than the analysis of the moving image and the means of textual analysis for non-media printed materiai can easily be transferred to the analysis of newspapers, magazines, leaflets, advertisements and so on. Nevertheless, this chapter is concerned with film and television and so the focus will remain on developing children's ability to understand, analyse and produce moving images.

Reading of images

As we have argued in previous chapters, literacy should incorporate the ability to read visual images. This skill is essential when deconstructing films and television. Children need to be able to analyse camera angles and their uses, how lighting affects scenes, use of iconography, body language of characters and so on in order to become effective readers of the moving image. The Film Education Working Group (FEWG, 1999) outlined a broad curriculum framework for work on the moving image which consists of five stages. At Stage 1, they suggest that children should have the opportunity to watch a range of film, video and television (FVT) from across a range of cultures and be able to talk about particular sections of videos, as well as discuss their viewing outside of school. In addition, the group suggested that learners should be able to work in three main areas: film language (ways in which moving image texts are internally constructed), producers and audiences (ways in which the texts circulate) and messages and values (interpretations of the world offered by the texts). Here, we outline the learning outcomes identified for the first two stages as exemplars (Tables 8.3 and 8.4).

At Stage 2, it is suggested that children should have opportunities to watch and deconstruct a range of complex narratives and extend the range to include silent and subtitled films. The outcomes build on those outlined in Stage 1.

Again, there is not space within this book to examine in any depth the ideas suggested by the Film Education Working Group. Instead, we refer you to the full report produced by the group, *Making Movies Matter* (FEWG, 1999) and materials produced by both Film Education (1999a, 1999b) and the British Film Institute.[1]

In addition to the study of the moving image, children need to be able to analyse how audiences are constructed in relation to films and television. Here, the concept of 'interpellation' has been used to describe this process. 'Interpellation' is a term introduced by the Marxist sociologist, Althusser, in order to demonstrate how ideology 'recruits' an audience:

I shall then suggest that ideology 'acts' or 'functions' in such a way that it 'recruits' subjects (it transforms them all) by that very precise operation which I have called interpellation or hailing, and which can be imagined along the lines of the most commonplace everyday police (or other) hailing: 'Hey, you there!'.

(Althusser, 1994, p. 162)

Table 8.3 Becoming cineliterate, Stage 1

Film language	Producers and audiences	Messages and values
• Identify and talk about structuring features such as music, changes in location, interior/ exterior settings, actors and presenters • Use key words to refer to elements of film language when describing events in a story • Use key words in talking about character types, as well as referring to clues such as dress, casting, performance, etc.	• Use credits, video covers and posters to identify titles and actors' names, likely audience category, and theme or genre • Identify broad categories of intended audience, e.g. 'this is for little children', and give reasons • Identify common features between FVT, book and game versions of generic texts, e.g. myth, fairy tale, space adventure, etc.	• Identify and talk about different levels of 'realism', e.g. naturalistic drama vs cartoon animation • Use key words to refer to elements of film language when explaining personal responses and preferences • Identify devices such as flashback, dream sequences, exaggeration – discuss why they are needed and how they are conveyed.

Key words:

shot	zoom	pan	videotape	camcorder
cut	close-up	track	cinema	programme
fade	mid-shot	focus	film	animation
mix	long-shot	soundtrack	television	video-recorder
				Special effects

Source: FEWG (1999, p. 74).

Table 8.4 Becoming cineliterate, Stage 2

Film language	Producers and audiences	Messages and values
• Describe how sound contributes to the overall meaning of a moving image sequence, using key words where appropriate • Use key words to explain how a FVT sequence is constructed	• Use key words to distinguish between different moving image delivery systems • Identify and distinguish some production roles, using key words • Suggest reasons why different people may have different responses to the same FVT text • Explain why some FVT may cost a lot of money to make	• Use key words to identify ways in which FVT can show things that have not 'really' happened e.g. violence, magic • Explore reasons for and against censorship, age classification and the broadcasting 'watershed'

Key words:

angle	sound effects	composer	release	short	recorded	'watershed'
frame	projector	director	exhibitor	documentary	censorship	star
sequence	scriptwriter	broadcast	trailer	live action	classification	satellite
dialogue	script	channel	feature	live	budget	cable

Source: FEWG (1999, p. 75).

Thus, we can see how television programmes such as *Blind Date* inter-pellate the viewer when the host, Cilla Black, says to the camera about one of the contestants, 'Ooh, isn't he gorgeous?' The viewer is inter-pellated as a heterosexual female who would have an opinion as to the desirability of a young male. She certainly wouldn't be expecting a gay male viewer to reply, 'Oh, yes!' However, the concept of inter-pellation has been criticized because of its rather abstract nature (O'Sullivan *et al.*, 1994) and the lack of attention to who is doing the hailing. A rather more useful concept might be that of Stuart Hall (1980) in which he proposes that media texts undergo an encoding and decoding process. Thus, the producers of a text *encode* certain ideological constructs into the text. These ideologies might be accepted by viewers when they *decode* the text according to their particular socio-cultural contexts and experiences, or they may be resisted to some degree. Whatever the processes involved in the construction of the viewer by the maker of media texts and the response of viewers to them, it is important that children are provided with opportunities to analyse critically these processes in order that the manipulation of the media is made transparent. Many people have underestimated children's skills in this area, believing them to be easily duped by media messages they receive. However, Messenger-Davies's work (1997) demonstrates how first-graders in American schools were able to understand how adverts worked by presenting a particularly rosy picture of the products. In addition, Tobin's research (2000), in which he analysed the responses of 6- to 12-year-old children to films, reveals the sophisticated understanding that many young children bring to the interpretation of media codes and conventions. It is essential that young children's skills in this area are not underestimated and that they are presented with relevant and challenging work.

Many proponents of media education stress the importance of children producing media texts as well as deconstructing them (Buckingham and Sefton-Green, 1994; FEWG, 1999). This is becoming much easier with the advent of digital technology, as digital video cameras are very light and portable in comparison with their older counterparts. Even if schools do not have access to editing facilities, much valuable work can be done with a video camera such as video diaries, video narratives based on favourite pop songs, animated films. In one class of 6- and 7-year-olds, children watched and analysed weather reports before writing and filming their own. This project promoted valuable media literacy skills as well as developing their understanding of the weather. Work on animated films can be undertaken in a variety of media as children paint scenes, create plastiscine figures or use the increasingly sophisticated software packages which are available. These activities can also provide rich opportunities for oracy and literacy work as children discuss plans, write scripts and read instructions. In the final part of the chapter, we consider other means of developing children's literacy skills in the context of work on television, video and film.

Television talk

In addition to reading, television and film can enhance children's oral skills. Carol Fox (1993) has demonstrated how children draw from their cultural repertoire in order to inform their oral storytelling. They take meaning from experiences with television, film and video as well as books in their play with language and their constructions of imaginary worlds. Chapter 3 demonstrated how children drew from televisual narratives in their play, which helped their oral skills. Because television is a medium which most children share, whatever their home culture, it can provide many opportunities for developing collaborative talk, either through play or more structured activities. We want to turn briefly here to the work of Bahktin and Volosinov in order to explore this concept further.

Bahktin and Volosinov were Russian literary theorists who were interested in the ways in which we create language communities. Bahktin and Volosinov both suggested that language is a two-way process between speaker and listener in that our words only become meaningful in relation to others: 'there is no reason for saying that meaning belongs to a word as such. In essence, meaning belongs to a words in its position between speakers; that is, meaning is realized only in the process of active, responsive understanding' (Volosinov, 1994, p. 35).

The dialogic process is also subject to socio-cultural factors. Words take on meaning because of historical contexts and also our anticipation of what a particular word might mean in the future. Thus synchronic and diachronic contexts shape the meaning of our discourse and the significance of any particular utterance is open to negotiation. If the meaning of utterances is fluid and contestable, then Bakhtin and Volosinov's work also has implications for social discourse. The dialogic process means that children create shared meanings as they speak about common experiences together and become 'interpretative communities' (Fish, 1980) in relation to oral discourse:

> The living utterance, having taken meaning and shape at a particular historical moment in a socially specific environment, cannot fail to brush up against thousands of living dialogic threads, woven by socio-ideological consciousness around the given object of an utterance, it cannot fail to become an active participant in social dialogue.
>
> (Bakhtin, 1994, p. 76)

Children's talk about television and film is a primary site for such discourse as children construct shared meanings based on common interests. In a study of a nursery which incorporated work on the *Teletubbies*, Marsh (2000b) found that the discourse encouraged 3- and 4-year-old children to exchange information regarding the programme and build dialogic communities:

Lianne: I'm Po, that red Teletubby.
Nasia: I'm Po red.
Shaun: I got Teletubby video. I got lots of videos.
Peter: And I got Tinky Winky.
Nasia: I'm Tinky Winky.
Ansa: I watch Teletubbies. I got Teletubbies on my bed.

These 3- and 4-year-old children were in the early stages of acquiring English as an additional language and so these opportunities for building shared discourses were very important. These occasions provided spaces in which children could share their 'cultural capital' (Bourdieu, 1977) with each other and demonstrate that they had common interests. Television and popular culture provide key sites for such processes as most children have some access to the texts, no matter what their socio-economic, cultural or linguistic background. Teachers can use film, video and television to stimulate similar kinds of oral work in a number of ways. Children could be asked to watch a sequence of a soap opera which had had the sound removed and record on tape their version of the dialogue. Groups could deliver formal oral presentations to the class in which they present their findings on a particular project e.g. an investigation into the types of characters found on police drama shows. Older members of the family could be interviewed about their viewing preferences and history. Younger children could retell stories experienced in films, video and television as they play with puppets based on the characters. These are only a few of the opportunities that work on the moving image can provide for those classrooms in which children are steeped in the language and lore of film, television and video.

Reading, writing and the moving image

Kerry, who was 4½-years-old, produced the story in Figure 8.6. Here, we can see that Kerry has been stimulated not only by a traditional world of fairy tales in which princesses marry princes, but also by the contemporary soap operas she watches in which couples indulge in pre-marital sex. In this world of 'Cinderella meets Coronation Street', children draw from a range of semiotic material in order to inform their writing. The work of Anne Haas Dyson (1996, 1997) has demonstrated how children use superhero narratives drawn from television and film in their classroom. She argues that 'our texts are formed at the intersection of a social relationship between ourselves as

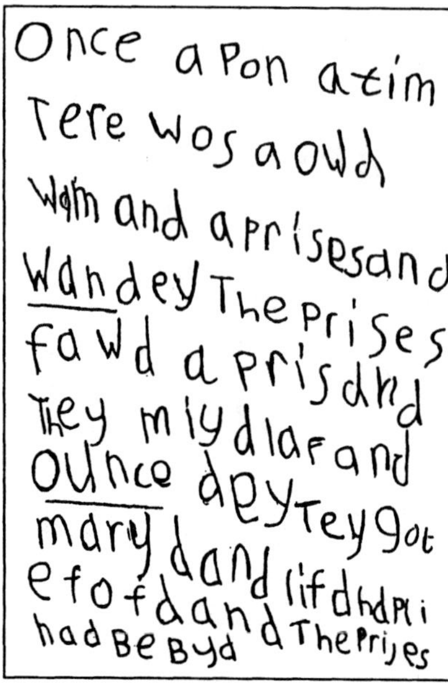

> Once a Pon a tim
> Tere wos a owd
> Wom and a prisesand
> Wandey The prises
> fawd a prisdh
> Tey mydlafand
> Ounce dpyTeygot
> mary dand lifdhdpi
> efofdaand lifdhdpi
> had Be Byd d The prijes

Figure 8.6 Kerry's story: *Text:* Once upon a time there was an old woman and a princess and one day the princess found a prince and they made love and one day they got married and lived happily ever after and the princess had a baby

composers and our addressees and an ideological one between our own psyches (or inner meanings) and the words, the cultural signs, available to us' (Dyson, 1996, p. 4).

Dyson introduces Figure 8.7 to illustrate this dynamic interplay. This deceptively simple diagram is a powerful way of looking at the process of children's writing. Children draw from 'available signs or words' and, as the work of Kress (1997) and Pahl (1999) has demonstrated, these can include three-dimensional materials as well as signs, symbols, images and letters. This store of semiotic material also includes children's cultural texts used in order to demonstrate their own inner meanings. These meanings are then negotiated between author and receiver of the text. Thus children use television and film narratives in their writing, but these are not always immediately recognizable to others and the dialogic processes involved in meaning-making are open to multiple interpretations. It is also the case that teachers do not always approve of the store of 'available signs and words' upon which children draw. Some would rather the store used consisted of semiotic material which is more readily recognized within the literary canon and discourage children from writing about their experiences with television and film. Yet, if

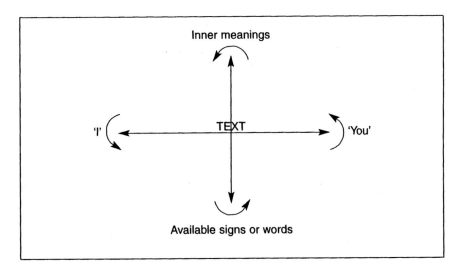

Figure 8.7 Composing as a dialogic process: its horizontal and vertical dimensions (from Dyson, 1996 p. 5)

children are allowed to mine the caverns of media material, their written compositions could be richer and more meaningful to them. Care has to be taken, however, in drawing children's attention to differences in the structure of film and print narratives, particularly in considering how setting and dialogue differ. Boys in particular draw heavily on film and television narrative in their own composition and this can be a disadvantage when conventional narratives are required for assessment (Millard, 1997).

Children's fascination with soap opera can be another source for writing in the classroom. A prime reason for the attraction of children to the genre is that soap operas are based in family life and so present real-life dilemmas to which they can relate. In addition, we would argue that the storylines of soap operas offer some of the attractions that fairy tales hold for children. Berger (1997) suggests five key reasons for children's love of fairy tales:

1 They generally begin with 'Once upon a time' and so situate the story away from the context of the child.
2 They often end with 'And they lived happily ever after', so offering satisfying closure.
3 They have a basic bipolar structure which children find attractive (good/evil; handsome/ugly; kind/cruel) – no ambiguity or ambivalence.

4 They centre on the actions of heroes and heroines who are typical, not specific and so children can relate to them.

5 Good and evil are omnipresent and the differences between them apparent (Berger, 1997, pp. 86–7).

If these factors are applied to soap operas, then one can begin to understand their attraction for children. The theme tunes of soap operas are often much more distinct than other types of programmes and act as 'Once upon a time' does in written texts; it draws the viewer into the 'make-believe' world of the soap opera. The episodes do not always end happily; cliff-hangers are often used as a means of ensuring viewers tune in next time, but storylines are generally always resolved in one way or another. In terms of the third point, it is clear that soap operas offer much potential for a paradigmatic analysis (Levi-Strauss, 1967) as dualistic discourses are often apparent. There are usually heroic characters within soap operas with whom children like to identify and so they offer narrative satisfaction. Finally, the tension between good and evil is as central a part of soap operas as it is of fairy tales and children are drawn to both because of this. However, soap operas are especially attractive to children because these fundamental features of narratives are set within a 'real-life' context – contemporary, recognizable fairy tales.

Soap operas offer the same opportunities for analytical work on narrative structure and characterization as printed texts do. Children can be asked to compare and contrast different soap operas in terms of setting, character types, typical storylines and so on. Using Propp's (1968) analysis of the functions of characters in fairy tales, (see Fig. 7.1) children could identify characters in soap operas who performed those functions. Children can devise their own soap operas. One class of 8-year-olds invented a street full of characters based on their experiences of living in an inner-city, multicultural neighbourhood and called it 'Soap Square'. The children then produced stories and plots which drew from these characters and which took their narrative cues from those soaps they watched regularly. Opportunities to film scripted sequences written as a result of such work can enable children to develop productive media skills in a meaningful context.

Quiz shows are another perennial children's favourite and can also be mined for opportunities to develop literacy skills. One class teacher exploited his children's interest in the programme *Who Wants to Be a Millionaire?* The phenomenal success of this programme is interesting and may be due to the fact that the questions are not situated within middle-class cultural domains as are the questions of other quiz shows such as *Mastermind* or *University Challenge*. Instead, the questions draw from a broad range of cultural knowledge which includes film, television and sport. The programme is also constructed within a more socially collaborative context than other quiz shows as contestants can 'ask the audience' a question or 'phone a friend'. In addition, the quiz master, Chris Tarrant, is a well-known presenter in other popular shows. Whatever the reasons, the class teacher realized that his class of children, who lived in a white working-class community which was hit by poverty and unemployment, could relate to this programme. He therefore asked the children to write three questions for their own class version of the quiz show as a homework task. The parents were as excited and committed to the task as the children, and they engaged in joint reading and writing activities as they researched and wrote the questions together. These questions were then sent back to school and placed in a class quiz booklet. The game was eventually played on the last day of the spring term, with Easter eggs as prizes. Each family was given a copy of the collectively-produced quiz booklet. This simple task engaged the interest of children and community alike, rooting the literacy experiences within their own cultural lives.

Media diaries are another valuable way of developing children's literacy skills. Children may be asked to keep a diary of their media consumption over a period of time, commenting on what they watched and their responses to it. These diaries can then be developed into interactive writing tasks with other adults. As children make comments on particular programmes or films watched, adults may insert a comment or question to promote further reflection by the child. Writing is, of course, inextricably linked to reading and so an activity such as this is useful in developing both skills. There are, however, specific activities which can be undertaken in order to promote reading.

Previously in the chapter, we examined how work which compares printed and film versions of the same text helps to develop children's literacy skills. There are many other opportunities for developing reading based on the moving image. Extracts from scripts of films and programmes can be used in shared reading sessions for work on aspects such as character, setting, genre, narrative and so on. Children can read schedules from magazines such as *Radio Times* and be asked to scan for particular information e.g. find all the programmes which relate to family life. Teachers may present children with descriptions of programmes which they need to place on a schedule (this would also provide a valuable means of working on concepts such as a 'watershed'). Texts related to favourite films, programmes or actors could be used to stimulate reading e.g. film reviews, magazines featuring television and film stars, related websites. Activities such as these promote an approach to literacy that involves children in a dynamic process in which they transform the texts around them and make them their own: 'Reading the word is not preceded merely by reading the world, but by a certain form of writing it or rewriting it, that is, transforming it by means of practical work. For me, this dynamic process is central to the literacy process' (Freire, 1972, p. 35).

This chapter has considered the use of video, television and film texts both as part of the intertextual frame in which the development of conventional reading is supported and as an important means of constructing meaning in their own right. We have argued that children need to be supported in developing their understanding of both processes. There are many more activities which could be undertaken in relation to children's experiences with film, television and video. This chapter can do no more than make a few suggestions that could be developed and adapted in relation to particular contexts and learning needs. Ultimately, there is an important role for educators in ensuring that children become competent and critical decoders, analysers and producers of televisual texts. In addition to the moving image, music is another important dimension in children's lives. The next chapter moves on to explore the world of popular music and examines ways in which it can inform the literacy curriculum.

Note:

1. See the website for both organizations for further details on resources: British Film Institute at http://www.bfi.org; Film Education at http://www.filmeducation.org

9

Popular Music and Literacy

Lara, the 4-year-old daughter of parents who are both teachers, had been asked to sing her favourite song. She performed a version of the Spice Girls' lyric, *Stop*, with appropriate actions, stretching her arms with her palms straight out in a gesture which signified the bringing of an issue to a complete standstill, as in the Spice Girls' own rendition of the song on video. She sang, 'Stop, right now, thank you very much, I need a bunny with a human face'. The unmodified version of the song's words is:

Stop right now, thank you very much,
I need somebody with a human touch.
Hey you, always on the run,
Gotta slow it down baby, gotta have some fun.

Lara's knowledge of the lyrics was a surprise to her parents, as she had been discouraged from listening to pop music at home. However, once in school, she was trying rapidly to absorb and join in the performances and snatches of songs and rhymes that she encountered in her playground. The phrase 'bunny with a human face' is her mishearing of the Spice Girls' lyric, in which the group express a longing for 'somebody with a human touch'. The latter phrase has very thinly disguised sexual overtones. Lara's version is of interest because it transforms the world of the sexually awakening adolescent girl, the original 'message' of the song, into that of the nursery and its host of accompanying anthropomorphic characters. She might have been imagining Miffy, Peter Rabbit or any one of the Flopsy Bunnies more prevalent within a middle-class, story-book world as she created her new version of the lyrics. It also, however, powerfully signifies Lara's desire to be part of the girls' 'club' attracted to 'girl power'. The performance could be seen as expressing the tension between her firm roots in her family's protective nursery culture and the seductions of the glamorous new world, encountered through playground activities with her peer group. The transformation of the materials available in the various aspects of their social worlds is common to all young children's play and Gunther Kress has shown the choice of signs to be dependent on both an awakened interest and available resources:

> The transformative action of childish meaning-making works relentlessly on their world. Their ravenous appetite for meaning-making leaves no object, no material untouched. All are drawn into structures which are both stable and novel. The voraciously analytical eyes of child sign-makers assess the semiotic possibilities of the world around them: 'reading' in the sense of detailed analytical scrutiny of all aspects of their world for their potential use in representation.
>
> (Kress, 1997, p. 33)

Lara's interest has been awakened by her friends, but the transformation is rooted in her own analysis of the supposed meaning.

Even more explicit in their underlying suggestiveness are the lyrics of the song which Lara chose to perform next, *Barbie Girl*. This is a parodic celebration of the ubiquitous American plastic doll and had been recorded by the pop group, Aqua, just after Lara's birth. Aqua deliver the lyrics through several levels of sexual ambiguity and include these lines in their full version:

> Come on Barbie – let's go party
> You're my doll – 'rock and roll' – feel the glamour in pink
> Kiss me here, touch me there
> – hanky panky.

For Lara and her 7-year-old brother, who rushed to join in the Barbie song, adding his own gestures and laughing wildly, the pleasure lay in the repetition of the lines, 'I'm a Barbie girl – in a Barbie world – life in plastic – it's fantastic'. The rhyme of 'fantastic' with 'plastic' seemed particularly delightful to both children and was the main focus of their interest. However, just as Lara's transformation of the Spice song embodied her desire to be one of the girls, her brother's sardonic rendering of the Barbie lyrics was clearly meant to express his disdain in general for all things girlish and for his sister's doll in particular. Their fascination with words and the desire to play with meaning is an important part of children's sign-making, to which popular music makes an important contribution. It is a process which the Australian academic, Garth Boomer, recorded in the pre-sleep monologue of his 3-year-old son, shortly after their arrival in Britain. His long, sleepy, rambling, sing-song recitation included the following lines:

Sing . . . yella
The ella sumporine
Ella sumporine,
We all live in the ella sumporine
ella sumporine, the ella sumporine
we all live in tile ella sum . . .

(and the rest is silence)

(Boomer, 1985, p. 6)

This snatch of the original sleep monologue contains what the child has remembered from the Beatles' hit song, *We All Live in a Yellow Submarine*. His monologue shows the potency of ambient music and the attraction of the key words. These examples underline the fascination young children have with the words of songs and the opportunities they provide for language play. They also demonstrate that children often appropriate cultural texts by transforming them and adapting the proffered social codes to ones which reflect their own interests, values and experiences. However, this transformation is not always apparent to their parents and carers, who would shudder at the thought of popular music as a component of children's school learning and are reluctant to allow their young children direct access to a world of overtly provocative language, accompanied by apparently lascivious body gyrations and gestures.

Yet, the world of popular music is inescapable for all but the most determined recluse. Songs, new and more dated, play a key role in both advertisements and film; they are a staple of radio programming and blare out from the doorways of shops in every major high street. In Chapter 4, we emphasized the ubiquity of print in the lives of young children. The same claim for children's early familiarity with words and their processes of signification, which we present in that chapter, can be made for the sounds and rhythms of popular music. Tapes and cassettes of nursery rhymes are frequently bought and played to infants from birth – indeed, some mothers deliberately try to expose their children to the soothing sounds of music in the womb. Toy-makers produce colourful, plastic versions of personal radios, CD-ROM players and other stereo systems, with knobs and buttons which many children learn to operate from infancy. In addition, there exist many varieties of popular music that are embedded deeply within specific cultural groups, like rap and reggae, or gospel music and blues and, for some children, modern versions of hymns. These are encountered in many community-based settings, including carnival, celebrations and worship, so that children may bring to school a rich tradition of musical experiences which are rarely recognized within the official curriculum. The potency of music transcends cultural boundaries and provides many instances of 'border crossings' (Giroux, 1992), places where culturally specific musical traditions cross over and are embedded within popular music. This has happened in recent years to rap, hip-hop and bhangra. Such musical forms are very popular with many young children, as well as the adolescent audiences that teachers more readily associate with them.

As is the case with the comics and popular novels that we have discussed in previous chapters, however, the music industry has attracted to itself a wide range of negative criticism. The first cultural dismissal of pop music was expressed by Adorno who, in discussing its 'standardization' of form and content, attacked its 'pseudo-individualisation', commented that, 'it induces relaxation because it is patterned and pre-digested' and therefore spares the masses the 'effort of participation' (Easthope and McGowan, 1992, p. 309). Adorno's dismissal is based on the fact that the music provided for mass consumption is mere entertainment ('people want to have fun') as a distraction from the miserable conditions of industrial production and is not educative, as, supposedly, is music in its classical forms. Popular music would, by his standards, offer few opportunities for intellectual stimulation, being merely emotive and sentimental at its best, trivializing and debased at its worst.

Second, some teachers have reservations about the expropriation of music from a particular culture, which is used without its roots or meanings being understood. Roland Barthes first commented about hearing a Hopi performance of ritual Native American music in Paris: 'Can we Westerners really consume a fragment of civilization totally isolated from its context?' (Barthes, 1985b, p. 121). It is this sense of deracination that makes some teachers of older pupils wary of studying popular music in class, because of the lack of historical background. Richards calls it 'an uncomfortably contradictory object of study' (Richards, 1998, p. 132). There is unease with the lack of context for the experience that lies behind this powerful form. Richards quotes a teacher explaining the influence of advertising on her own son's music: 'My little son who's nine, for Christmas wanted tapes . . . wanted a Beethoven tape, blues and jazz tapes and this seems to have been because, is it Budweiser? . . . have been using, is it John Lee Hooker? And the Heineken one' (Richards, 1998, p. 145). Richards comments:

The concern here is partly that the reappropriation of black music by the media, and particularly by advertising, is compromised in that it does successfully create some awareness and enthusiasm for the music but does so, of course, without acknowledging the larger context of the production of such music or the longevity of the musical traditions from which such tiny fragments are taken.

(Ibid.)

Although the last point may be of central concern in the secondary school, where popular music is studied as part of a media course, in the context of the primary school the important point seems to be that pupils from all communities should be able to identify and contribute to the discourses created by the music that is brought to school.

There are other issues to consider, however. Commentators have bridled at the misogynistic content of some lyrics, most notably seen in the dismissive terminology 'bitches', which is present in some forms of 'gangsta rap'. A feminist reading of popular music can find a host of material which promotes misogyny and we would not wish to suggest that all lyrics should be welcomed into the classroom to be treated uncritically. Indeed children could engage in a study of the roles ascribed to men and women in a range of musical genres. Opera, no less than musicals or popular music, portrays both men and women in stereotypical roles. The overreaction of many journalists, media analysts and politicians often fails to discern the patriarchal and offensive messages contained within more mainstream forms of music and also ignores the alternative songs produced by young women which offer a challenge to female subordination, including the Spice Girls' lyrics. It would appear that racism may underpin much of the furore against some popular musical forms, in that critics who do little to challenge sexism within white discourses, for example in the lyrics of the Rolling Stones' music, suddenly become very vocal in relation to such forms as rap or reggae.

This is not to deny the offensive nature of some of the 'gangsta rap' material, nor to suggest that any of it should be used with young children in the classroom, rather it is to suggest that we need to examine reactions to popular music in greater depth and understand the complex forces that are at work. For example, some of the rap music enjoyed by adolescents has presented fantasies of violence against racists. One cultural critic argues that this should be seen in context: 'Rappers' fantasies about killing white people in general, or policemen in particular, are no more than the letting off of steam about the most unbearable racist pressure under which most of us live; these fantasies are not the ones acted upon' (Williams, 1992, p. 171). In relation to the supposed harm to which children are exposed in hearing sexually explicit and violent lyrics, (Johnson, Jackson and Gatto, 1995) some research has suggested that young children reinterpret lyrics (as was seen in the case of Lara cited at the beginning of the chapter) and so they are not therefore necessarily absorbing the messages about which there is such concern (Greenfield *et al.*, 1987; Hall, 1998). This does not mean, however, that we are advocating the exposure of young children to music which has been created for an adult audience, rather it points to the dangers of a knee-jerk reaction which is inherent within the oversimplification of such issues. Put simply, lyrics for use in the classroom need to be selected particularly carefully with close attention to their words and the range of meanings suggested. However, when inappropriate material has been weeded out, there still remains a wide range of possibilities for interesting work.

Rap music offers rich opportunities for classroom analysis of linguistic forms, as well as a black cultural heritage. In addition, it is clear that children's interest in rap has been widespread and has crossed cultural groupings. Children's natural enthusiasm for the rhythms and structures of the genre has been recognized by many publishers and raps on various topics of interest to children abound in poetry anthologies:

Baby-K Rap Rhyme
My name is Baby-K
An dis is my rhyme
Sit back folks
While I rap my mind;

Ah rocking with my homegirl,
My Mommy
Ah rocking with my homeboy,
My Daddy
My big sister, Les an
My Granny,
Hey dere people – my posse
I'm the business
The ruler of the nursery

poop po-doop
poop-poop po-doop
poop po-doop
poop-poop po-doop

(from *Baby-K Rap Rhyme*, in Nichols, 1991, p. 39)

In fact, the National Literacy Strategy for Year 5 suggests that both modern music in general and rap in particular can help children to identify patterns of rhythm and rhyme. There is a further suggestion that children might be asked to compose their own verse for a popular modern song. In the case of the *Baby-K Rap*, children could add a verse to introduce members of their class to the baby.

In addition to their concerns about the words of songs, many parents are made anxious by the superficial glamour of the popular music industry, which they fear lures their children into a precocious sexual awareness. Magazines for young girls promote a fascination with heterosexual romance in relation to young male pop stars. Further, it is the case that the popular music industry in developed countries has begun to target younger and younger children in its desire to create new markets. 'Boy bands' and 'girl bands' have often been thrown together in a hurry in order to exploit the craze for the products of such icons and they then have been surrounded by the 'commercialised superstar system' (Clarke, 1995) associated with other popular cultural texts. Such aggressive marketing strategies sit uneasily with primary school values, which can find sex education difficult.

However, it is no new phenomenon; generations of children have been attracted by the popular musical icons of their day, with Frank Sinatra creating the first mass-adoring young female following, called 'bobby soxers'. Springhall (1998) demonstrates how popular music aimed at children and young people has always discomfited many groups in society and created 'moral panics' in which certain genres of music, such as rock and roll in the 1950s, punk music in the 1970s and 'gangsta rap' in the 1990s, have provoked oppositional media responses. We have analysed these reactions in previous chapters, where we have argued that part of the discomfort many adults feel in relation to children's culture may arise because of their alienation from children's current interests, their lack of understanding of what is involved and a longing for a mythical past of innocent childhoods. However, talking about music in school can help pupils to think through some of these difficult issues. Reviews of current hits and a survey of how particular groups are presented and targeted at certain types of audiences can be part of classroom discussions. Such analyses can be used gradually in the upper part of the primary school to make pupils more aware of how the industry works and what the system suggests about what it is to be a man, what it is to be a woman. Pop stars themselves can offer a critique of the glamour of their profession through their other roles, so that former Spice Girl Geri Halliwell's work with children for the United Nations might also be discussed.

The final criticism which needs to be examined in relation to popular music is an accusation about the industry's commercial manipulation of children. What has been interesting in recent years is the increasing tendency to wrap popular music more firmly within the intertextual web of popular cultural forms. Some years ago, popular songs were linked with the children's cartoon characters, the Smurfs, and the CDs sold in their thousands. Now we see the launch of computer games (Pokémon) linked with the screening of a related film, which features pop songs. The accompanying CD then becomes as desirable as some of the other texts and artefacts which surround the phenomenon. This is a measure of the widening consumerist net which engulfs the children's market and creates new opportunities for enterprising music producers.

We can see, therefore, that teachers need to consider all these issues carefully when devising appropriate work for school that incorporates popular songs and their related texts. However, we may be helped to think more clearly about the processes involved in children's reception of lyrics by considering the role played by nursery rhymes, many of which began their lives in more adult forms. If pop lyrics cause alarm, nursery rhymes are everybody's favourite childhood medium, whether sung or chanted, and their messages are therefore often left unexamined. They have been rightly acknowledged as helping to develop a phonemic awareness of onset and rime (Maclean, Bryant and Bradley, 1987) and are a staple item in every nursery and reception class's language curriculum. Yet, as Peter and Iona Opie (1951) found in their exhaustive compilations and study of the genre, most of the little rhymes we now consider as appropriate for children did not begin their lives in this way, but had circulated amongst adult popular audiences in more robust forms. Thus, they write in the preface to *The Oxford Dictionary of Nursery Rhymes*: 'It can be safely stated that the overwhelming majority of nursery rhymes were not in the first place composed for children; in fact many are survivals of an adult code of joviality, and in their original wording were, by present standards, strikingly unsuitable for those of tender years' (Opie and Opie, 1951, p. 3).

One rhyme that Opie and Opie identify as carrying hidden adult messages is 'One misty moisty morning', a section from a longer traditional ballad called *The Wiltshire Wedding*. Like *The Foggy Dew*, the subject of the rhyme is that of a child conceived outside of marriage. Another example of innuendo is provided by 'Little robin redbreast sat upon a rail', which the Opies record as 'a rude little jest'. Commenting further, they suggest that, 'latter day editors have shown ingenuity in making it suitable for their collections' (Opie and Opie, 1951, p. 174). The Opies show also, how in a reversal of the process that brought adult songs to the nursery, advertisers reappropriate the rhythms and language of nursery rhymes to constitute an adult text, as in this 1947 advertisement:

There was a little man
And he felt a little glum,
He thought that a Guinness was due, due, due.
So he went to the Plough
And he feels better now,
For a Guinness is good for you, you, you.

The point is that adults and children use the same kinds of material for different purposes and children's interests are not necessarily focused on adult meanings. The relationship, then, between children's and adults' songs, rhymes and jingles is far more complex than can be arrived at by a simple designation of child-appropriate or adult-appropriate material. In their access and replication of modern popular lyrics in playground rituals, children are transforming meanings to shape their own emergent sense of self and creating different forms of agency. Lara's version of the sexy Spice Girls' lyrics, which we cited in the opening paragraphs, can be seen both as continuous with her childlike preoccupations with small fluffy animals and as a rite of passage into the world of school, rather than a corruption of innocence which her parents fear.

Moreover, children's tastes in music in the primary years are very eclectic. Pop songs compete with nursery rhymes and traditional tunes written for children, such as *The Wheels on the Bus* and *Miss Polly had a Dolly*, as examples offered by pre-school children when their favourite songs were requested in a play-corner version of a karaoke session. Similarly, when asked for their favourite pop songs, 10-year-old children produced a wide range of examples spanning both time and place, including Chubby Checker's *Let's Twist Again*, Madness's *Our House* and several well-known Beatles' lyrics, in addition to a topical cover version of *American Pie* by Madonna and the latest hit from the teenie-bop idol, Britney Spears. The point is that interest in pop music traverses age as well as class and 'race', and children were happy to join in the singing of other children's choices. The songs which accompany the Disney animations are well known, as are songs from musicals and stage shows. As previously noted with popular authors, like Blyton, and in the sharing of comics, popular music can be seen to provide points of continuity and communication between generations, as well as heralding difference and challenge.

In addition to the rich tradition of rhymes and songs which form a part of every culture, young children are exposed daily to the newer forms of music which may play a powerful role in their lives. Children's television exploits the power of the combination of music and words to embed themselves in memory, presenting each of its programmes in the frame of a repetitive lyric. Thus each new children's programme has its own recognisable jingle, such as the jolly jog of 'Postman Pat and his black and white cat'.

Alongside the songs of the shows themselves are advertisements which also contain memorable lyrics. Words coupled to music or rhythmic chant have the power to linger in the memory long after a particular campaign or programme has ended. Test out on mature colleagues their response to being told the Milky Bar Kid is big and strong song; give the prompt: 'The Milky Bar Kid just . . .' and you will probably get the answer . . . 'can't go wrong!' It is the memorability of texts that makes them a good medium for early shared reading, because, just as in the case of nursery rhymes, memory can be linked to prediction of meaning from minimal cues. The pervasive power of advertising and the ability of its jingles to capture the imagination of children can be seen in this vignette:

> After each had brought in a cuddly toy, pupils in an infant class were asked to imitate the sound the animal would make. Jake brought in a lion and made a great impression with his 'roar!'. Annie's dog was easily imitated with a 'woof-woof!' When asked what he had brought in, Nicholas showed his frog. 'And what sound does a frog make, Nicholas?' 'Budweiser, Miss!'
>
> (Bolton, 2000, p. 3)

Nicholas's interest had obviously been captured by the Budweiser song, as chorused by frogs in a recent advertisement. There have been many other stories recounted to us by teachers of children bursting into song as they write or paint, chanting the words to the latest jingles or advertisements which had caught their attention.

It can therefore be seen that the songs and recitations of popular culture which children enjoy derive from a range of sources which include traditional lyrics, ballads, nursery rhymes, advertising jingles and songs. All of these genres may be used to inform the literacy curriculum. Indeed, Suzi Clipson-Boyles advocates the use of popular culture in the teaching of poetry, arguing that:

> Children's own language can be used as a useful starting-point for creating poetry and rhyme. Likewise, the multi-faceted world of popular culture and the media offer tremendous potential for creating language activities which have the additional benefits of using children's own literacy worlds.
>
> (Clipson-Boyles, 1999, p. 41)

Using popular music in school

Because of the many challenges to parental and academic values which we have outlined above, very little has been written to date about the use of lyrics in the primary classroom. Older pupils have sometimes been asked to study the pop music industry as part of Media Studies (Richards, 1995, 1998; Archer, 1996) and teachers of literature in the secondary school have occasionally combined the study of lyrics with a study of modern poetry; Bob Dylan and the poetry of T. S. Eliot being a perennial favourite combination. A careful analysis of the words of pop songs can also be a useful antidote to those cultural critics who may dismiss the words of popular songs as 'cheap', 'trite' or 'sentimental' (Hoggart, 1995). However, as we have discussed earlier, the introduction of material which is so close to the emergent and contested identities of young people can cause problems in the formal setting of the classroom:

> Where people are being taught more or less compulsorily or have a strong instrumental understanding of education, the orientation is one which is likely to define boundaries between what is personal and what is a matter of personal skill or competence . . . Being taught may be something in which people acquiesce or concede almost on condition that it does not undermine, or weaken, or challenge the boundaries between 'private' and 'public' regions of subjectivity.
>
> (Richards, 1998, p. 136)

There is a danger of appropriating the cultural worlds of children for educational ends in ways which work to negate the pleasures derived from texts which they claim as their own (Buckingham and Sefton-Green, 1994). However, with sensitivity, educators can utilize children's interests in popular music. In an American study, Hagood and Ash (1999) used karaoke within reading lessons in order to orientate adolescents towards schooled reading practices. Working with a group of children identified as having reading difficulties, they created karaoke sessions in which children were required to read the words of the song lyrics as they sang their favourite tunes. This proved to be very motivating for the children. In the UK, the practice of reading popular songs in chorus from shared texts has been used with older 'catch-up' groups and, with a careful selection of materials, could be used for shared reading in the literacy hour.

Moreover, in the primary school, competing personal taste in music is likely to be less of a problem than with teenage pupils whose choices and interests are often promoted and defended at the expense of those of other class members. This is particularly understandable because of the powerful role music plays in identity formation and friendship group cohesion, a process which begins from an early age, but is at its most potent in adolescence. Pop music has a real power because of this and, as can be shown with aspects of film and television, pupils from ethnic minorities often have easier access to it than the lore and language of traditional English culture. Nevertheless, teachers need to take care that all their pupils' choices are represented in selections for the classroom and that no one's tastes are discounted or ridiculed, as should be the case with all aspects of personal interest when they are introduced into school. Providing opportunities to share their tastes with others will also allow the teacher to develop a wider knowledge of each individual child's interests.

As an extension of this sharing, children could conduct their own survey of the class or school's musical tastes and, over a period of a few weeks, compile their own list for a Top of the Pops. The opportunity to research older people's tastes and collect examples of parents' and grandparents' choices could be used for a Golden Oldie chart of all-time favourites. This is particularly useful if the class are researching a particular period of culture, in relation to a book or other topic. The 1960s or 1970s are periods which are especially accessible in terms of musical taste of parents and grandparents.

Popular songs, lyrics and rhymes may be used in exactly the same way as traditional nursery rhymes with the youngest classes in order to develop an understanding of analogy, through a focus on onset and rime and prediction of line endings (see Chapter 4 for a more detailed account of this). We asked one teacher to explain how she had used popular songs to develop creative and lively work on phonics and rhymes with her infant class in the previous academic year:

> The songs . . . well, I didn't plan anything in advance, just kept an eye on the new singles on *Top of the Pops*, Radio 1 etc., and when they sounded like fun, and worked in well with what we were doing, we

learnt the lyrics. One example was '*The Witchdoctor*' (ooh eeh ooh ah ah ting tang walla walla bing bang . . .). The children loved then substituting their own phonemes/digraphs/ blends etc. They sang them and wrote them down, like: th, th, ar, ar, ar, ar, oo, oo, sh, sh, sh, sh. Actually, I wasn't that bothered about the written bit, it was really the aural skills it developed. The children who hadn't accessed nursery rhymes had good rhyming/predicting skills on pop songs. When we did the techno *King of my castle* song this year, the conversation about 'What is a trastle/why is the word there?' (I still don't know) prompted far more interest than dry discussions about rhyming words in nursery rhymes. Lately, I haven't done much, but the revamped *Jerusalem* (Euro 2000) song means reading those lyrics . . . I have to check out any dodgy lyrics with my daughter!

A verse from a song that is currently popular could provide the focus for handwriting as children enjoy copying familiar lyrics and with older children this could turn into the structuring of a compilation album with a particular theme. In addition, some song lyrics embody a central metaphor and can be used to explore figurative language when these are the focus for analysis in a close reading. The National Literacy Framework suggests that Year 4 children should look for figurative language in poetry and compare narrative and poetic phrases. Elton John's two versions of *Candle in the Wind* for example, would be appropriate for this focus as would the folk song, *Where Have All the Flowers Gone*? Personification, alliteration and onomatopoeia can all be explored just as easily as imagery and thematic structures, although the songs need to be carefully selected for their images. Songs can be collected on a particular theme: rain and sunshine, cars and highways spring to mind as being common subjects of many pop lyrics. These ideas can be pursued either as a stand-alone activity or used in conjunction with poetry. A primary teaching student decided to compare and contrast the poet's use of rhyming couplets in *The Highwayman* with the use of such a device in S Club 7's *Bring It All Back*. The children were asked to analyse both texts and identify the rhymes and the figurative language in each text. In addition, children were asked to find parts of the song lyrics which needed to be sung in a particular way in order for the rhyming couplets to work effectively.

Some song lyrics, such as the currently popular *American Pie*, or *Starry, Starry Night* have a narrative structure which can be analysed in the classroom. The settings, characters and the narrative structure of song can form a focal point of study. Beatles' lyrics have often provided such a starting point and songs like *Hey, Jude* and *She's Leaving Home*, which are centred on a main character, can provide a number of opportunities for comparative work with characters in books. Bob Marley's reggae lyrics, like *Buffalo Soldier*, provide a starting point for examining prejudice and slavery when these are the focus of study in history or personal and social education. In addition, songs on a particular theme can be compared and contrasted. For example, many popular songs have addressed the theme of the environment and the threats to the world from nuclear disaster and global warming, as in Michael Jackson's *Earth Song*. They also sometimes address social issues; Elvis Presley's *In the Ghetto*, for example, raises the issue of poverty and could be set alongside Charles Causley's poem, *Timothy Winters*, to begin a discussion or increase children's awareness of poverty. A popular song based on the theme of loss or death, such as Puff Daddy's *I'll Be Missing You*, can be a useful way into the study of a children's text on the same theme.

We are not suggesting, however, that popular songs should only be analysed in relation to more conventional texts. Popular songs and their related artefacts also offer the opportunity for the development of critical literacy skills. Children can be asked to analyse songs and identify the way in which the texts have been framed to position the listener, what role is given to girls in the song, what other values are being promoted. This work, as we have suggested before, needs to be carefully managed so that children's pleasures in the songs are not diminished or ridiculed or a particular community's tastes rejected. This, of course, is easy to say; difficult to do. One way of approaching the task would be to allow children to express their pleasures in the song, both before and after the analysis of the text. Pleasure can then be seen as one of the acknowledged positions within the discourse. In addition, it may be useful to discuss ways in which all of us can enjoy texts of which we are also critical in some way, with teachers presenting honest appraisals of their own popular tastes.

As well as the study of well-established lyrics, alternative versions of well-known songs are also an interesting area, as are the misheard lyrics of old and new favourites. Perhaps not everyone has heard of 'Gladly, the cross-eyed bear' as the hymn of which it is a corruption is specific to the English Christian tradition, but every group of children can produce their own examples of corruptions, parodies and adaptations. Football anthems provide a lively set of parodies and could lead on to a discussion of why particular songs are chosen for particular teams. In addition, playground chants and rhymes are often parodies and adaptations of popular lyrics and songs, and children could compile a list of the current favourites. The link between songs, lyrics, jingles, rhymes and chants is not straightforward and the genres cross nowhere as completely as in the playground. Children delight in word-play and especially enjoy the rhythmic pleasures that singing along to tunes can give. The rhymes children devise often make wry comments on topical issues, as in the skipping rhyme collected in 1997 at the time when boys' 'underachievement' was being much discussed in the popular press:

> Girls go to Mars, collect more stars
> Boys go to Jupiter to get more stupider.

Grugeon (1999) argues that children's oral cultural traditions are rich in such parodies and her Bachelor of Education students collected a range of examples of songs, rhymes, jokes, chants, skipping and clapping games which were steeped in intertextual references. She notes that some of these rhymes provide opportunities for children to subvert imposed notions of childhood and gender:

> Among the clapping rhymes recorded was a version of My boyfriend gave me an apple with the final verse:
>
> I took him to the pictures
> To buy some bubble gum
> And when he wasn't looking
> I shoved some up his bum.
>
> This rhyme is typical of the way taboo topics are used by young girls to subvert rhymes which originally put the girlfriend in a powerless position.
>
> (Grugeon, 1999, p. 15)

Similarly, children subvert the naïve lyrics of songs and rhymes in order to reject adult notions of childhood innocence and non-agency, often substituting innocuous verses with stanzas which celebrate violence, blood and gore, as in this adaptation of a song featuring the Teletubbies:

> I love Po
> Po loves me
> Let's hang Laa-Laa from a tree
> With a knife in his back and a gun to his head
> Ha-Ha, Dipsy, Laa-Laa's dead.

This notion of parody is a strong thread within children's culture and has often been seen as a Bakhtinian form of 'the carnivalesque' in which traditional forms are dragged from their pedestal, usurped by a playful need to challenge traditional notions of authority and hegemony through the production of irreverent travesties of these forms. Carnivals are a strong tradition from the Middle Ages and provide opportunities for people to celebrate in a range of ways which challenge established notions of 'acceptable' behaviour and standards. Thus Bahktin emphasized the bawdy and irreverent nature of much carnival activity. Some argue that such carnivalesque behaviour offers the opportunity for children to transgress imposed boundaries: 'These carnivalesque moments foreground freedom, pleasure and desire. They unsettle the existing order of things. They use satire and laughter to imagine how things might be otherwise' (Grace and Tobin, 1998, p. 48).

The parodying of current pop lyrics and other rhymes can therefore be considered to offer opportunities for children to create worlds in which established notions of childhood are turned upside down and mocked in an assertive move toward self-determination. However, it may sometimes be difficult to see how the chants of children, which often reinforce hegemonic and patriarchal attitudes in their celebration of violence and sexism, can offer emancipatory opportunities. Perhaps what they can do is provide spaces for children to play with other identities, identities which are both alluring and frightening to them at the same time. They may also, at times, help teachers to approach a difficult issue, such as bullying, from children's own constructs.

Children's authors and publishers are well aware of young children's attraction to popular music and some have drawn on this in imaginative ways. Vivian French and Korky Paul (1997) have produced *Aesop's Funky Fables*, which draw on the rhythms of rap and song:

Oh me
(Plod plod)
Oh my
(Plod plod)
Could it be
That I spy Hare
Over there?
(Trudge trudge)

from 'The Hare and the Tortoise'

Saturday Night at the Dinosaur Stomp (Shields, 1998) draws on the rock and roll songs popular in the era of Bill Haley and the Comets:

Word went out 'cross the prehistoric slime:
'Hey, dinosaurs, it's rock 'n' roll time!

Slick back your scales and get ready to romp
On Saturday night at the Dinosaur Stomp!

Brachio-, Suoer-, and Ultrasaurus
Sang, 'Doo-bop-a-loo-bop,' all in a chorus.
Ankylosaurus drummed on his hard-shelled back,
Boomalcka boomalacka Whack! Whack! Whack!

(Shields, 1998, p. 3)

These are just a few snippets from texts that draw on children's love of songs and rhythms, texts which have been enormously popular in infant classrooms.

However, as in relation to other forms of media, some teachers do have questions about using this genre. Analysing song lyrics in class can pose difficult questions. Should teachers confront the gender, racial and class stereotypes found in a large proportion of lyrics? Are Spice Girl power, the world of Madonna, the violent sexism of 'gangsta rap' or even the fighting ethics of the Pokémon song, values that teachers should be seen to endorse? The issue is a sensitive one. Sometimes it must appear to older students of popular cultural forms that teachers' only interest in youth culture comes from a desire to undermine their interest and divest the medium of its particular appeal. For us, the issue is not one either of censorship, i.e. choosing so carefully that much of popular culture is excluded from the classroom, or of unmasking ideologies in a confrontational way, rather our approach depends on creating opportunities for dialogue and discussion of emerging issues. It seems important to us that the debates should take place within school where all can be given a voice.

Another concern that some may have is that of knowledge of the genre. If teachers are to incorporate popular music into the curriculum, they need to take time to keep up with trends and the traditions that feed them. Popular songs enter children's cultural spaces very quickly and leave almost as quickly again. Hard-pressed teachers, unless modern music is their own passion, rarely have the time or the inclination to follow the popular music charts in a concerted way. However, we are not suggesting that such texts should become a permanent feature of the literacy curriculum; rather, that teachers might provide spaces within the curriculum to use the songs for short, concentrated periods of time, perhaps using the lyrics as a way in to studying other texts. In addition, this is an area in which teachers can rely on children to keep them updated, asking them to bring in favourite CD-ROMS and pop magazines.

Producing media texts

So far, we have talked primarily of the analysis of popular songs and rhymes. Media studies courses often stress the importance of production (Richards, 1998; Archer, 1996). This may be approached by creating a class music magazine with reviews and comments in the manner of fanzines, perhaps also incorporating the star profiles which are a regular feature of such publications. Alternatively, pupils can mock-up their own hosted music programme, where class members 'write in' with requests and are encouraged to script the running commentary, using a popular radio programme as their model. Scripting will also allow pupils to use more formal and considered language as part of their Speaking and Listening targets. The use of a tape-recorder and where available a microphone will add some degree of authenticity to this activity.

Children's interest in particular pop stars can also be exploited to investigate and develop websites relating to these icons, or a critical appraisal of sites which already exist. Children, often young girls, spend much time in their bedroom writing fan letters to pop stars. Their interest could be developed into a study of letter writing as a social phenomenon and children could be encouraged to analyse the difference between fan letters and other types of letters. As in the manner of the Ahlbergs' *The Jolly Postman* (1999), the children could produce fan letters which are a parody of other styles (e.g. a fan letter to Madonna written in the style of a formal solicitor's letter to a client). Sometimes, fanzines give details of pop stars' favourite books. This can be a useful means of promoting reading amongst otherwise reluctant readers and in fact can be used to stimulate book writing. For example, children may be interested in analysing the tastes of a particular pop star and then creating a book which would please them.

This chapter has explored both the problems and possibilities posed by the decision to use popular songs when working with children. It is perhaps the facet of popular culture which is used least often in primary schools, where teachers often prefer to draw their ideas from the wide range of specialist compositions available for children's singing, or more traditional lyrics and ballads. In making recommendations for ways of approaching the use of the lyrics, we have drawn on a very limited number of titles that will appear very dated to some readers. They are meant to act only as exemplification, rather than as key recommendations, as it is preferable for those wanting to use the media to examine the current tastes of children and the more recent shows and videos that may be informing their choice. As with the other media we have discussed in previous chapters, there is much to be gained in terms of motivation and interest from their inclusion, but teachers need to be thoughtful about both the choices and interventions they make. The emphasis must be on helping children to be more considered about the symbolic materials they use in everyday exchanges. Dyson describes the teacher as helping children 'to deliberately manipulate textual material – composed words or symbols – in order to deliberately assert, resist, rework both ideological "truths" and social relations . . . (through) the interplay of unofficial and official worlds' (Dyson, 1997 p. 16). The emphasis must be on the 'deliberately'. In all our recommendations, there is an emphasis on the underlying planning strategy which guides use, rather than a carnivalesque abandonment of the prevailing values and norms established for the classroom. This does not mean that delight, pleasure and even moments of *jouissance* may not emerge from children's engagement; it is our experience that they always do.

10

Conclusion

In 1990, Paul Willis presented the readers of *Common Culture* with an interesting set of statistics:

> 5% of the UK population attend the theatre, opera or ballet.
> 4% of the UK population attend museums or art galleries.
> 2% of the UK working class attend any of the above . . .
> 98% of the population watch TV on average for over 25 hours a week.
>
> (Willis, 1990, p. ix)

Comparative figures from the 1998 edition of *Social Trends* suggests that this picture has changed somewhat, as it reports that 11 per cent of the UK working-class now attend the theatre and art galleries. However, this increase is not enough to suggest that the working classes are at last, as Arnold, Leavis and Hoggart might have wished, seeing the error of their ways and wholeheartedly embracing high culture (they would, perhaps, be dismayed to learn that the percentage of people in social groups D and E visiting a betting shop was marginally higher, at 12 per cent). Despite all those years in which the working classes endured a school curriculum that discounted their culture and exulted the artistic output of a privileged minority, it would appear that the majority of the population has their own idea about what provides them with narrative pleasure.

We have argued, throughout this book, that the recognition of working-class children's 'cultural capital' (Bourdieu, 1977) in the literacy curriculum is essential if children are to feel that schooled literacy practices are meaningful reflections of home experiences. This is not to suggest that this strategy would be enough to alleviate poverty, poor housing, unequal access to facilities and so on. We do not suppose for a moment that placing *The Beano* on the classroom shelves will facilitate an increase in the percentage of children from social classes D and E achieving five A–C grades or more at General Certificate of Secondary Education (GCSE), for example, or lead to more children from state schools being accepted at Oxford or Cambridge universities. The causes of inequality in society are deep, complex structures which cannot be addressed by changes to the texts studied in school classrooms. Nonetheless, we tentatively suggest that recognizing the social and cultural worlds of children and allowing such discourses to creep under the classroom door will encourage their literacy development in a number of important ways.

First, it will provide children with the message that they do not have to cast off the identity of home and community as they enter the classroom and become consumers of a cultural universe in which they have to search for glimmers of familiar narratives. Recognizing children's cultural capital and placing it on classroom walls and shelves will create a space in which children can feel more comfortable within school. Various studies have suggested that older children can become particularly disaffected and disenfranchised from school (Elliott et al., 1999). When asked about the reasons for this, children often cite the fact that school holds little of interest for them and that it represents values which are completely dislocated from the rest of their lives (Corrigan, 1979). Some working-class children manage to adapt to the requirements of a middle-class education system and become successful within it, but this is often at a cost. For the minority of children from the working class who do manage to enter university, the price to pay is usually a sense of movement away from their roots and the formation of a fissure between their interests and lifestyles, and those of their families. Educational success brings with it profound changes to social and cultural identities, which may result in an individual feeling neither a part of a working-class nor a middle-class milieu, an issue tentatively explored in the play *Educating Rita* (Russell, 1985). This seems to be an unnecessary, but inevitable, process.

When the cultural capital of working-class communities does become the focus of academic study, as we see in the increasingly popular communication studies, cultural studies and media studies degrees, then the establishment responds by attempting to debase it, calling into question its integrity and value. The *Guardian* reported that 'In a recent radio interview, the Chief Inspector of Schools, Chris Woodhead, derided the pretensions of media studies to be a degree subject' (Low, 2000, p. 11) and the historian, Christopher Lee, suggested that 'at its best, media studies is a good post-graduate diploma' (Lee, 1999). Yet, it is the very growth of such courses which has resulted in a more thorough understanding of the way in which cultural exclusion occurs, in addition to providing a forum in which marginalized groups can give their own texts currency. The development of many courses in black studies, for example, provides a space in which the extensive range of literature produced by black people and ethnic minorities can be fully recognized. However, this work needs to move from the margins to the central arena of the curriculum. There is an urgent need to reconsider the exclusion of some cultural forms from primary schools, in order to ensure that the education system belongs to all and that all can have access to the breadth of work available. This last point is an important one. We are not suggesting the inclusion of popular culture in the school curriculum will benefit only working-class children. Most children engage with popular culture to a greater or lesser extent and all who do so find great satisfaction from the discourses available. Valuing this culture in the classroom will provide a means of engaging with material which works across boundaries of class, gender and 'race'. However, as many middle-class children also have access to other cultural forms which are valued in school, the inclusion of popular cultural texts will provide only additional benefits. For working-class children, it may serve more essential purposes.

Second, using popular cultural texts can provide motivation for literacy. Motivation is one of the key ingredients needed if learning is to be effective. It has been argued that intrinsic motivation (Meece, Blumenfeld and Hoyle, 1988) is essential if learning is to be made real. Intrinsic motivation can be related to the interest children have in the tasks with which they are presented in the classroom (Hidi, 1990; Schiefele, 1991; Guthrie *et al.*, 1996). Studies have shown that if children have a genuine interest in the reading and writing tasks in which they engage, it has a positive effect on their learning (Hidi, 1990; Turner, 1995; Guthrie *et al.*, 1996). It is obviously the case that interest will be related to children's previous experiences and socio-cultural backgrounds. Indeed, Smogarinsky and O'Donnell-Allen (1998) note that educators should develop a notion of motivation: 'that takes into account learners' cultural and social histories and views their relationships with texts in terms of this vast web of experience that they bring to particular classroom episodes' (Smogarinsky and O'Donnell-Allen, 1998, p. 552). Certainly, previous studies do indicate that incorporating popular cultural texts into the literacy curriculum has enhanced the motivation of specific groups of children (Dyson, 1996, 1998, 1999; Marsh, 1999, 2000a). Children have responded with delight when given an opportunity to use their cultural knowledge in an informed way in the classroom, as

Cathy Pompe notes on her work in primary schools: 'I was myself always popular simply for carrying around a few Batman figures and Sindy dolls ("You always do such interesting things, Cathy!"): frenzied children in the playground squashed their noses against the windows of the library where we worked amongst mouth-watering plastic treasures' (Pompe, 1996, p. 102). Drawing on this delight in such pleasurable narratives can provide riches untold, as children rush to share their joy and excitement, with both each other and the adults who work with them. Some may be concerned that this process is little more than exploitation on the part of adults, who wish to do nothing more than find another way to impose their agendas on unsuspecting minors. One of the pleasures of popular culture, after all, is that it usually has nothing to do with school and the more formal elements of children's lives; indeed, it provides an escape route from their restrictive discourses. In this case, there is a danger that appropriating children's cultural interests for educational ends could take away the gratification gained from out-of-school activities. However, children's engagement with popular culture is so extensive that one could not possibly exhaust the supply and leave children with no secret pleasures. Educators need only draw on small elements in this intertextual universe in order to enliven their literacy curriculum. Not to do so runs higher risks in that children may not only be less motivated within school, but left feeling that literacy practices outside of school are meaningless and irrelevant. In a study of working-class adolescents' literacy experiences, Nagle (1999) found that:

> The pleasure that some of the participants found in literacy outside school was killed by the emphasis of school literacy practices. Bianca's poetry and Kevin's comics had no place in a lesson on writing. Jayne's romance novels were of no value in a literature class. Jim summed up the frustration of many of the participants when he talked about the way he was introduced to school literacy.
> 'You know what I think? I think schools work hard at convincing you that you aren't smart. Before I got to school I loved books. I remember my mom reading me the dinosaur books all the time. I couldn't get enough of them. Then school starts and not one dinosaur book. There are all these "See Jane run," "See Dick run." I remember always praying I could go to the school library where they had dinosaur books. You can't tell me that they can't teach a kid to read with dinosaurs.'
>
> (Nagle, 1999, p. 178)

Here, Jim is pleading for an opportunity to bring home interests into school and have them recognized within the curriculum. He perceives no danger of his interests being taken over and therefore extinguished. Jim's experience was clearly unfortunate, but things have changed. Most teachers, of course, do now provide a rich range of texts to encourage early reading, some of which focus on dinosaurs. Most teachers are aware of the need to incorporate children's interests into the curriculum and want nothing more than to engage their pleasure in literacy activities both within and outside of school. However, if this wish is to be fulfilled, we need to embrace *The Dandy* and Digimon as well as dinosaurs.

In addition, there have been profound changes to the nature of literacy in recent years as technological changes impact on the ways in which we communicate with one another. Chapter 7 detailed how the Internet, video technology and mobile phones are transforming literacy practices. If schools focus on increasingly outmoded forms of literacy, then children's motivation toward the literacy diet offered in the classroom will be affected further. This is not to berate teachers for a continuing focus on traditional print literacy; teachers constantly struggle with overdeterministic curriculum frameworks which themselves reflect outmoded forms of communication and schools have long suffered a lack of funding for the appropriate resources. Both these factors militate against change and it is a measure of teachers' continuing commitment to children's learning that, despite these difficulties, they strive constantly to orientate the children they teach toward meaningful literacy practices.

Third, the use of popular culture to capture children's interest can be a means of introducing them to the recognized canon of texts. Children need to be able to discern which cultural forms accrue specific symbolic capital in any situation. Bourdieu explained that there are four types of capital: economic, cultural, social and symbolic. Symbolic capital is that which has been legitimated and thus carries power within any given discourse (Bourdieu, 1979). In this way, the cultural capital of the dominant classes becomes symbolic capital in education, government and the courts. It is this symbolic capital which working-class children will need to access if they are to progress through the system. Working-class children will not be empowered if they are allowed to enjoy superhero stories in the classroom, but not given access to Shakespeare, Keats or any of the other texts which they will meet in examinations. However, literature from the monolithic canon is often presented in ways which do little to locate it within the cultural worlds children inhabit. Yet children will have more interest in Greek mythology, for example, if their attention is drawn to the way in which contemporary authors draw on it in their work. Wilson (2000) outlines how the cover of Peter Lerangis's *The Yearbook*, a horror fiction for children, 'shows Pytho, the huge serpent from Greek mythology who delivered the Delphic Oracle and who, in this story, has reappeared many centuries later to cause havoc in small town Middle America' (Wilson, 2000, p. 8). Drawing children's attention to this fact and encouraging them to research the original myth will provide a stimulating way into the study of Greek texts. Similarly, Anne Haas Dyson (1996) reports that an elementary schoolteacher, Kristin, provided opportunities for her class to explore the links between the stories of the Greek gods and the superheroes with which they were more familiar from their engagement in everyday popular culture.

These are just two examples which indicate the potential for weaving texts together in a meaningful way. After all, narratives have served a particular function for humans over centuries and it is inevitable that we can trace particular themes throughout a range of texts, including popular texts. As Stuart Hall has stated, popular culture 'is an arena that is *profoundly* mythic' (Hall, 1992, p. 32). The mass media is the repository of our fears, hopes and dreams and in it, we find old stories refashioned in new forms. Thus soap operas deal daily with traditional themes and storylines and there are rich opportunities for teachers to make the links between one of the women characters in an episode of *Brookside* and Shakespeare's Lady Macbeth, or a character's anger in *EastEnders* and Max's responses in Maurice Sendak's *Where the Wild Things Are*. This continuous movement between a range of discourses will enable children to bring their previous experiences and understanding to new texts and take from traditional narratives those elements which reflect contemporary life. In addition, children can create new, exciting cultural forms, which arise from interaction with a wide range of discourses, including popular culture (Dyson, 1997, 1999, 2000).

The fourth reason why we should make every effort to embrace the potential of popular culture to inform the literacy curriculum is that it can be a useful means of developing critical literacy skills. Social discourses often contain conflicting messages and children need to be able to deconstruct these texts in order to tease out the complexities. Nowhere are these dualistic discourses more clearly demonstrated than in the media. Television offers a powerful means of educating us about ourselves and the world, through its mixed diet of soap operas, quiz programmes, documentaries and films. There is more information in one edition of a broadsheet newspaper than the average person living in the seventeenth century consumed in a lifetime. Yet both of these media have the potential for propaganda, polemic and manipulative persuasion. Children need to be able to navigate this terrain in a critical, alert manner. Work on popular culture can provide a successful means of developing these skills, as it often is easier for them to trace personal responses to what is presented within the discourses. This can be done in a climate which recognizes that, 'Binary distinctions between "ideology" and "pleasure" or "reason" and "emotion" ultimately lead to quite one-dimensional understandings of the process' (Buckingham, 1993b, p. 290) and that children can both express a pleasure in these texts and analyse them in a way which leads to greater understanding.

It is also important that children are able to transfer their ability to analyse discourses critically to a wide range of texts, for popular culture does not hold a monopoly on manipulation. Throughout this book, we have seen that the greatest threats to the use of popular culture in the classroom have arisen from concerns over the levels of violence, racism, sexism and other ideologically unsound messages which reside in the texts. Yet these features are not absent from texts which are more commonly accepted as good quality 'literature'. Racism, anti-Semitism, homophobia and sexism are so rife within the 'great works' of literature that it is difficult to single any authors out for particular mention – Ezra Pound, T. S. Eliot, Rudyard Kipling, Kingsley Amis and Mark Twain are some of the myriad writers who managed to express ideas which lead to oppression and discrimination, whilst receiving numerous literary accolades. Nevertheless, the outcry over the potential to debase and corrupt is usually only ever raised in relation to popular culture, although there have been some notable literary exceptions; D. H. Lawrence's *Lady Chatterley's Lover* being the most notorious example.

Another criticism which is often voiced is that popular culture is ephemeral and therefore an insufficiently stable medium for the curriculum. Children's interests come and go and a carefully crafted lesson on a particular phenomenon could be out of date before a teacher is provided with an opportunity to deliver it. This, to a certain extent, is a danger, but there are other arguments which get lost in such assertions. There are many other cultural forms that are as transient. New children's fiction titles appear monthly and, of those which are considered to be of high quality (in contrast to the popular forms on supermarket shelves), only a small percentage remain in publication for years, becoming modern children's classics. In addition, many iconic works in children's popular culture enjoy longevity. The trajectory throughout this century of Disney's *Snow White* was used as an example in the introduction to this book. There are other well-established popular icons. Batman was first introduced in the opening pages of Detective Comics no. 27 in May 1939. Bob Kane was the artist, Bill Finger the writer and in 'Creating a figure who, like the criminals, operated outside the law, on their own terms, yet did so on behalf of the status quo, Kane and Finger originated a popular myth that has lasted for over half a century' (Boichel, 1991, p. 7).

Similarly, Superman and Barbie have been around for decades and still enjoy widespread appeal. Other cultural forms become popular for a number of years before disappearing and even then they might resurface at some point, albeit as a kitsch icon, as we have seen recently with the Smurfs. Some aspects of popular culture mutate over the years, retaining the same essential features but reforming themselves for new audiences. This appears to be the case with wrestling figures. The World Wrestling Federation phenomenon, which currently stirs great passion in many young boys, first appeared in the early 1990s, sporting such plastic doll heroes as Ultimate Warrior and Sgt. Slaughter. Indeed, as Fleming reminds us, these early fighting figures themselves 'revived the basic idea of the Marx company's 1930s Popeye boxing toy' (Fleming, 1996, p. 49). It is, perhaps, inevitable that some aspects of popular culture endure and others experience transmutability. For what such icons do is to draw on the basic and persistent interests of human beings themselves, interests which have been relatively unchanged since the days before mass media. The interests in wrestlers can be traced back to Ancient Greece and a fascination with Hercules and Vulcan. As Springhall reminds us, reporting an interview with a young boy: ' "I like beat-em ups. As nasty as you can get and with lots of blood and guts," claimed 16 year-old Mark Nolan, dismissing as "rubbish" suggestions that violent games induce violence. Adolescent boys were ever thus' (Springhall, 1998, p. 154).

This is not to suggest, of course, that we are proposing an unquestioning acceptance of hegemonic masculinist discourses which privilege patriarchal power, aggression and violence. Just because there have always been a number of boys who have been attracted to warrior-fantasies through their play with war toys and fighting dolls, does not mean that violent narratives should become a naturalized and accepted part of the iconography of childhood. However, the issues are complex (see Urquhart, 1996) and a feminist reading of the discourse would suggest that, instead of a simplistic ban on such play, we need to accept that 'The challenge for educators is to deconstruct these seemingly *natural* responses with children and enable them to see that there are other positions they can take within discursive practice' (Lowe, 1998, p. 219).

Finally, popular culture can provide opportunities for creating social communities in which children and teachers can engage in discourses that cement shared understanding and interests. Richards comments that 'Participation in popular culture reaffirms the containing social matrix of which we are a part, to which we belong and which belongs to us' (Richards, 1998, p. 7). It is this social aspect of popular culture which is the defining feature for children. Through popular culture, they can forge identities which are shared by a group, mark out their common cultural territories and feel part of a network which extends beyond the immediate home environment. As argued in Chapter 3, the appeal of popular cultural texts for many children is their place within a narrativized, semiotic system which knits disparate aspects of their lives together.

In addition, popular culture can provide a means of placing ourselves within a public discourse which offers reflections on our own identities. When children buy a *Batman* or a *Barbie* comic, they are buying into a set of hegemonic discourses which tell them comforting and familiar stories about the complex world which surrounds them and provide them with a set of common patterns they can share with others. As Paul Willis has said about popular music, popular culture can provide children with 'a set of public discourses . . . which play back to people their own situations and experiences, and provide a means of interpreting those experiences' (Willis, 1990, p. 69). We make sense of ourselves in relation to others and popular culture presents us with opportunities to get to know those others, or at least representations of them. Therefore, when we acquire particular texts or artefacts, we are acquiring a set of social practices. The challenge for educators is to enable children to deconstruct the ways in which these social practices encourage participation in the world 'as a gendered, classed and ethnic subject' (Alloway and Gilbert, 1998, p. 96).

The relationship of popular culture to identity construction can be seen most easily in an area of popular culture which we have had no space within this book to explore: that of the body. Clothes, shoes, hairstyles, hair accessories, body tattoos, decoration, piercings, make-up and jewellery, all provide means by which children can forge individual identities that have deliberate commonalities and differences from others. It is not just goods which relate to the outside of the body that become social markers; food and drink serve this purpose as well.

Thus, we can see that popular culture plays a significant role in many children's lives. It provides a forum in which they can explore questions of identity and positioning in relation to others, although, as we have seen throughout this book, this exploration is channelled into hegemonic discourses in which what it means to be a girl or boy, black or white, rich or poor is set in stone. Popular culture can also provide a meeting ground for children, a space where childhood interests overlap and form lines of communication between disparate groups and individuals. It is a place where fundamental narratives of desire, fear and pleasure are played out in a space which is bounded by straightforward binaries and seemingly unquestionable truths about life, a reassurance which is welcome in the uncertain and unstable discourses of childhood. Popular culture imparts untold pleasures as children weave their dreams and aspirations into a rich tapestry of interlocking threads, engaging in a 'symbolic creativity' (Willis, 1990) that can be profoundly fulfilling. Educators must grasp some of these threads and pull them into the fabric of the classroom, in order to weave together the disparate strands of children's lives more effectively and provide them with a coherent and affirming framework for learning. Not to do so is to open ourselves up to staunch challenge, for as Luke and Roe (1993) suggest:

> What Bart Simpson, Madonna, M.C. Hammer, or New Kids on the Block have to say about the world is far more important to youth than the social and moral lessons teachers extract from literature and basal readers. One way of viewing culture is that it consists of complex and often contradictory narratives by which people negotiate in and make sense of the world. And since schooling is all about inducting the young into specific encultural knowledge and practices, the lack of attention to today's most pervasive and powerful narrative sources of culture is difficult to justify pedagogically and politically.
>
> (Luke and Roe, 1993, p. 115)

Ultimately, literacy is a social practice (Barton, 1994; Barton and Hamilton, 1998). Through literacy, we communicate with each other, cement existing discourses, shape new ones and fashion out the structure of our lives. Some communities do this to a greater or lesser extent than others, but all communities do use literacy, in its broadest sense, to build common structures. Even those communities which do not rely on print-based means of communication often use signs and symbols to supplement the spoken word. If literacy is a such a widespread social practice, then it is inevitable that it will draw from cultural landscapes in its meaning-making. Throughout this book, we have argued for the exploration of terrains whose boundaries are as wide as possible, in order to ensure that all children have a voice in shaping the social practices of schooled literacy. Such work will not only enrich the lives of children, it will provide teachers with potent opportunities to share in the wider discourses that are located on the margins of classroom life and which are usually hidden away from them in secret childhood worlds.

References

Abbot, C. (1998) Making connections: young people and the Internet, in J. Sefton-Green (ed.) *Digital Diversions: Youth Culture in the Age of Multimedia*, London, University of Central London Press.

Adams, M. J. (1990) *Beginning to Read: Thinking and Learning about Print*, Cambridge, MA, MIT Press.

Adorno, T. W. (1991) *The Cultural Industry: Selected Essays on Mass Culture*, ed. J. M. Bernstein, London, Routledge.

Al-Eidan, A. A. (1999) The impact of computer games on children's development. Unpublished M.Ed dissertation, University of Sheffield.

Allan, A. and Ahlberg. J. (illustrator) (1999) *The Jolly Postman or Other People's Letters*, London, Viking Books.

Alloway, N. and Gilbert, P. (1998) Video game culture: playing with masculinity, violence and pleasure, in S. Howerd (ed.) *Wired Up: Young People and the Electronic Media*, London, UCL Press.

Althusser, L. (1994) Ideology and ideological state apparatuses, in J, Storey (ed.) *Cultural Theory and Popular Culture: A Reader*, London, Prentice Hall.

Alvermann, D., Moon, J. S. and Hagood, M. C. (1999) *Popular Culture in the Classroom: Teaching and Researching Critical Media Literacy*, Newark, DE, IRA.

Ang, I. (1985) *Watching Dallas: Soap Opera and the Melodramatic Imagination*, trans. D. Couling, London, Methuen.

Archer, S. (1996) Pop, pleasure and pedagogy: the challenges of teaching pop music for Media Studies GCSE, *The English and Media Magazine*, no. 34, pp. 39–44.

Ariès, P. (1966) *Centuries of Childhood*, London, Pimlico (first published in France in 1960).

Arnold, M. (1963) *Culture and Anarchy*, (ed. J. Dover Wilson,) Cambridge, Cambridge University Press.

Bakhtin, M. M. (1994) Extract from 'The Dialogic Imagination', in P. Morris (ed.) *The Bakhtin Reader: Selected Writings of Bakhtin, Medvedev, Volosinov*, London, Arnold.

Balzagette, C. (2000) A stitch in time: skills for the new literacy, *English in Education*, Vol. 34, no. 1, pp. 42–9.

Bardsley, D. (1991). *Factors Relating to the Differential Reading Attitudes, Habits and Interests of Adolescents*, Research Affiliateship Report No. 1, New Zealand, Department of Education, Massey University.

193

Barker, M. and Brooks, K. (1998) *Knowing Audiences: Judge Dredd, its Friends, Fans and Foes*, Luton, University of Luton.

Barker, M. and Petley, J. (eds) (1997) *Ill Effects: The Media-Violence Debate*, London, Routledge.

Barrs, M. (1988) Maps of play, in M. Meek and C. Mills (eds) *Language and Literacy in the Primary School*, London, Falmer Press.

Barthes, R. (1973) *Mythologies*, trans. A. Lavers, New York, Hill and Wang (original work published 1970, Paris, Seuil).

Barthes, R. (1974) *S/Z: An Essay*, trans. R. Miller, New York, Hill and Wang; London, Collins, Fontana Press (original work published 1970).

Barthes, R. (1977) The death of the author, in S. Heath (ed. and trans.), *Image Music Text*, London, Fontana.

Barthes, R. (1985) How to spend a week in Paris, in M. Blonsky (ed.) *On Signs* pp. 118–21, Oxford, Blackwell.

Barton, D. and Hamilton, M. (1998) *Local Literacies: Reading and Writing in One Community*, London, Routledge.

Barton, R. (1994) *Literacy: An Introduction to the Ecology of Written Language*, Oxford, Blackwell.

Baudrillard, J. (1983) *Simulations*, trans. P. Foss, P. Patton and P. Beitchman, New York, Semiotext.

Beano website at http://www.beano.com accessed 6 May 2000.

Beavis, C. (1998) Computer games, culture and curriculum, in I. Snyder (ed.) *Page to Screen: Taking Literacy Into the Electronic Era*, London, Routledge.

Bennett, A. (1994) *Writing Home*, London, Faber and Faber.

Benson, R. (2000) The joy of text, *Guardian*, Weekend Supplement, 3 June 2000, p. 23–7.

Benton, P. (1995). Recipe fictions: literary fast food? Reading interests in Y8, *Oxford Review of Education*, Vol. 21, pp. 108–11.

Berger, A. A. (1997) *Narratives in Popular Culture, Media, and Everyday Life*, London, Sage.

Berger, A. A. (2000) Arthur's computer (narrative) adventure, *TelevIZIon*, vol. 13, 1, p. 40.

Bloch, L. R. and Lemish, D. (1999) Disposable love: the rise and fall of a virtual pet, *New Media and Society*, Vol. 1, no. 3, pp. 283–303.

Blyton website at http://www.btinternet.com/~ajarvis/blyton/blyton.htm accessed 6 January 2000.

Boichel, B. (1991) 'Commodity as myth' in R. E. Pearson and W. Uricchio, *The Many Lives of the Batman*, London, Routledge.

Bolton, C. (2000) Soundbites, *Times Educational Supplement*, 3 March, p. 3.

Bolton, E. (1998) Introduction: why books matter, in B. Cox (ed.) *Literacy is Not Enough: Essays on the Importance of Reading*, Manchester, Manchester University Press.

Boomer, G. (1985) *Fair Dinkum Teaching and Learning: Reflections on Literacy and Power*, Upper Montclair, NJ, Boynton Cook.

Bourdieu, P. (1977) *Outline of a Theory of Practice*, Cambridge, Cambridge University Press.

Bourdieu, P. (1979) Symbolic power, *Critique of Anthropology*, Vol. 4, pp. 77–85.

Bourdieu, P. (1990) *The Logic of Practice*, trans. R. Nice, Cambridge, Polity Press (original work published in 1980).

Britton J. (1977) Response to literature, in M. Meek, A. Warlow and G. Barton (eds) *The Cool Web: The Pattern of Children's Reading*, London, Bodley Head.

Bromley, H. (1996) 'Did you know that there's no such thing as Never Land?' Working with video narratives in the early years, in M. Hilton (ed.) *Potent Fictions: Children's Literacy and the Challenge of Popular Culture*, London, Routledge.

Bromley, H. (1999) Storytelling, *Primary English Magazine*, Vol. 4, no. 5, pp. 22–5.

Bromley, H. (2000) Never be without a Beano: comics, children and literacy, in A. Andersen and M. Styles (eds) *Teaching through Texts*, London, Routledge.

Brooks G., Schagen, I. and Nastat, P. (1998) *Trends in Reading at Eight*, Slough, NFER.

Brooky, M. (1998) Television and children, *Raphael House Newsletter*, 30 April, pp. 1–4, accessed 4 June 2000 at http://www.rh.steiner.school.nz/article18.htm.

Browne, N. (1999) *Young Children's Literacy Development and the Role of Televisual Texts*, London, Falmer Press.

Buckingham, D. (1993a) *Changing Literacies: Media Education and Modern Culture*, London, Tufnell.

Buckingham, D. (1993b) *Children Talking Television: The Making of Television Literacy*, London, Falmer Press.

Buckingham, D. (ed.) (1998) *Teaching Popular Culture: Beyond Radical Pedagogy*, London, UCL Press.

Buckingham, D. and Sefton-Green, J. (1994) *Cultural Studies Goes to School: Reading and Teaching Popular Media*, London, Taylor and Francis.

Burkeman, O. (2000) Pokemon power, *Guardian*, 20 April, pp. 2–3.

Carter, R. (1990) The new grammar teaching, in R. Carter (ed.) *Knowledge about Language and the Curriculum: The LINC Reader*, London, Hodder and Stoughton.

Cassell, J. and Jenkins, H. (1998) Chess for girls? Feminism and computer games, in J. Cassell and H. Jenkins (eds) *From Barbie to Mortal Kombat: Gender and Computer Games*, Cambridge, MA, MIT Press.

Chall, J. (1983) *Stages of Reading Development*, New York, McGraw-Hill.

Christensen, P. and James, A. (eds) (2000) *Research with Children: Perspectives and Practices*, London, Falmer Press.

Christie, J. F. (ed.) (1991) *Play and Early Literacy Development*, Albany, NY, State University of New York Press.

Clark, E. (1995) Popular culture: images of gender as reflected through young children's story. Paper presented at Annual Joint Meeting of the Popular Culture Association/American Culture Association, Philadelphia. ERIC document no. ED 388966.

Clark, M. (1976) *Young Fluent Readers*, Oxford, Heinemann Educational.

Clay, M. (1979). *Reading: the Patterning of Complex Behaviour*, 2nd ed, Auckland and London, Heinemann.

Clipson-Boyles, S. (1999) Poetry, in J. Marsh and E. Hallet (eds) *Desirable Literacies: Approaches to Language and Literacy in the Early Years*, London, Paul Chapman.

Coffin, T. P. and Cohen, H. (1978) *The Parade of Heroes*, New York, Anchor Press and Doubleday.

Cohen, S. (1987) *Folk Devils and Moral Panics: The Creation of the Mods and Rockers*, 2nd edn, Oxford, Blackwell.

Coleridge, S. T. (1976) On the constitution of the church and state, in J. Colmer (ed.) *Collected Works Volume 10: On the Constitution of the Church and State*, Princeton, NJ, Princeton University Press.

Connell, R. W. (1987) *Gender and Power: Society, the Person and Sexual Politics*, Cambridge, Polity Press/Blackwell.

Considine, D. M. (1986) Visual literacy and children's books: an integrated approach, *School Library Journal*, September, pp. 38–42.

Corrigan, P. (1979) *Schooling the Smash Street Kids*, London, Macmillan.

Cox, B. (ed.) (1998) *Literacy Is Not Enough: Essays on the Importance of Reading*, Manchester, Manchester University Press.

Craggs. C. E. (1992) *Media Education in the Primary School*, London, Routledge.

Cross, G. (1997) *Kid's Stuff: Toys and the Changing World of American Childhood*, Cambridge, MA, Harvard University Press.

Cunningham, V. (1998) Reading now and then, in B. Cox (ed.) *Literacy Is Not Enough: Essays on the Importance of Reading*, Manchester, Manchester University Press.

Dahl website at http://www.roalddahl.org/whoami.htm accessed 6 January 2000.

Davies, B. (1990) Agency as a form of discursive practice: A classroom scene observed, *British Journal of Sociology of Education*, Vol. 11, no. 3, pp. 341–61.

Davies, B. (1992) The gender trap: a feminist poststructuralist analysis of primary school children's talk about gender, *Journal of Curriculum Studies*, Vol. 24, no. 1, pp. 1–25.

Davies, B. (1993) *Shards of Glass: Children Reading and Writing beyond Gendered Identities*, Cresskill, NJ, Hampton Press.

Davies, B. (1997) Constructing and deconstructing masculinities through critical literacy, *Gender in Education*, Vol. 9, no. 1, pp. 9–30.

Davies, B. (1989) *Frogs and Snails and Feminist Tales: Preschool Children and Gender*, Sydney, Allen and Unwin.

Davies, J. and Brember, I. (1993) Comics or stories? Differences in the reading attitudes of boys and girls in Years 2, 4, 6, *Gender and Education*, Vol. 5 no. 3, pp. 305–20.

Denzin, N. (1987) Postmodern children, *Caring for Children/Society*, March–April, pp. 25–25.

Department for Education and Employment (DfEE) (1999) *The National Curriculum: Key Stages 1 and 2*, London, DfEE/QCA.

Department for Education and Employment (DfEE) (2000) *National Curriculum for England, Key Stage 1–4*, London, HMSO.

Department of Education and Science (DES) (1988) *National Curriculum*, London, HMSO.

Department of Education and Science (1989) *Report of the English Working Group* (The Cox Report), London, HMSO.

Derrida, J. (1967) *Speech and Phenomena*, Evanston, IL, Northwest University Press.

Dodwell, E. (1999) 'I can tell lots of Punjabi': developing language and literacy with bilingual children, in J. Marsh and E. Hallet (eds) *Desirable Literacies: Approaches to Language and Literacy in the Early Years*, London, Paul Chapman.

Dyson, A. (1994) The Ninjas, the X-Men and the ladies: playing with power and identity in an urban primary school, *Teachers College Record*, Vol. 96, no. 2, pp. 219–39.

Dyson, A. H. (1989) *Multiple Worlds of Child Writers: Friends Learn to Write*, New York, Teachers College Press.

Dyson, A. H. (1996) Cultural constellations and childhood identities: on Greek gods, cartoon heroes, and the social lives of schoolchildren, *Harvard Educational Review*, Vol. 66, no. 3, pp. 471–95.

Dyson, A. H. (1997) *Writing Superheroes: Contemporary Childhood, Popular Culture and Classroom Literacy*, New York and London, Columbia University Teachers College Press.

Dyson, A. H. (1998) Folk processes and media creatures: reflections on popular culture for literacy educators, *The Reading Teacher*, Vol. 51, no. 5 pp. 392–402.

Dyson, A. H. (1999) Coach Bombay's kids learn to write: children's appropriation of media material for school literacy, *Research in the Teaching of English*, Vol. 33, no. 4, pp. 367–402.

Dyson, A. H. (2000) On reframing children's words: the perils, promises and pleasures of writing children, *Research in the Teaching of English*, Vol. 34, pp. 352–67.

Eagleton, T. (1983) *Literary Theory: An Introduction*, Oxford, Blackwell.

Eagleton, T. (1996) *Literary Theory: An Introduction*, 2nd edn, Oxford, Blackwell.

Eagleton, T. (2000) *The Idea of Culture*, Oxford, Blackwell.

Easthope, A. and McGowan, K. (eds) (1992) *A Critical and Cultural Theory Reader*, Buckingham, Open University Press.

Eco, U. (1981) *The Role of the Reader*, London: Hutchinson.

Eliot, T. S. (1974) *Collected Poems 1909–62*, London, Faber and Faber.

Elliot, J., Hufton, N., Hildreth, A. and Illushin, L. (1999) Factors influencing educational motivation: a study of attitudes, expectations and behaviour of children in Sunderland, Kentucky and St Petersburg, *British Educational Research Journal*, Vol. 25, no. 1, pp. 75–94.

Epstein, D. (1993) *Changing Classroom Cultures*, Stoke-on-Trent: Trentham Books.

Farver, J. M. (1992) An analysis of young American and Mexican children's play dialogues: illustrative study no. 3, in C. Howes and C. C. Matheson (eds) *The Collaborative Construction of Pretend*, Albany, NY, State University of New York Press.

Fein, G. G. and Stork, L. (1981) Socio-dramatic play: social class effects in integrated preschool classrooms, *Journal of Applied Developmental Psychology*, Vol. 2, pp. 267–79.

Field, C. (2000) Metropolis Street Racer, *Mr Dreamcast*, June, pp. 16–19.

Film Education (1999a) *Film and Literacy Pack: Part 1*, London, Film Education.

Film Education (1999b) *Film and Literacy Pack: Part 2*, London, Film Education.

Film Education Working Group (FEWG) (1999) *Making Movies Matter: Report of the Film Education Working Group*, London, British Film Institute.

Fish, S. (1980) *Is There a Text in This Class? The Authority of Interpretive Communities*, Cambridge, MA, Harvard University Press.

Fisher, M. (1964) *Intent Upon Reading: A Critical Appraisal of Modern Fiction for Children*, 2nd edn, Leicester, Brockhampton Press.

Fiske, J. (1989) *Understanding Popular Culture*, London, Unwin Hyman.

Fleming, D. (1996) *Powerplay: Toys as Popular Culture*, Manchester, Manchester University Press.

Flesch, R. (1955) *Why Johnny Can't Read*, New York, Harper and Row.

Formanek-Brunell, M. (1998) The politics of dollhood in nineteenth-century America, in H. Jenkins (ed.) *The Children's Culture Reader*, New York, New York University Press.

Foucault, M. (1979) *The History of Sexuality, Vol. 1: An Introduction*, London, Allen Lane and Penguin.

Fox, C. (1993) *At the Very Edge of the Forest: The Influence of Literature on Storytelling by Children*, London, Cassell.

Francis, B. (1998) *Power Plays: Primary School Children's Constructions of Gender, Power and Adult Work*, Stoke-on-Trent, Trentham Books.

Frater, G. (1997) *Improving Boys' Literacy*, London, Basic Skills Agency.

Freebody, P. (1992). A socio-cultural approach: resourcing four roles as a literacy learner, in A. Watson and A. Badenhop (eds), *Prevention of Reading Failure*, Sydney, Ashton Scholastic.

Freebody, P. and Luke, A. (1990) Literacies programs: debates and demands in cultural context, *Prospect: Australian Journal of TESOL*, Vol. 5, no. 7, pp. 7–16.

Freeman Davidson, J. I. (1998) Language and play: natural partners, in D. P. Fromberg and D. Bergen (eds) *Play from Birth to Twelve and Beyond: Contexts, Perspectives and Meanings*, New York, Garland.

Freire, P. (1972) *The Pedagogy of the Oppressed*, Harmondsworth, Penguin.

French, J. (1987) *A Historical Study of Children's Heroes and Fantasy Play*. Research report. School of Education, Boise State University, Idaho, ERIC Document No. ED 310885.

French, V. and Paul, K. (1997) *Aesop's Funky Fables*, London, Puffin.

Frith, U. (1985) Developmental dyslexia, in K. E. Paterson *et al.* (eds) *Surface Dyslexia*, Hove, Lawrence Erlbaum Associates.

Funk, J. B., Behmann, J. N. and Buchman, D. D. (1997) Children and electronic games in the United States, *Trends in Communication*, Vol. 2, pp. 111–26.

Gagnon, D. (1985) Videogames and spatial skills: an exploratory study, *Educational Communication and Technology Journal*, Vol. 33, no. 4, pp. 263–75.

Gailey, C. W. (1993) Mediated messages: gender, class and cosmos in home video games, *Journal of Popular Culture*, Vol. 27, no. 1, pp. 81–98.

Garvey, C. (1977) *Play*, London, Fontana and Open Book.

Gaut, B. (1993) The paradox of horror, *British Journal of Aesthetics*, Vol. 37, no. 4, pp. 333–45.

Giroux, H. (1992) *Border Crossings: Cultural Workers and the Politics of Education*, London, Routledge.

Giroux, H. (1998) Are Disney movies good for your kids?, in S. R. Steinberg and J. L. Kincheloe (eds) *Kinderculture: The Corporate Construction of Childhood*, Boulder, CO, Westview Press.

Giroux, H. A. (1981) *Ideology Culture and the Process of Schooling*, London, Falmer Press.

Giroux, H. A. (1988) *Schooling for Democracy: Critical Pedagogy in the Modern Age*, London, Routledge.

Godzich, W. (1985) The semiotics of semiotics, in M. Blonsky (ed.) *On Signs*, Oxford, Blackwell.

Goodman, K., Smith, E. B., Meredith, R. and Goodman, Y. (1987) *Language and Thinking in School: A Whole Language Curriculum*, Katonah, NY, Richard C. Owen.

Goodman, Y. (1980) *The Roots of Literacy*. Claremont Reading Conference yearbook, Vol. 44, pp. 1–32.

Goodman, Y. (1986) Children coming to know literacy, in W. H. Teale and E. Sulzby (eds) *Emergent Literacy: Writing and Reading*, Norwood, NJ, Ablex.

Goodman, Y. M. (1989) Roots of the whole-language movement, *Elementary School Journal*, Vol. 90, pp. 113–27.

Goosebumps website: at http://place.scholastic.com/goosebumps/indexa.htm accessed on 6 January 2000.

Goswami, U. (1988) Orthographic analogies and reading development, *Quarterly Journal of Experimental Psychology*, Vol. 40A, pp. 239–68.

Goswami, U. and Bryant, P. (1990) *Phonological Skills and Learning to Read*, Hillsdale, NJ, Erlbaum.

Grace, D. and Tobin, J. (1998) Butt jokes and mean-teacher parodies: video production in the elementary classroom, in D. Buckingham (ed) *Teaching Popular Culture: Beyond Radical Pedagogy*, London, UCL Press.

Green, B., Reid, J. and Bigum, C. (1998) Teaching the Nintendo generation? Children, computer culture and popular technologies, in S. Howerd (ed.) *Wired Up: Young People and the Electronic Media*, London, UCL Press.

Greenfield, P. M. (1984) *Mind and Media: The Effects of Television, Computers and Video Games*, London, Fontana.

Greenfield, P. M., Bruzzone, L., Koyamatus, K., Satuloff, W., Nixon, K., Brodie, M. and Kingsdale, D. (1987) What is rock music doing to the minds of our youth? A first experimental look at the effects of rock music, *Journal of Early Adolescence*, Vol. 28, no. 4, pp. 315–29.

Griffiths, M. (1995) *Feminisms and the Self*, London, Routledge.

Griffiths, M. D. (1993) Are computer games bad for children? *The Psychologist: Bulletin of the British Psychological Society*, Vol. 6, pp. 401–7.

Griswold, W. (1994) *Cultures and Societies in a Changing World*, Thousand Oaks, CA, Pine Forge Press.

Grugeon, E. (1999) The state of play: children's oral culture, literacy and learning, *Reading*, Vol. 33, no. 1, pp. 13–16.

Guardian (2000) In brief, *Guardian*, 3 June, p. 22.

Gunter, B. and Harrison, J. (1997) Violence in children's programmes on British television, *Children and Society*, Vol. 11, no. 3, pp. 143–56.

Gunter, B. and McAleer, J. (1997) *Children and Television*, 2nd edn, London, Routledge.

Guthrie, J. T., Van Meter, P., Dacey Mcanu, A. Wigfield, A., Bennett, L., Poundston, C. C., Rice, M. E., Faibisch, F. M., Hunt, B. and Mitchell, A. M. (1996) Growth of literacy engagement: changes in motivations and strategies during concept-oriented reading instruction, *Reading Research Quarterly*, Vol. 31, no. 3, pp. 306–25.

Hagood, M. C. and Ash, G. E. (1999) 'I Want My MTV!' Reading fluency, student motivation, karaoke and pop music. Paper presented at AERA, Montreal, Canada, April.

Hall, C. and Coles, M. (1999) *Children's Reading Choices*, London, Routledge.

Hall, N. (1987) *The Emergence of Literacy*, Sevenoaks, Hodder and Stoughton, in association with the United Kingdom Reading Association Literacy Development.

Hall, N. (1991) Play in the emergence of literacy, in J. Christie (ed.) *Play and Early Literacy Development*, Albany, NY, State University of New York Press.

Hall, N. (1999) Young children, play and literacy: engagement in realistic uses of literacy, in J. Marsh and E. Hallet (eds) *Desirable Literacies: Approaches to Language and Literacy in the Early Years*, London, Paul Chapman.

Hall, N. and Robinson, A. (1995) *Exploring Writing and Play in the Early Years*, London, David Fulton.

Hall, P. (1998) The relationship between types of rap music and memory in African-American children, *Journal of Black Studies*, Vol. 28, no. 6, pp. 802–14.

Hall, S. (ed.) (1980) *Culture, Media, Language: Working Papers in Cultural Studies*, 1972–79, London, Hutchinson in association with the Centre for Contemporary Cultural Studies, University of Birmingham.

Hall, S. (1992) What is this 'black' in black popular culture?, in G. Dent, (ed.) *Black Popular Culture*, Seattle, Bay Press.

Halliday, M. A. K. (1993) *Explorations in the Functions of Language*, London, Edward Arnold.

Hannon, P. (1995). *Literacy, Home and School Research and Practice in Teaching Literacy with Parents*, London, Falmer Press.

Harris, S., Nixon, J. and Rudduck, J. (1993) Schoolwork, homework and gender, *Gender and Education*, Vol. 5, no. 1, pp. 3–15.

Heath, S. B. (1983) *Ways With Words: Language, Life and Work in Communities and Classrooms*, Cambridge, Cambridge University Press.

Her Majesty's Inspectorate (HMI) (1991) *The Teaching and Learning of Reading in Primary Schools 1990: a Report by HMI*, Stanmore: DES.

Hidi, S. (1990) Interest and its contribution as a mental resource for learning, *Review of Educational Research*, Vol. 60, pp. 549–71.

Hilton, M. (1996) Manufacturing make-believe: notes on the toy and media industry for children, in M. Hilton (ed.) *Potent Fictions: Children's Literacy and the Challenge of Popular Culture*, London, Routledge.

Hoggart, R. (1958). *The Use of Literacy, Aspects of Working-Class Life with Special Reference to Publications and Entertainments*, Harmondsworth, Penguin.

Hoggart, R. (1995) *The Way We Live Now*, London, Pimlico.

Holdaway, D. (1979) *The Foundations of Literacy*, Gosford, NSW, Ashton Scholastic.

Hutt, S. J., Tyler, C., Hutt, C. and Christopherson, H. (1989) *Play, Exploration and Learning*, London, Routledge.

Ineson, J. and Marsh, J. (2000) Comic capers, *Primary English*, Vol. 5, no. 2, pp. 6–10.

Isenberg, J. and Jacob, E. (1983) Literacy and symbolic play: a review of the literature, *Childhood Education*, Vol. 59, no. 4, pp. 272–6.

Iser, W. (1978) *The Act of Reading, a Theory of Aesthetic Response*, Baltimore, The Johns Hopkins University Press, and London, Routledge and Kegan Paul.

James, A. and Prout, A. (1997) *Constructing and Reconstructing Childhood: Contemporary Issues in the Sociological Study of Childhood*, 2nd edn, London, Falmer Press.

Jenks, C. (1993) *Culture*, London, Routledge.

Johnson, J., Jackson, L. A. and Gatto, L. (1995) Violent attitudes and differed academic aspirations: deleterious effects of exposure to rap music, *Basic and Applied Psychology*, Vol. 16, pp. 27–41.

Johnson, J. C. (1990) The role of play in cognitive development, in E. Klugma and S. Smilansky (eds) *Children's Play and Learning: Perspectives and Policy Implications*, New York, Teachers College Press.

Johnson, S. (1755) *A Dictionary of the English Language*, 3rd edn, London, W. Strahan.

Jones, A. (1997) Teaching post-structuralist feminist theory in education: student resistances, *Gender and Education*, Vol. 9, no. 3, pp. 261–9.

Jordan, E. (1995) Fighting boys and fantasy play: the construction of masculinity in the early years of school, *Gender and Education*, Vol. 7, no. 1, pp. 69–86.

Kessler, S., Ashenden, D. J., Connell, R. W. and Dowsett, G. W. (1985) Gender relations in secondary schooling, *Sociology of Education*, Vol. 58, no. 1, pp. 34–48.

Ketch, A. (1991) The delicious alphabet, *English in Education*, Vol. 25, no. 1, pp. 1–4.

Kincheloe, J. (1998) Home alone and 'Bad to the Bone': the advent of a postmodern childhood, in S. R. Steinberg and J. L. Kincheloe (eds) *Kinderculture: The Corporate Construction of Childhood*, Boulder, CO, Westview Press.

Kinder, M. (1991) *Playing with Power in Movies: Television and Video Games from Muppet Babies to Teenage Mutant Ninja Turtles*, Berkeley, CA, University of California Press.

Kline, S. (1993) *Out of the Garden: Toys and Children's Culture in the Age of TV Marketing*, London, Verso.

Kline, S. (1998) The making of children's culture, in H. Jenkins (ed.) *The Children's Culture Reader*, New York, New York University Press.

Kostelnick, M. J., Whiren, A. P. and Stein, L. C. (1986) Living with he-man: managing superhero fantasy play, *Young Children*, Vol. 41, no. 4, pp. 3–9.

Kress, G. (1997) *Before Writing: Rethinking the Paths to Literacy*, London, Routledge.

Kress, G. and van Leeuwen, T. (1996) *Reading Images: The Grammar of Visual Design*, London, Routledge.

Kroeber, A. L. and Kluckholn, C. (1952) *Culture: A Critical Review of Concepts and Definitions*, New York, Vintage Books.

Lakoff, G. (1980) *Metaphors We Live By*, Chicago, University of Chicago Press.

Lankshear, C. and Mclaren, P. L. (eds) (1993) *Critical Literacy, Policy, Praxis and the Post-modern*, Albany NY, State University of New York Press.

Lankshear, C. with Gee, J. P., Knobel, M. and Searle, C. (1997) *Changing Literacies*, Buckingham, Open University Press.

Leavis, F. R. (1962) *The Great Tradition*, Harmondsworth, Penguin (first published 1948).

Lee, C. (1999) War exposes futility of media degrees, *Times Educational Supplement*, 7 May.

Lessing, D. (1994) *Under My Skin. Volume One of My Autobiography to 1949*, London, HarperCollins.

Levi-Strauss, C. (1967) *Structural Anthropology*, New York, Doubleday.

Levin, D. E. and Carlsson-Paige, N. (1995) The Mighty Morphin Power Rangers: teachers voice concern, *Young Children*, Vol. 50, no. 6, pp. 67–72.

Lewis, D. (1996) Pop-ups and fingle-fangles: the history of the picture book, in V. Watson and M. Styles (eds) *Talking Pictures: Pictorial Texts and Young Readers*, London, Routledge.

Livingstone, S. and Bovill, M. (1999) *Young People, New Media*, London, London School of Economics.

Lloyd, S. (1992) *The Phonics Handbook*, Chigwell, Jolly Learning.

Loftus, G. R. and Loftus, E. E. (1983) *Mind at Play: The Psychology of Video Games*, New York, Basic Books.

Low, G. (2000) The concept of traditional degrees is changing radically, *Guardian*, 2 May, p. 11.

Lowe, K. (1998) Gendermaps, in N. Yelland (ed.) *Gender in Early Childhood*, New York and London, Routledge.

Luke, A. (1993) *The Social Construction of Literacy in the Primary School*, Melbourne, Macmillan Education Australia.

Luke, C. (2000) What next? Toddler netizens, Playstation thumb, technoliteracies, *Contemporary Issues in Early Childhood*, Vol. 1, no. 1, pp. 95–100.

Luke, C. and Roe, K. (1993) Introduction to special issue: media and popular cultural studies in the classroom, *Australian Journal of Education*, Vol. 37, no. 2, pp. 115–18.

Lyness, P. (1952) The place of mass media in the lives of boys and girls, *Journalism Quarterly*, Vol. 29, pp. 43–54.

Mac an Ghaill, M. (1994) *The Making of Men: Masculinities, Sexualities and Schooling*, Buckingham, Open University Press.

Maclean, M., Bryant, P. and Bradley, L. (1987) Rhymes, nursery rhymes and reading in early childhood, *Merrill-Palmer Quarterly*, Vol. 33, no. 3, pp. 255–81.

Macmillan, B. (1997) *Why Schoolchildren Can't Read*, Studies in Education no. 2, London, Institute of Economic Affairs.

MacNaughton, G. (1997) Who's got the power? Rethinking gender equity strategies in early childhood, *International Journal of Early Years Education*, Vol. 5, no. 1, pp. 57–66.

Marriott, S. (1998) Picture books and the moral imperative, in J. Evans (ed.) *What's in The Picture? Responding to Illustrations in Picture Books*, London, Paul Chapman.

Marsh, J. (1998) Gender and writing in the infant school: Writing for a gender-specific audience, *English in Education*, Vol. 32, no. 1, pp. 10–18.

Marsh, J. (1999) Batman and Batwoman go to school: popular culture in the literacy curriculum, *International Journal of Early Years Education*, Vol. 7, no. 2, pp. 117–31.

Marsh, J. (2000a) 'But I want to fly too!' Girls and superhero play in the infant classroom, *Gender and Education*, Vol. 12, no. 2, pp. 209–20.

Marsh, J. (2000b) Teletubby tales: popular culture in the early years literacy curriculum, *Contemporary Issues in Early Childhood*, Vol. 1, no. 2, pp. 119–36.

Marx, K. (1963) *Selected Writings in Sociology and Social Philosophy*, eds T. Bottomore and M. Rubel, Harmondsworth, Penguin.

McLaren, P. and Morris, J. (1998) Mighty Morphin Power Rangers: the aesthetics of phallo-militaristic justice, in S. R. Steinberg and J. L. Kincheloe (eds) *Kinderculture: The Corporate Construction of Childhood*, Boulder, CO, Westview Press.

McLeod, F. (1991) Down the chippy, in N. Hall and L. Abbott (eds) *Play and the Primary Curriculum*, London, Hodder and Stoughton.

McLuhan, M. and Fiore, Q. (1967) *The Medium is the Message*, Harmondsworth, Penguin.

McRobbie, A. (1994) *Postmodernism and Popular Culture*, London, Routledge.

Medhurst, A. (1991) Batman, deviance and camp, in R. E. Pearson and W. Uricchio, *The Many Lives of the Batman*, London, Routledge.

Meece, J. L., Blumenfeld, P. C. and Hoyle, R. (1988) Students' goal orientations and cognitive engagement in classroom activities, *Journal of Educational Psychology*, Vol. 80, pp. 514–23.

Meek, M., Warlow, A. and Barton, G. (eds) (1977) *The Cool Web: The Pattern of Children's Reading*, London, Bodley Head.

Meek, M. (1991) *On Being Literate*, London, Bodley Head.

Messenger-Davies, M. (1997) *Fake, Fact and Fantasy: Children's Interpretations of Television Reality*, Norwood, NJ, Erlbaum.

Metz, C. (1994) *Film Language: A Semiotics of the Cinema*, trans. M. Taylor, New York, Oxford University Press.

Millard, E. (1994) *Developing Readers in the Middle Years*, Buckingham, Open University Press.

Millard, E. (1997) *Differently Literate: The Schooling of Boys and Girls*, London, Falmer Press.

Millard, E. (2000) New technologies. Old Inequalities, in E. Millard (ed.) *Enquiring into literacy*. Papers from the literacy research centre, Department of Educational Studies, University of Sheffield.

Millard, E. and Marsh, J. (2000) Sending Minnie the Minx home: comics and reading choice. Paper presented at the *Education for Social Democracies* Conference, London Institute of Education, July.

Minns, H. (1990) *Read It to Me Now! Learning at Home and at School*, London, Virago.

Minns, H. (1993) 'Don't tell them daddy taught you': the place of parents or putting parents in their place? *Cambridge Journal of Education*, Special Issue, Vol. 23, no. 1, pp. 25–32.

Moss, G. (1999) Boys and non-fiction: cause or effect? *Literacy Today*, Vol. 21, p. 19.

Nagle, J. P. (1999) Histories of success and failure: working class students' literacy experiences, *Journal of Adolescents and Adult Literacy*, Vol. 43, no. 2, pp. 172–85.

Neuman, S. (1995) *Literacy in the Television Age: The Myth of the TV Effect*, 2nd edn, Norwood, NJ, Ablex.

Neuman, S. (1988) The displacement effect: assessing the relation between television viewing and reading performance, *Reading Research Quarterly*, Vol. 23, no. 4, pp. 414–40.

Neuman, S. B. and Roskos, K. (1992) Literacy objects as cultural tools: effects on children's literacy behaviours in play, *Reading Research Quarterly*, Vol. 27, no. 3, pp. 202–35.

Neuman, S. B. and Roskos, K. (1993) Access to print for children of poverty: differential effects of adult mediation and literacy-enriched play settings on environmental and functional print tasks, *American Educational Research Journal*, Vol. 30, no. 1, pp. 95–122.

Nichols, G. (ed.) (1991) *Can I Buy a Slice of Sky? Poems from Black, Asian and American Indian Cultures*, London, Hodder Children's Books.

Nutbrown, C. (2000) Alex's story: literacy and literacy: teaching in the earliest years, in E. Millard (ed.) *Enquiring into Literacy*. Papers from the literacy research centre, Department of Educational Studies, University of Sheffield.

Nutbrown, C. and Hannon, P. (1997) *Preparing for Early Literacy Education with Parents: A Professional Development Manual*, Nottingham, REAL Project and NES Arnold.

Nwokah, E. E. and Ikekeonwu, C. (1998) A sociocultural comparison of Nigerian and American children's games, in M. C. Duncan, G. Chick, and A. Aycock (eds) *Play and Culture Studies, Volume 1: Diversions and Divergences in Fields of Play*, Greenwich, CT, Ablex.

O'Sullivan, T., Dutton, D. and Rayner, P. (1994) *Studying the Media: An Introduction*, London, Edward Arnold.

Opie, I. and Opie, P. (eds) (1951) *The Oxford Dictionary of Nursery Rhymes*, London, Oxford University Press.

Orellana, M. F. (1994) Appropriating the voice of the superheroes: three preschoolers' bilingual language uses in play, *Early Childhood Research Quarterly*, Vol. 9, pp. 171–93.

Pahl, K. (1999) *Transformations: Meaning Making in Nursery Education*, Stoke-on-Trent, Trentham Books.

Paley, V. G. (1984) *Boys and Girls: Superheroes in the Doll Corner*, Chicago, University of Chicago Press.

Palmer, P. (1986) *The Lively Audience: A Study of Children Around the TV Set*, Sydney, Allen and Unwin.

Parker, D. (1999) You've read the book, now make the film: moving image media, print literacy and narrative, *English in Education*, Vol. 33, no. 1, Spring, pp. 24–35.

Phillips, A. (1993) *The Trouble with Boys*, London, Pandora Press.

Pidgeon, S. (1993) Learning reading and learning gender, in M. Barrs and S. Pidgeon (eds) *Reading the Difference*, London, Centre for Language in Primary Education.

Pompe, C. (1996) 'But they're pink!' – 'Who cares!': popular culture in the primary years, in M. Hilton (ed.) *Potent Fictions: Children's Literacy and the Challenge of Popular Culture*, London, Routledge.

Postman, N. (1983) *The Disappearance of Childhood*, London, W. H. Allen.

Propp, V. (1968). *Morphology of the Folk-Tale*, trans. L. Scott, Austin, TX, and London, University of Texas Press.

Pumfrey, P. (1991) *Improving Children's Reading in the Junior School: Challenges and Responses*, London, Cassell.

Purcell-Gates, V. (1996) Stories, coupons and the TV guide: relationships between home literacy experiences and emergent literacy experiences, *Reading Research Quarterly*, Vol. 31, no. 4, pp. 406–28.

Ramsey, P. (1998) Diversity and play: influence of race, culture, class and gender, in D. P. Fromberg and D. Bergen (eds) *Play from Birth to Twelve and Beyond: Contexts, Perspectives and Meanings*, New York, Garland.

Rand, E. (1998) Older heads on young bodies, in H. Jenkins (ed.) *The Children's Culture Reader*, New York, New York University Press.

Richards, C. (1995) Popular music and media education, *Discourse in the Cultural Politics of Education*, 163 Carfax/University of Queensland, Australia.

Richards, R. (1998) Beyond classroom cultures, in D. Buckingham (ed.) *Teaching Popular Culture, Beyond Radical Pedagogy*, London, UCL Press.

Richler, M. (1977) The great comic book heroes, in M. Meek, A. Wardlow and G. Barton (eds) *The Cool Web: The Pattern of Children's Reading*, London, Bodley Head.

Rieber, L. P. (1992) Computer-based microworlds: a bridge between construction and direct instruction. *Educational Technology Research and Development*, Vol. 40, no. 1, pp. 93–106.

Ritzer, G. (1998) *The McDonaldization Thesis: Explorations and Extensions*, London, Sage.

Robinson, M. (1997) *Children Reading Print and Television*, London, Falmer Press.

Roe, K. and Muijs, D. (1998) Children and computer games: a profile of the heavy user, *European Journal of Communication*, Vol. 13, no. 2, pp. 181–200.

Rogers, M. F. (1999) *Barbie Culture*, London, Sage.

Rose, J. (1984) *The Case of Peter Pan, or, the Impossibility of Children's Fiction, Language, Discourse and Society*, London, Macmillan.

Rosen, M. (1996) Reading *The Beano*: a young boy's experience, in V. Watson and M. Styles (eds) *Talking Pictures: Pictorial Texts and Young Readers* London, Hodder and Stoughton.

Roskos, K. (1990) A taxonomic review of pretend play among four- and five-year-old children, *Early Childhood Research Quarterly*, Vol. 5 no. 4, pp. 495–572.

Rotundo, E. A. (1998) Boy culture, in H. Jenkins (ed.) *The Children's Culture Reader*, New York, New York University Press.

Rowe, D. (1995) *Popular Cultures: Rock Music, Sport and the Politics of Pleasure*, London, Sage.

Rumelhart, D. (1977) Towards an interactive model of reading in S. Dornic (ed.) *Attention and Performance VI: proceedings of the 6th International Symposium*, Hillsdale, NJ, New York and London: Lawrence Erlbaum Associates.

Ruskin, J. (1985) *Unto this Last, and Other Writings*, Harmondsworth, Penguin.

Russell, W. (1985) *Educating Rita*, Harlow, Longman.

Salomon, G. (1979) *Interaction of Media, Cognition and Learning*, San Francisco, Jossey-Bass.

Sanger, J. with Willson, J., Davies, B., and Whitaker, R. (1997) *Young Children, Videos and Computer Games*, London, Falmer Press.

Schiefle, U. (1991) Interest, learning and motivation, *Educational Psychologist*, Vol. 26, pp. 299–323.

Searle, C. (1993, Words to a life-land, in C. Lankshear and P. L. Mclaren (eds) *Critical Literacy, Policy, Praxis and the Post-Modern*, Albany, NY, State University of New York Press.

Sefton-Green, J. (1999) review article, Playing the game: the critical study of computer games, *Convergence*, Vol. 5, no. 4, pp. 114–20.

Sefton-Green, J. and Buckingham, D. (1998) Digital visions: children's 'creative' uses of multimedia technologies, in J. Sefton-Green (ed.) *Digital Diversions: Youth Culture in the Age of Multimedia*, London, UCL Press.

Seiter, E. (1993) *Sold Separately: Children and Parents in Consumer Culture*, New Brunswick, NJ, Rutgers University Press.

Seiter, E. (1998) Children's desires/mothers' dilemmas: the social contexts of consumption, in H. Jenkins (ed.) *The Children's Culture Reader*, New York, New York University Press.

Shields, C. D.(1998) *Saturday Night at the Dinosaur Stomp*, London, Walker Books.

Singer, J. L. and Singer, D. G. (1981) *Television, Imagination and Aggression: A Study of Preschoolers*, Hillsdale, NJ, Erlbaum.

Singer, J. L. and Singer, D. G. (1990) *The House of Make-Believe: Children's Play and the Developing Imagination*, Cambridge, MA, Harvard University Press.

Smilansky, S. (1968) *The Effects of Socio-Dramatic Play on Disadvantaged Preschool Children*, New York, John Wiley.

Smith, D. (1987) *The Everyday World as Problematic: A Feminist Sociology*, Boston, Northeastern University Press.

Smith, F. (1984) *Reading that Helps Us Teach: Joining the Literacy Club*, Reading, Reading Centre.

Smogarinsky, P. and O'Donnell-Allan, C. (1998) The depth and dynamics of context: tracing the sources and channels of engagement and disengagement in students' response to literature, *Journal of Literary Research*, Vol. 30, no. 4, pp. 515–59.

Soler, J. (2000) Past and present technocratic solutions to teaching literacy: implications for New Zealand primary teachers and literacy programmes, *Curriculum Studies*, Vol. 7, no. 3.

Solsken, J. (1993) *Literacy, Gender, and Work in Families and in School*, Norwood, NJ, Ablex.

Sousa, C. and Schneiderman, J. (1986) Preschoolers and superheroes: a dangerous duo, *Early Years*, November–December, pp. 75–7.

Springhall, J. (1998) *Youth, Popular Culture and Moral Panics: Penny Gaffs to Gangsta Rap*, Basingstoke, Macmillan.

St Clair, W. (1989) William Godwin as children's bookseller, in C. Avery and J. Briggs (eds) *Children and their Books*, Oxford, Oxford University Press.

Storey, J. (1993) *An Introduction to Cultural Theory and Popular Culture* , 2nd edn, London, Harvester Wheatsheaf.

Storkey, A. (1999) *Media Addiction: Children and Education*. Movement for Christian Democracy, discussion paper 99/4, London, Mayflower C.

Strinati, D. (1995) *An Introduction to Theories of Popular Culture*, London, Routledge.

Strinati, D. and Wagg, S. (eds) (1992) *Come on Down? Popular Media Culture in Post-War Britain*, London, Routledge.

Stutz, E. (1996) Is electronic entertainment hindering children's play and social development? in T. Gill (ed.) *Electronic Children: How Children are Responding to the Information Revolution*, London, National Children's Bureau.

Sutton-Smith, B. (1986) *Toys as Culture*, New York, Gardner Press.

Swift, J. (1726) *Gulliver's Travels and Other Works* (1906 edn, exactly reprinted from the first edition), London, Routledge.

Swingewood, A. (1998) *Cultural Theory and the Problem of Modernity*, London, Macmillan Press.

Taylor, C. (1999) 'I like it when my mum comes to school with me': family literacy, in J. Marsh and E. Hallet (eds) *Desirable Literacies: Approaches to Language and Literacy in the Early Years*, London, Paul Chapman.

Taylor, D. and Dorsey-Gaines, C. (1988) *Growing Up Literate: Learning from Inner-City Families*, Portsmouth, NH, Heinemann.

TES (2000a) Pocket monsters provoke fights, *Times Educational Supplement*, 14 April, p. 4.

TES (2000b) Beanies' power to bend our minds, *Times Educational Supplement*, 19 May 19, p. 3.

TES (2000c) Letter from Twining on Letters page, *Times Educational Supplement*, 2 June, p. 16.

Thomas, H. (1998) *Reading and Responding to Fiction*, Leamington Spa, Scholastic.

Thompson, D. (ed.) (1970) *Discrimination and Popular Culture*, Harmondsworth, Penguin.

Thorne, B. (1993) *Gender Play: Girls and Boys in School*, Buckingham, Open University Press.

Tobin, J. (2000) *'Good Guys Don't Wear Hats': Children's Talk about the Media*, New York, Teachers College Press.

Todorov, T. (1977) *The Poetics of Prose*, trans. R. Howard, Minneapolis, MN, University of Minnesota Press.

Turner, G. (1994) Film languages, in D. Graddol and O. Boyd-Barrett (eds) *Media Texts: Authors and Readers*, Milton Keynes and Cleveland, Multilingual Matters.

Turner, J. (1995) The influence of classroom contexts on young children's motivation for literacy, *Reading Research Quarterly*, Vol. 30, no. 3, p. 410–40.

Twitchell, J. B. (1985) *Dreadful Pleasures: An Anatomy of Modern Horror*, Oxford, Oxford University Press.

Urquhart, I. (1996) Popular culture and how boys become men, in M. Hilton (ed.) *Potent Fictions: Children's Literacy and the Challenge of Popular Culture*, London, Routledge.

Volosinov, V. N. (1994) Extract from 'Marxism and the philosphy of language', in P. Morris (ed.) *The Bakhtin Reader: Selected Writings of Bakhtin, Medvedev, Volosinov*, London, Arnold.

Vukelich, C. (1991) Materials and modelling: promoting literacy during play, in J. F. Christie (ed.) *Play and Early Literacy Development*, New York, State University of New York Press.

Vukelich, C. (1994) Effects of play interventions on young children's reading of environmental print, *Early Childhood Research Quarterly*, Vol. 9, pp. 153–70.

Vygotsky, L. S. (1978) *Mind in Society: The Development of Higher Psychological Processes*, Cambridge, MA, Harvard University Press.

Vygotsky, L. S. (1986) *Thought and Language*, Cambridge, MA, MIT Press.

Walkerdine, V. (1999) Violent boys and precocious girls: regulating childhood at the end of the millennium, *Contemporary Issues in Early Childhood*, Vol. 1, no. 1, pp. 3–22.

Waterland, L. (1988) *Read with Me*, London, Thimble Press.

Watson, V. (1992) The possibilities of children's fiction, in Styles, M., Bearne, E. and Watson, V. *After Alice: Exploring Children's Literature*, London, Cassell.

Weedon, C. (1987) *Feminist Practice and Poststructuralist Theory*, Oxford, Blackwell.

Weinberger, J. (1996) *Literacy Goes to School: The Parents' Role in Young Children's Literacy Learning*, London, Paul Chapman.

Wells, G. (1987) *The Meaning Makers: Children Learning Language and Using Language to Learn*, London, Hodder and Stoughton.

Whitehead, F., Capey, A., Maddren, W. and Wellings, A. (1977) *Children and their Books. The Final Report of the Schools Council Project on Children's Reading Habits 10–16*, Basingstoke, Macmillan Education.

Whitehead, M. (1997) *Language and Literacy in the Early Years*, 2nd edn, London, Paul Chapman.

Whyte, J. (1983) *Beyond the Wendy House: Sex Role Stereotyping in Primary Schools*, York, Longman for the Schools Council.

Willis, P. (1990) *Common Culture*, Buckingham, Open University Press.

Wilson, M. (2000) The point of horror: the relationship between teenage popular horror fiction and the oral repertoire, *Children's Literature in Education*, Vol. 31, no. 1, pp. 1–9.

Witty, P. (1967) Children of the television era, *Elementary English*, Vol. 44, pp. 528–35.

Wood, E. and Attfield, J. (1996) *Play, Learning and the Early Childhood Curriculum*, London, Paul Chapman.

Worthy, J., Moorman, M. and Turner, M. (1999) What Johnny likes to read is hard to find in school, *Reading Research Quarterly*, Vol. 34, no. 1, pp. 12–27.

Index

Printed in the United Kingdom
by Lightning Source UK Ltd.
108843UKS00004B/64-90